Creations from the Garden

Creations from the Garden
Growing Plants for the
Art of Flower Arranging

Kaye B. Vosburgh

fm

First Printing, 2021

ISBN 978-05-78974-62-0

Book production by Foxtown Murphy, Charlottesville, VA

Table of Contents

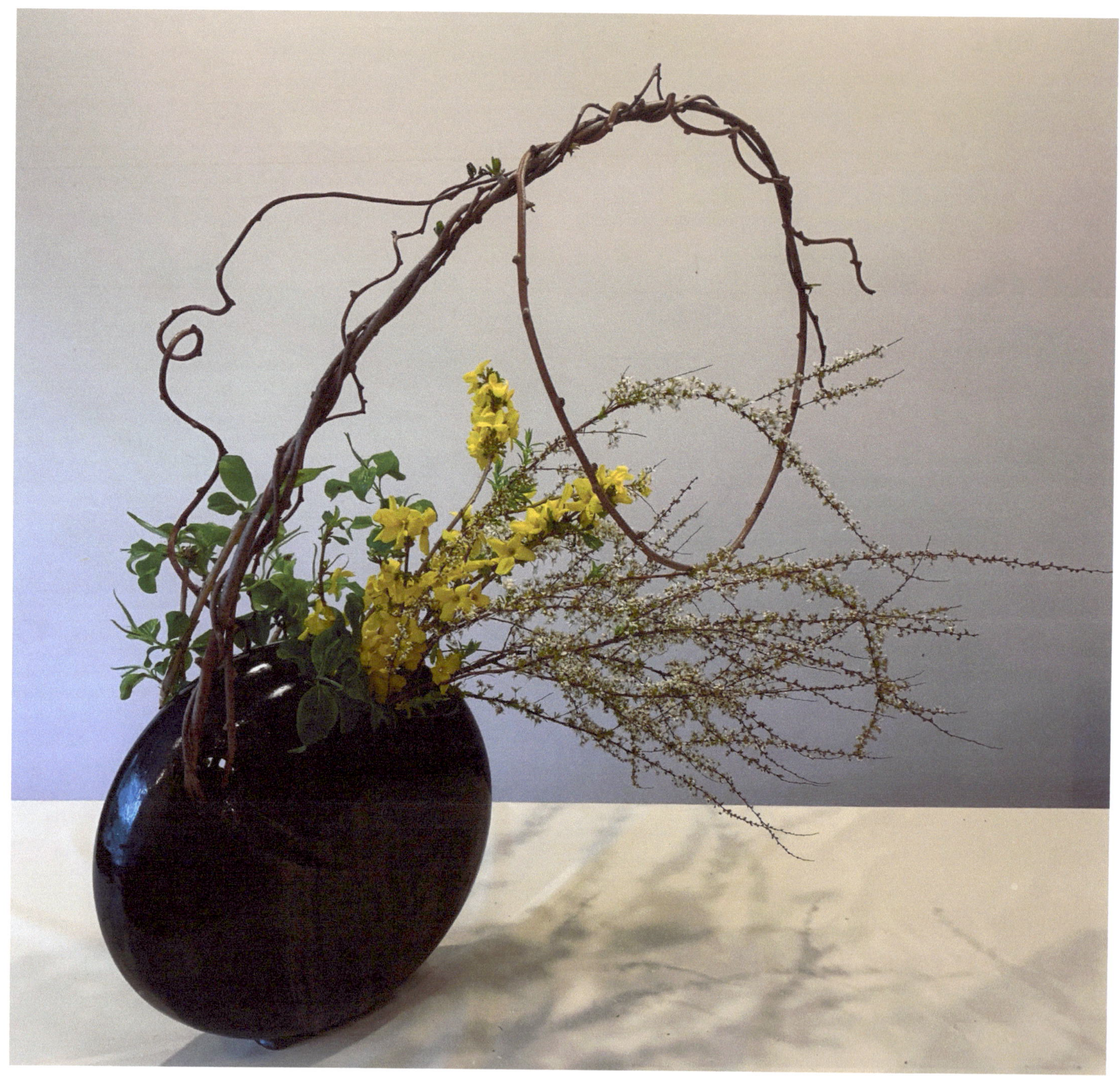

Introduction

This book was inspired by my ikebana students, who have asked what to plant in their yards for flower arranging. One of them said to me: "I see that having the right materials for arrangements makes all the difference." While flowers are generally available commercially, the branches are often gathered by the arranger. Ikebana arrangers use branches and other line material more frequently than traditional and creative American designers. I teach Sogetsu ikebana, Japanese flower arranging, and I am also a judge in the National Garden Clubs, Inc., where I teach student judges to evaluate designs in flower shows.

In this book, I provide a short introduction to the trees, shrubs and vines from my own garden, then examples of my flower arrangements using these materials. I include examples of both Eastern and Western designs using the plant materials that we grow. Common names are used to organize the plants; you will find the scientific name on the top right of each page. We grew some of the flowers, but many were purchased from local grocery stores and garden centers.

One of my students said to me, "I see that having the right materials for arrangements makes all the difference."

This past year I have stayed close to home because of the pandemic, so I have relied on my garden to provide most of the plant material for my in-person teaching, online lessons, and demonstrations. I was inspired to plant seeds and order small plants to enhance my garden and to provide more selections for designing. By the end of the summer in 2020, we had planted a whole new shrub garden. The value of a varied garden has proved itself.

We live in the Northeast of the United States in zone 6b. You may want to research the plants that interest you to see if they will grow in your area. Successful cultivation depends on the amount of sun, soil type, moisture, winter temperatures, local pests and care that you are willing to provide. Study your environment carefully and consult gardening centers and garden designers for help planning your garden. I usually just add wonderful plants when I see them or when someone suggests a certain variety. Some garden club members and ikebanists share plants from their gardens or have plant sales to raise money for good causes. Take advantage of these offerings from experienced gardeners.

Terminology

<u>Definitions</u>

Ikebana is the Japanese word for flower arranging. *Bana* means flower and the verb *ikeru* means to set (arrange) or to live or to create.

Freestyle Arranging is a type of Japanese creative design. The beginning lessons in the Sogetsu School and the traditional styles in other schools are rigorously prescribed. Sofu Teshigahara felt constrained by the many rules, so he developed a new style of arranging called "freestyle"; less prescriptive, it allows for more expression and creativity. Freestyle has become popular with the other ikebana schools today.

Traditional Design is a term the Garden Clubs use to describe arrangements that have a geometric form, that are naturalistic in placement, and that have few or no abstract qualities.

Creative Design is a term in the Garden Clubs which refers to non-traditional arranging. This includes abstract design and naturalistic design that incorporates and often features a lot of space. Sometimes it is hard to distinguish between creative design and freestyle ikebana.

<u>Techniques</u>

Conditioning is a method to ensure your plant material is as good as it can be, by making sure it is as full of water (turgid) as possible. Take your bucket of water and pruners out to the garden in the early morning or early evening. Cut stems and branches when the plants aren't suffering from the heat of the day and place them immediately into the bucket. Bring them inside and re-cut them under water. Then find a cool place to store the bucket out of drafts and out of the sun. Let them rest overnight or for several hours to give them time to soak up the water. Some plants are more delicate than others and need more conditioning care. Well-conditioned plant material will last longer before wilting.

Forcing Branches in the winter is a way to accelerate their blooming before spring. You can cut flowering shrub branches that have buds and bring them in to sit in water near a sunny window. In a few weeks, they will burst into bloom.

<u>Materials</u>

A **Kenzan** is a mechanic for holding branches and flowers. It has several brass pins that stick up, upon which stems can be impaled. It is called a pin holder by English-speaking arrangers.

Moribana containers are low-sided and flat-bottomed. They are named after the moribana-style arrangements done in them which are usually arranged in a kenzan. Moribana means "piled up flowers" in Japanese.

Nageire containers are usually tall cylindrical vases. In Japanese it means "thrown in," but usually today a variety of techniques are used to organize what is put in the vase. They frequently involve cutting and splitting the stems. Throughout this book, I note when branches are not well-suited to this technique, since they may be too thin or too brittle.

Tsubo containers are rounded. They require more sophisticated mechanics to position the plant material.

In Sogetsu ikebana the containers play a significant part in the design. Often they are the inspiration for the lines, colors, or moods of the design. I have listed the potters and craftsmen whose containers I have used in the designs in this book whenever I could. Many containers were purchased at the Sogetsu Headquarters in Tokyo; the designers are unknown unless they were created by one of the four iemotos (Headmasters) of the school. Skidmore College ceramics classes for me and my husband started our journey of creating and collecting usable containers.

The ikebana school that I teach was founded recently (1927) compared to some of the other schools, which are hundreds of years old. In Sogetsu we teach basic styles and eight variations, all of which have prescribed angles and designs. These give the student experience working with the plant material: cutting, bending, and placing the stems. Then the student is guided through many freestyle designs which encourage creativity. The founder of this school was the first ikebanist to encourage individual expression and creativity. In this book, you will see examples of these basic arrangements as well as freestyle creations.

Japanese flower arranging is known for asymmetrical designs and for line designs. In Japanese tradition, there is much attention to the seasons and their symbolism in our lives. Nature, spirit, and religion are intertwined in Japanese culture. Ikebana is one of the means of expression. Unlike the decorative purpose of most Western arrangements, ikebana often places more emphasis on meaning than decoration.

Shortly after beginning classes in ikebana, I joined a garden club and began studying to become a judge. The basis for evaluating designs and in fact creating them, are the Principles of Design we use in the National Garden Clubs: Dominance, Contrast, Scale, Proportions, and, of course, Balance and Rhythm. I find these concepts valuable in understanding designs. I use the vocabulary to communicate with people in design competitions in the garden clubs as well as with my students in ikebana.

People are often reluctant to cut plant material because it is no longer growing, but as I go to the garden to cut flowers, leaves, and branches I know that they will have a second life in my flower arrangements.

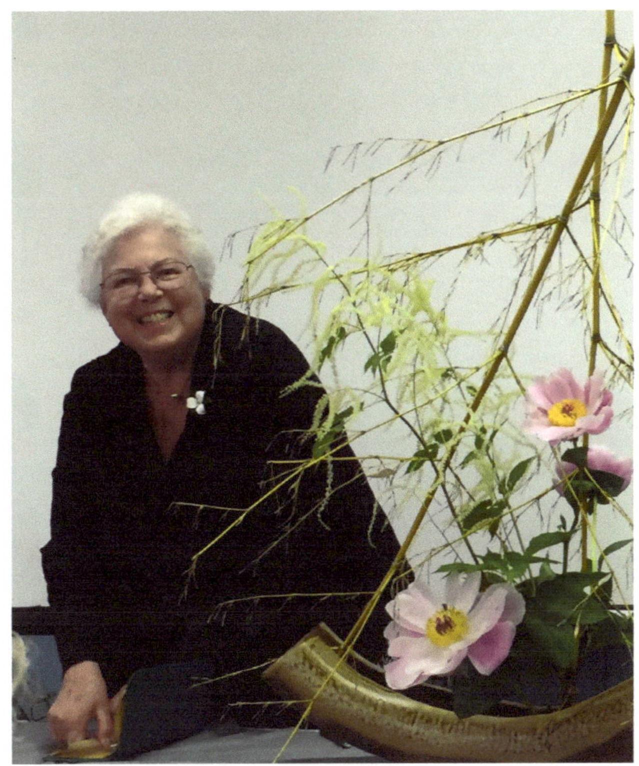

Aralia, Fiveleaf

1   This variegated shrub is a vigorous grower with thorns. The arching branches are nice to use in arrangements. It requires regular pruning. Be aware that it may be considered invasive.

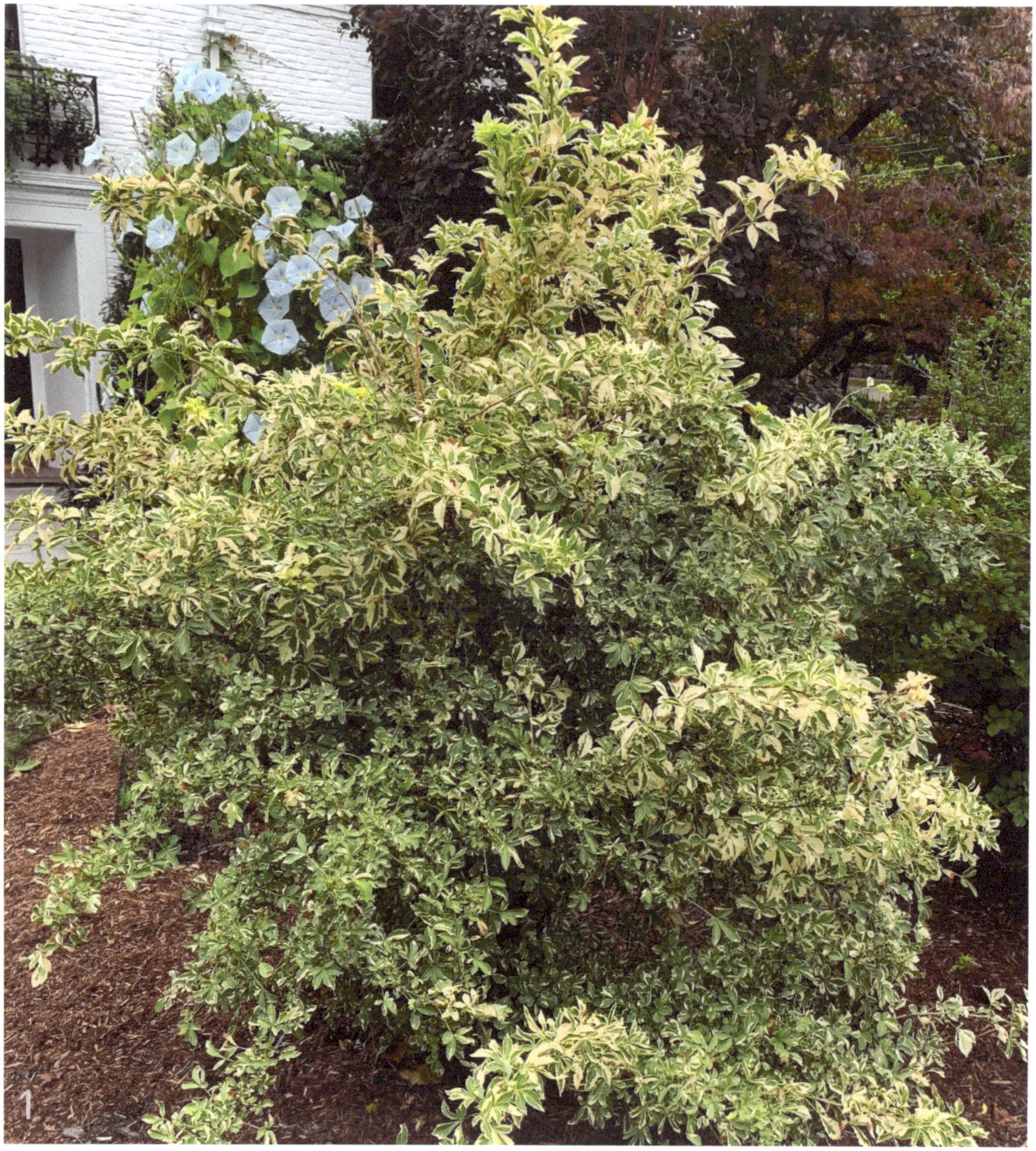

2   In this close-up, you can see the five leaflets and the variegation.

3   This is a Sogetsu School variation two slanting arrangement and it is my favorite. It is the only variation where the flowers—this case roses—stand upright. We always study these prescribed forms before we begin our freestyle designs. In this way we learn about managing the plant material, the mechanics, and the distinctively Japanese aesthetics.

4   This horizontal arrangement, seen from above, can be used on a dining table because it can be viewed from all sides and is not too tall to obstruct conversations.

5   The aralia and the foxtail lily have been tightly grouped to form a vertical mass design.

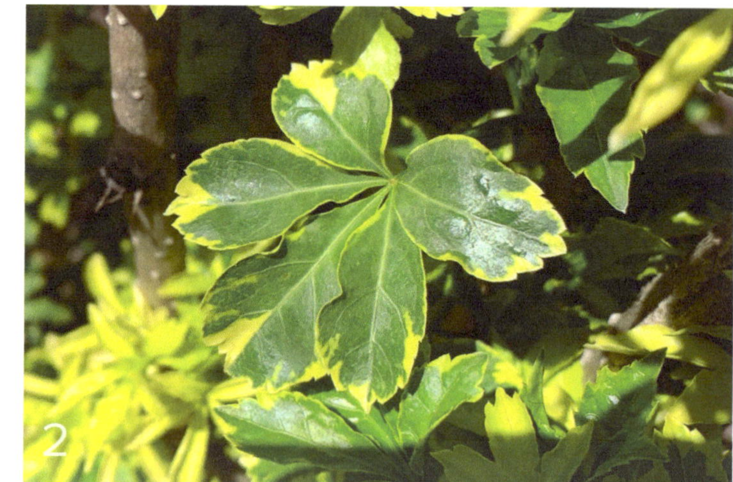

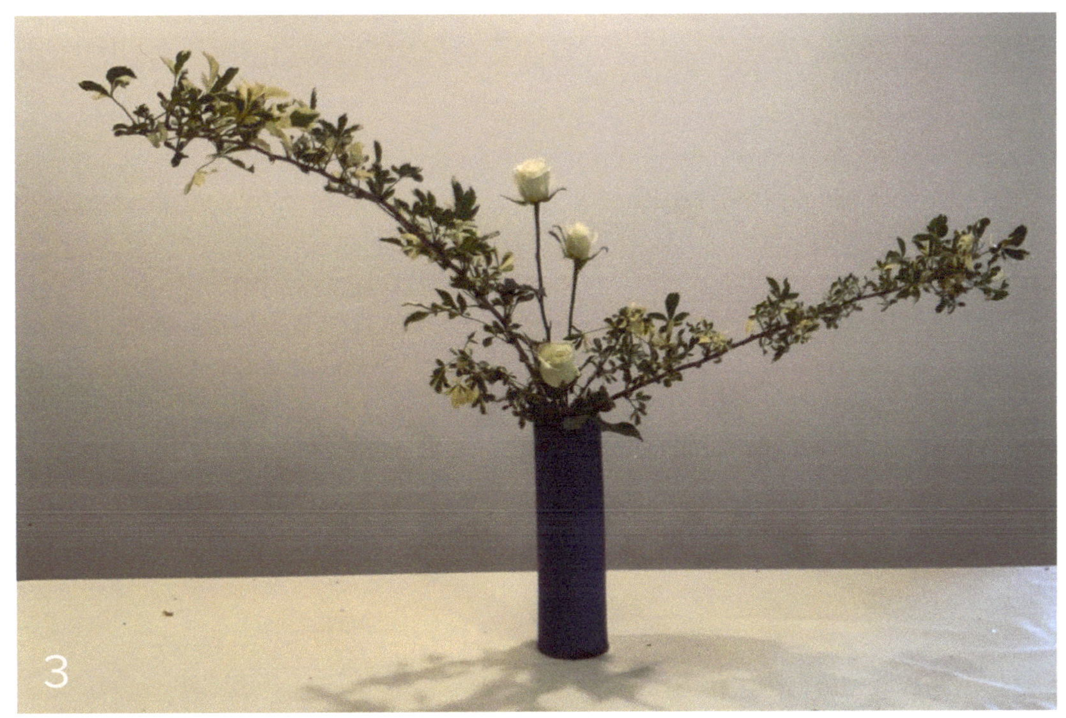

3

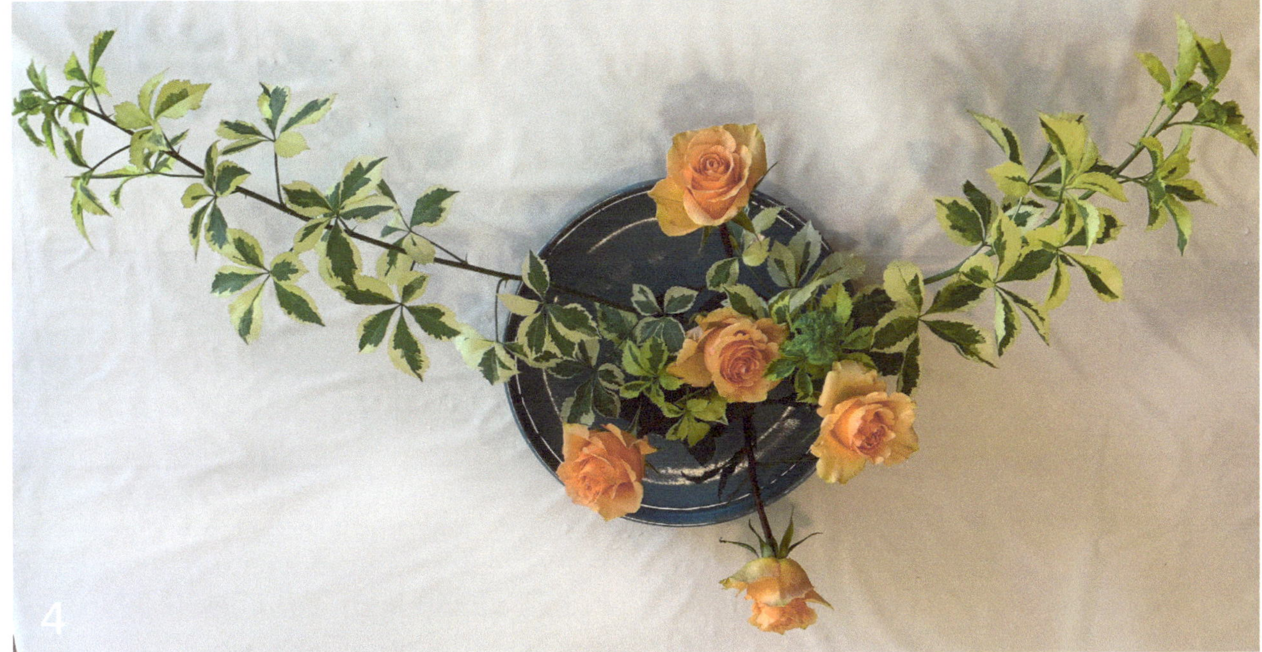

4

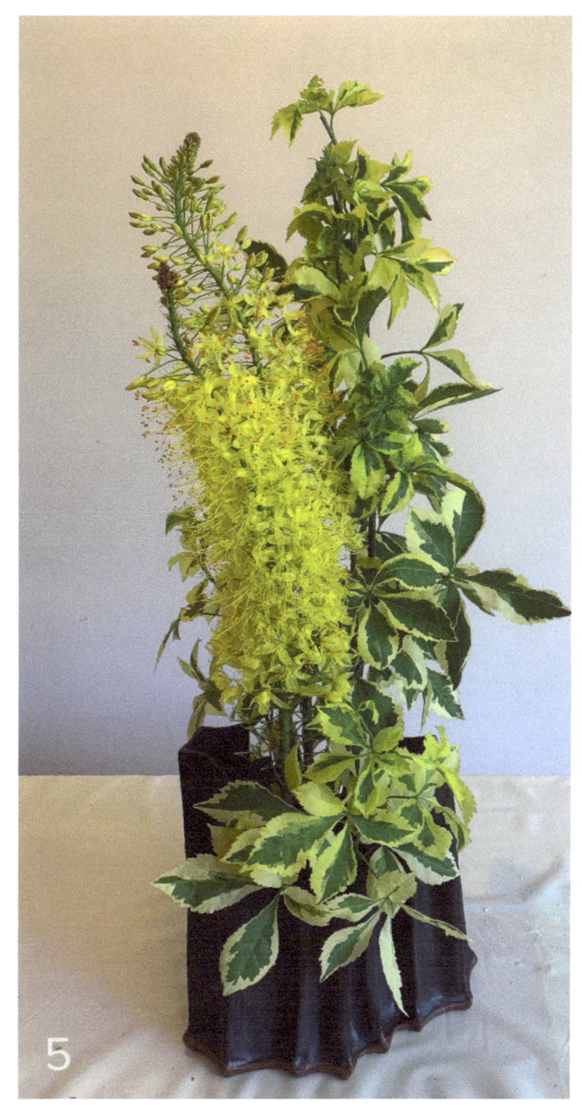

5

11

Bamboo, Yellow Groove *Phyllostachys aureosulcata*

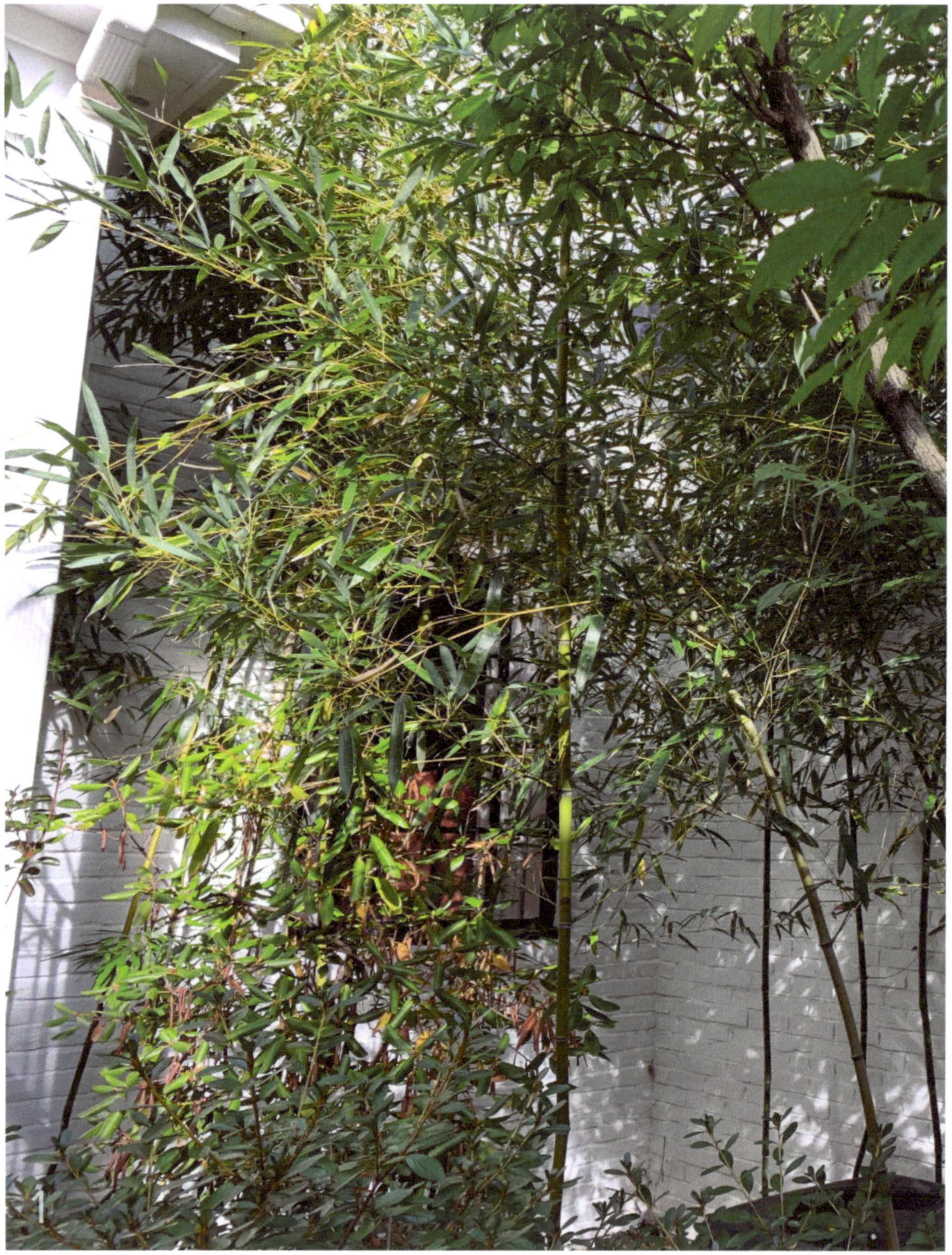

1   This vigorous plant is hard to keep under control. I love having it for its many uses. It grows to a height of 20 feet or more and is always expanding its footprint. The stolons travel underground far, wide, and fast. Before you plant it, have a plan for controlling it. Some varieties stay in a clump. Bamboo is often used in New Year's arrangements; it symbolizes resiliency. Even though snow will bend it to the ground, it will return to upright when released.

2   The characteristic bent branches of yellow groove are shown here next to new shoots still wrapped in their sheathing.

3   A tall bamboo with a damaged tip grows new leaves just below the damage. A festive look is achieved by adding tiny strips of bamboo painted gold to surround the lily and pine.

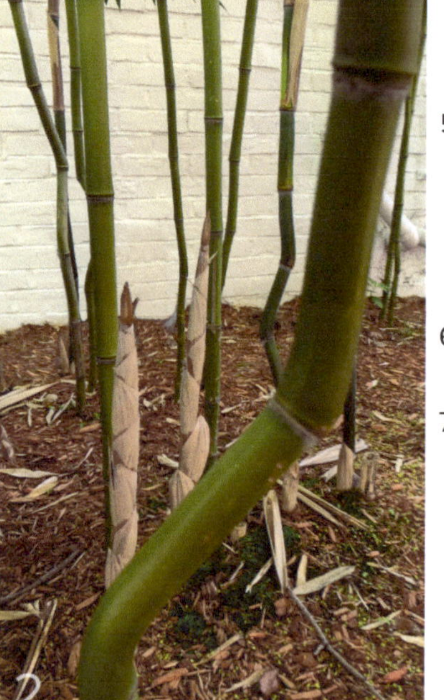

4   The dried yellow bamboo placed upside-down represents the path of the busy bee flying from sunflowers to honeycomb heliconia (beehive ginger).

5   This abstract form is created by weaving thin dried bamboo branches. Thicker pieces of bamboo, chrysanthemum, and pine are added for interest.

6   The newly-emerging shoots are combined with yellow tree peonies.

7   These bamboo poles are tied together with red cord and embellished with pine. Clementine fruit is balanced on top of the bamboo and gold leaf is floating in the water, both representing our wishes for prosperity in the new year.

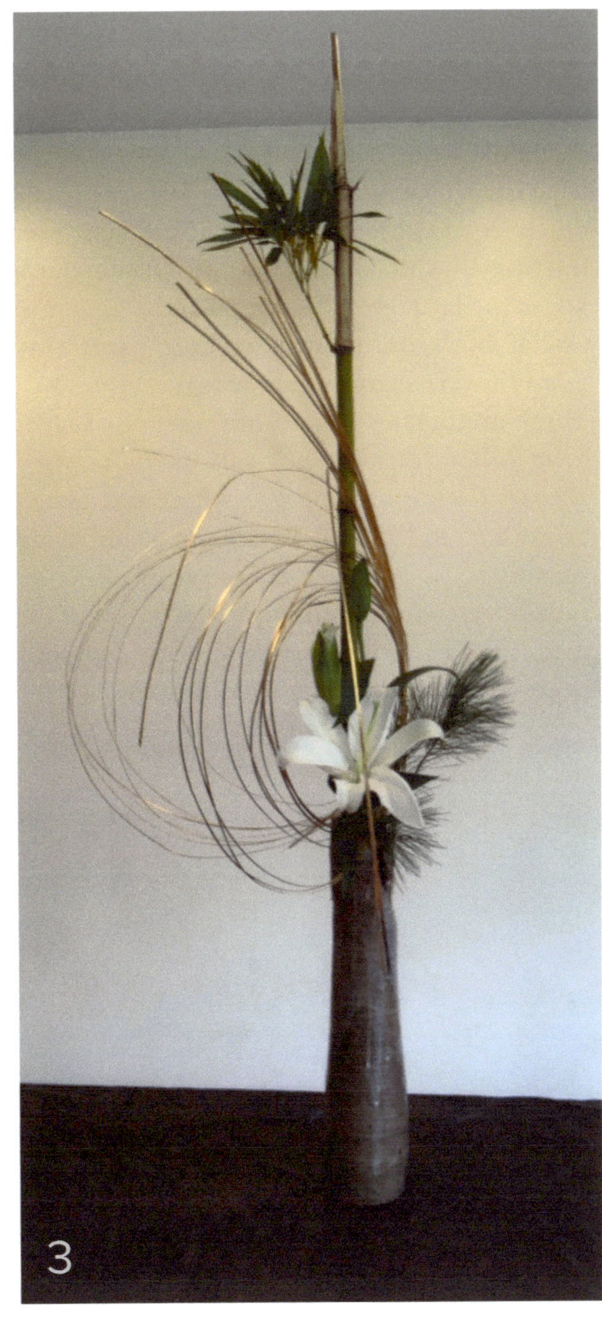

3

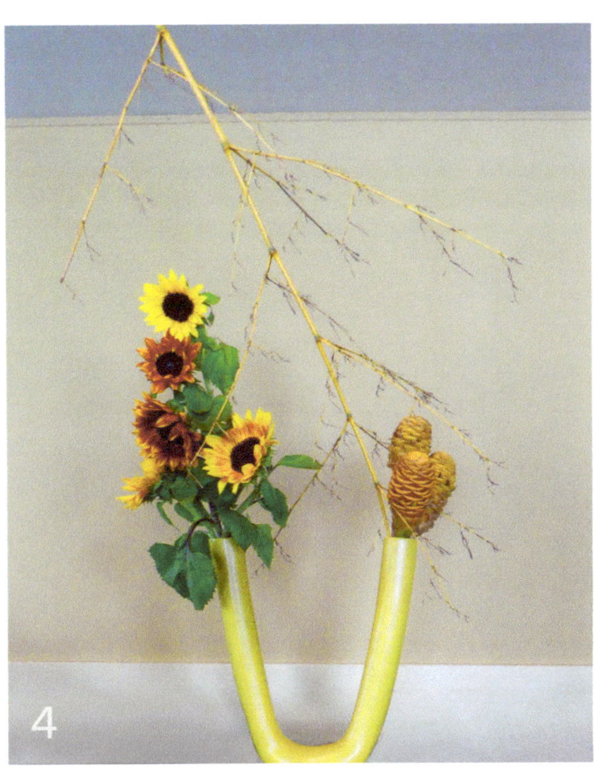

4

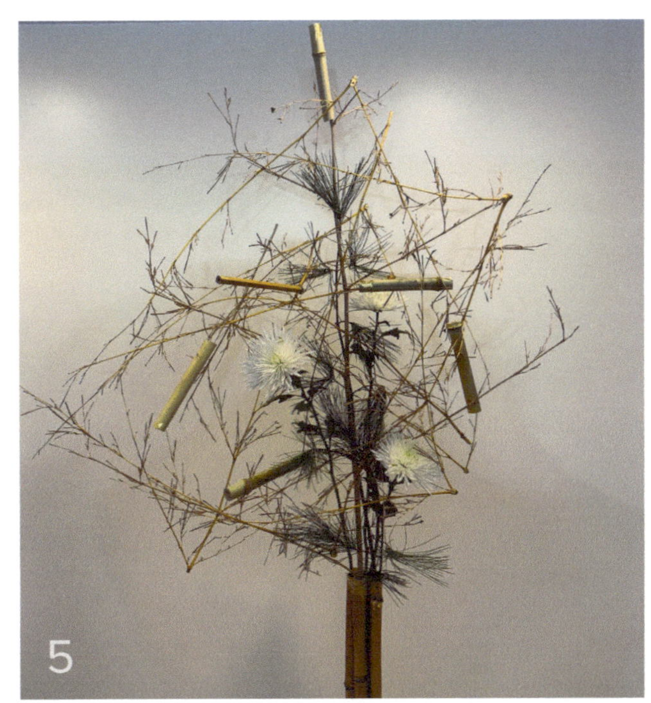

5

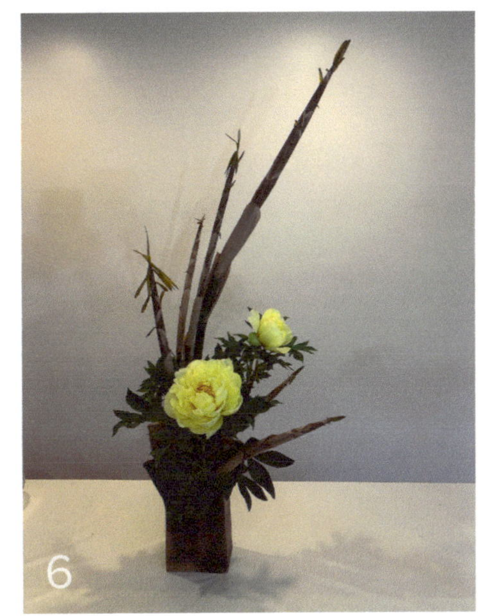

6

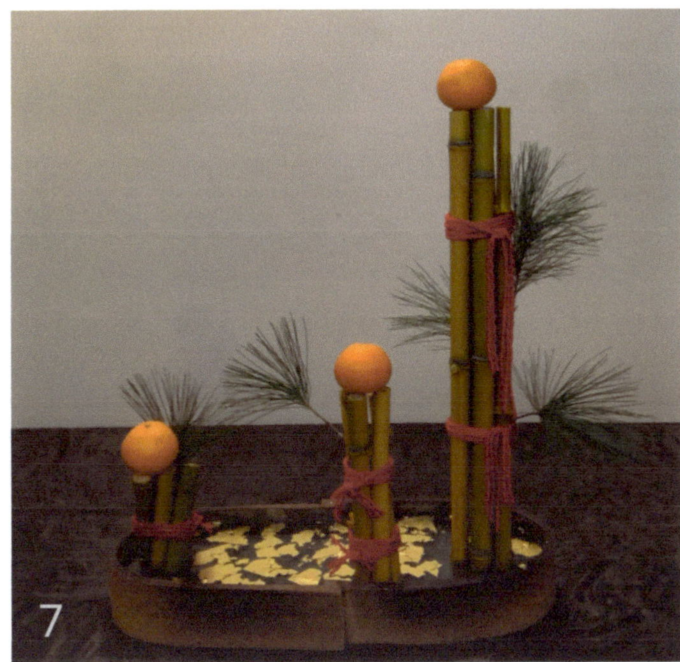

7

Beautyberry, Japanese (Purple)

Callicarpa japonica

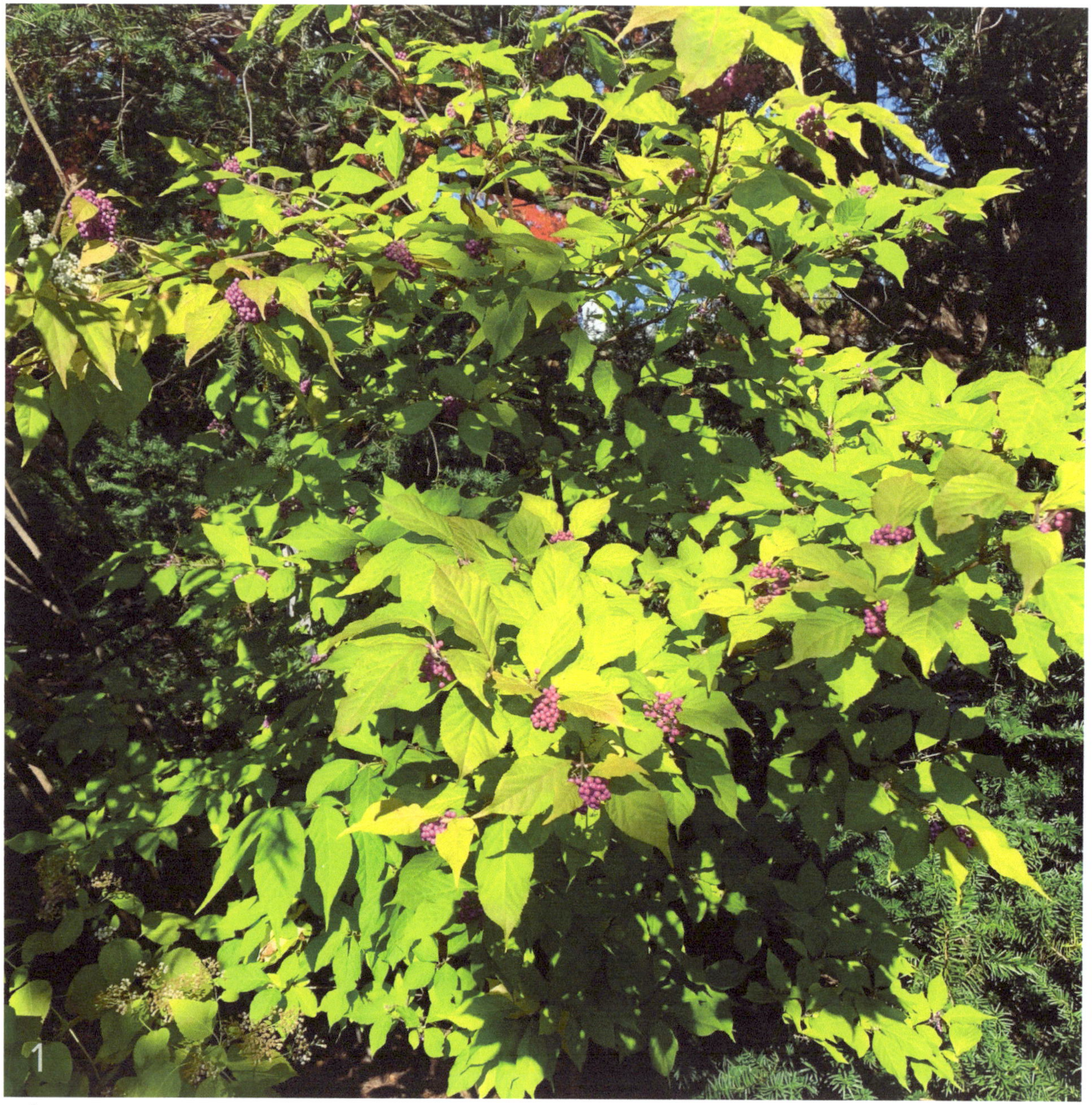

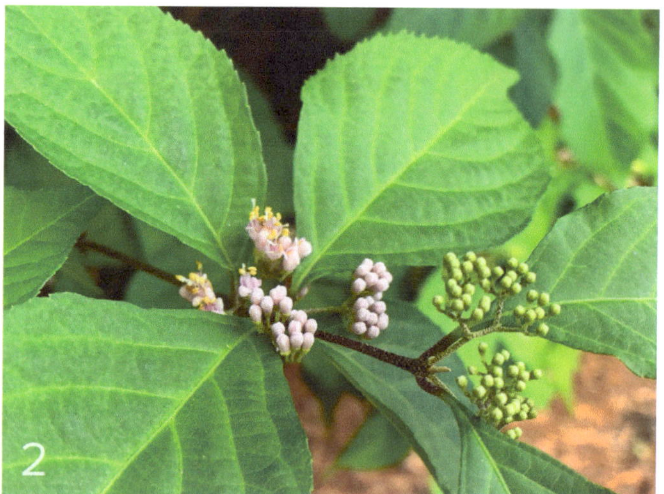

1. The purple beautyberry is more common than the white. This shrub has bunches of berries at the ends of the stems, whereas most varieties have berries along the stem. In Japan this is a much loved plant, called 'Lady Murasaki' after the woman who wrote *The Tale of Gengi*. Murasaki is the Japanese word for purple.

2. Green buds, more mature buds, and tiny open flowers surrounded by leaves.

3. These are berries in autumn after the leaves have fallen. A simple, basic ikebana with chrysanthemum, Monte Casino, and leatherleaf fern to hide the kenzan in a self-made container.

4. Purple berries and red sugar maple leaves express fall. The snowberries peeking out connect with the white of the container.

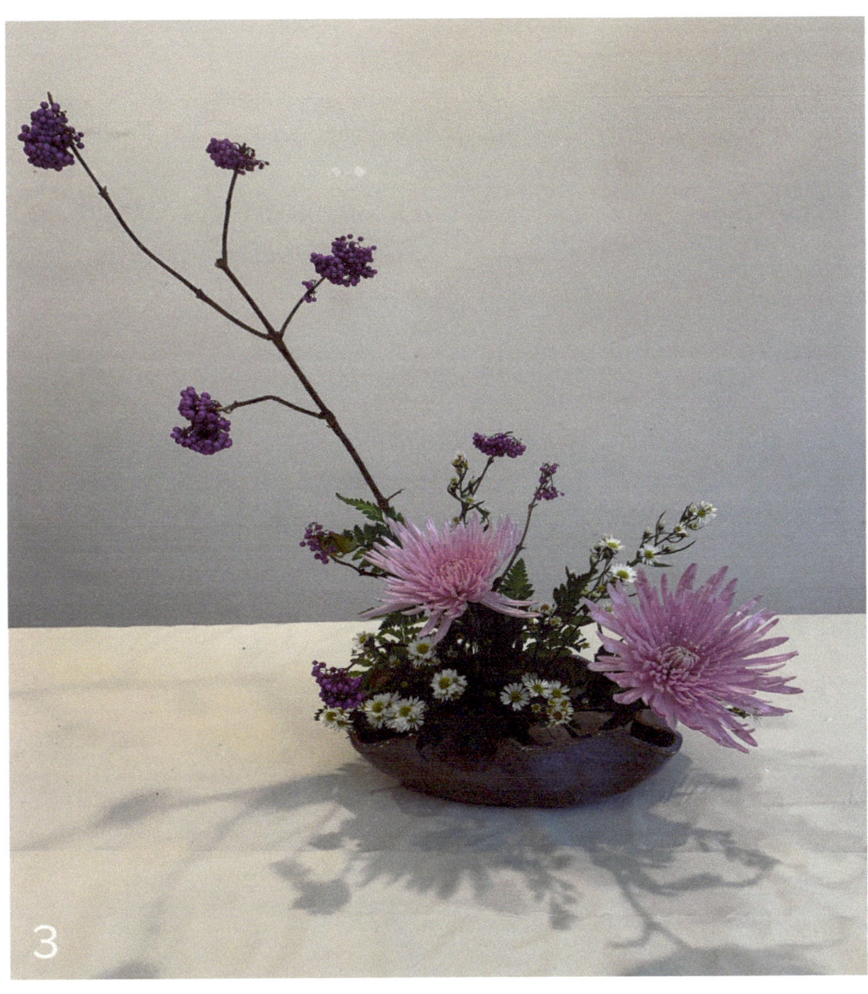

3

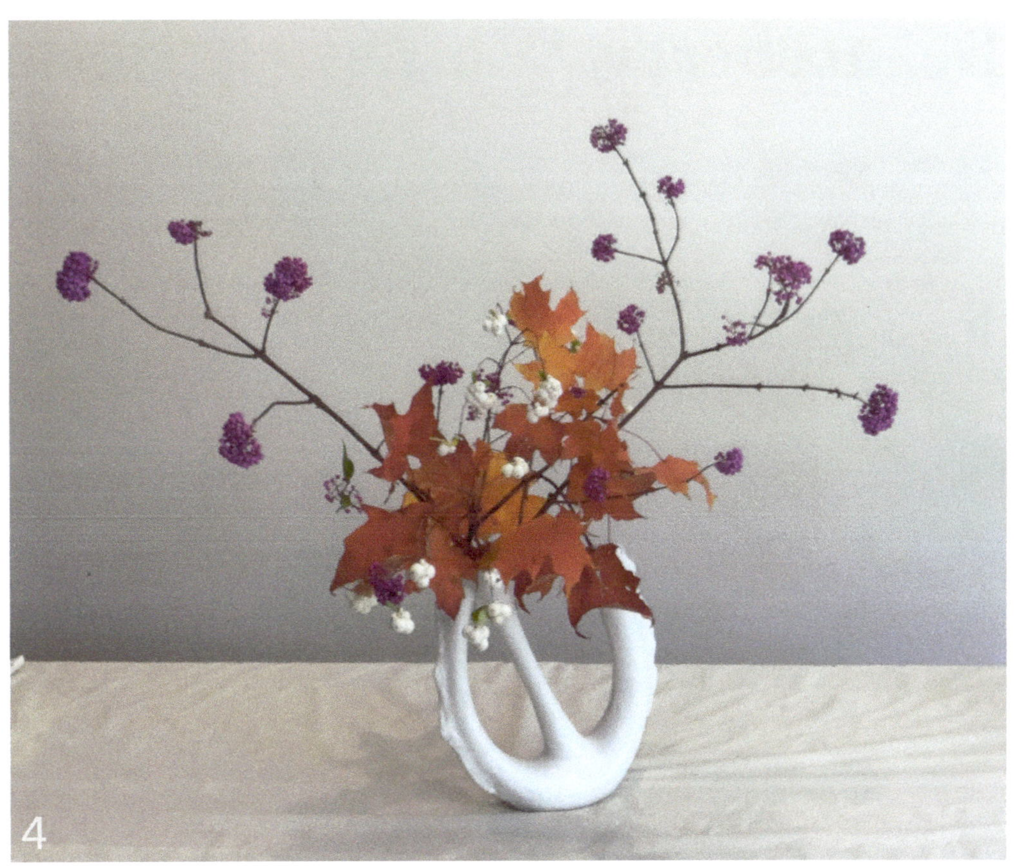

4

Beautyberry, White

Callicarpa japonica 'Leucocarpa'

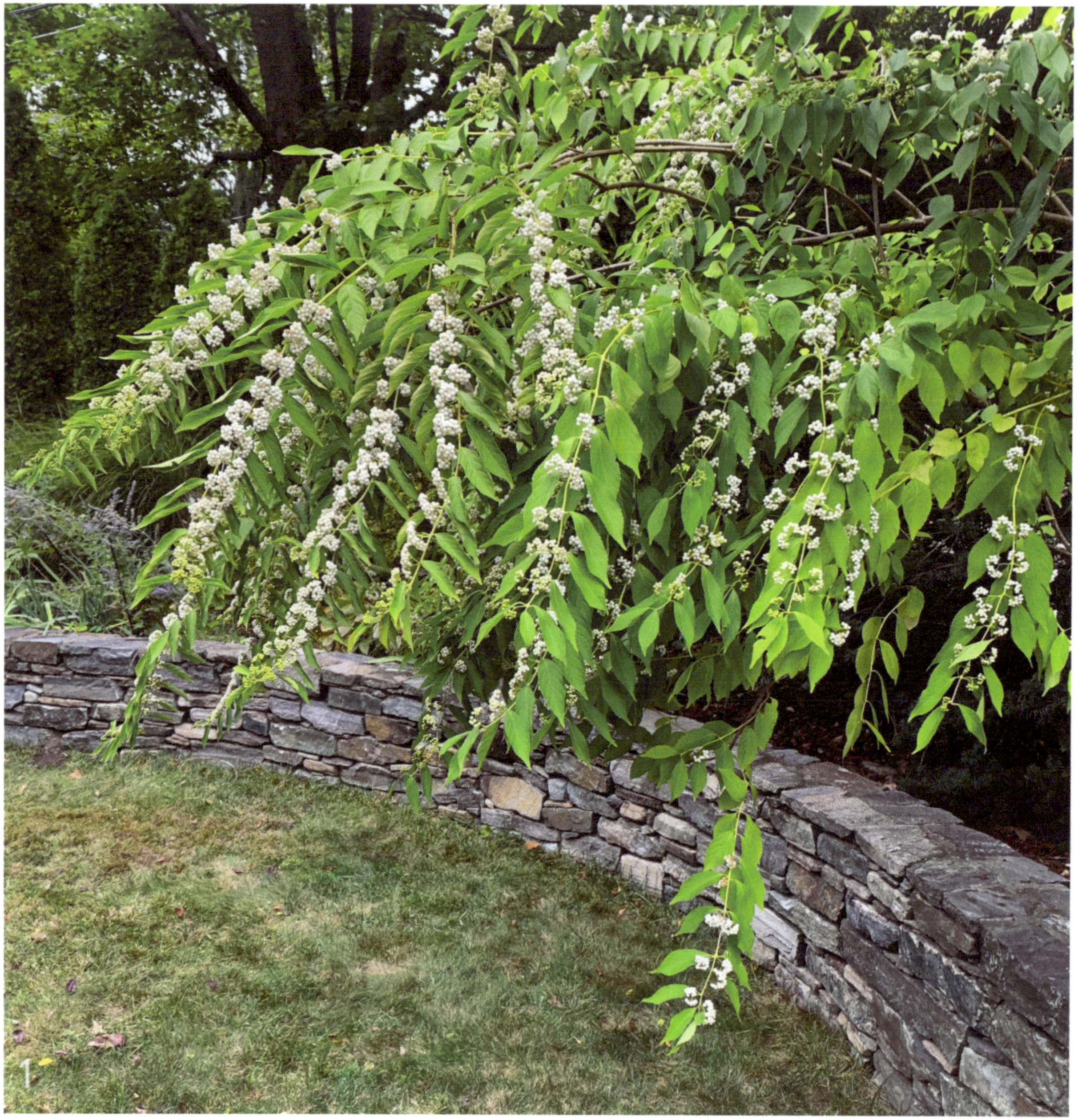

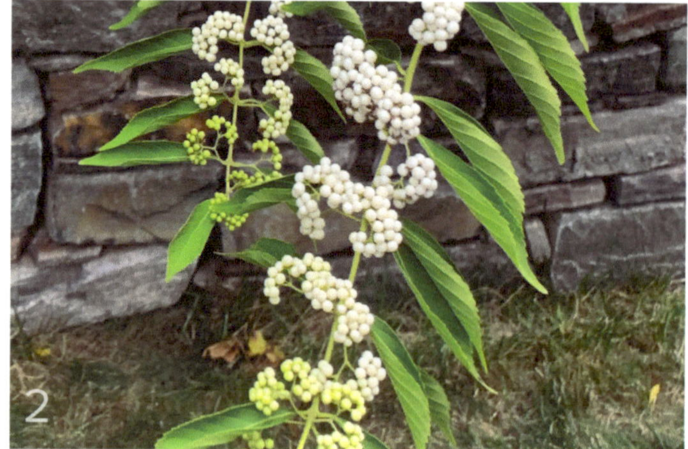

1. The white 'leucocarpa' beautyberry is not very common. I acquired mine as a gift from Harvard University's Arnold Arboretum when I joined, twenty years ago. I love it. In the fall, if it has been well watered during the summer, it has tiny white berries along each stem. I take the leaves off before I use it in arrangements.
2. Here you see the berries in a line along the branch with the leaves.
3. A miniature composition of immature berries upside-down, wedged in a shell.
4. The berries emerge from the basket, repeating its curved silhouette. The pomegranates, lily, Solomon's seal, viburnum, and miscanthus complete the mixed materials (*maze-zashi*) design.
5. In this arrangement, I imagine horses galloping off to the right with riders of hydrangeas bearing streamers of berries arching behind them.

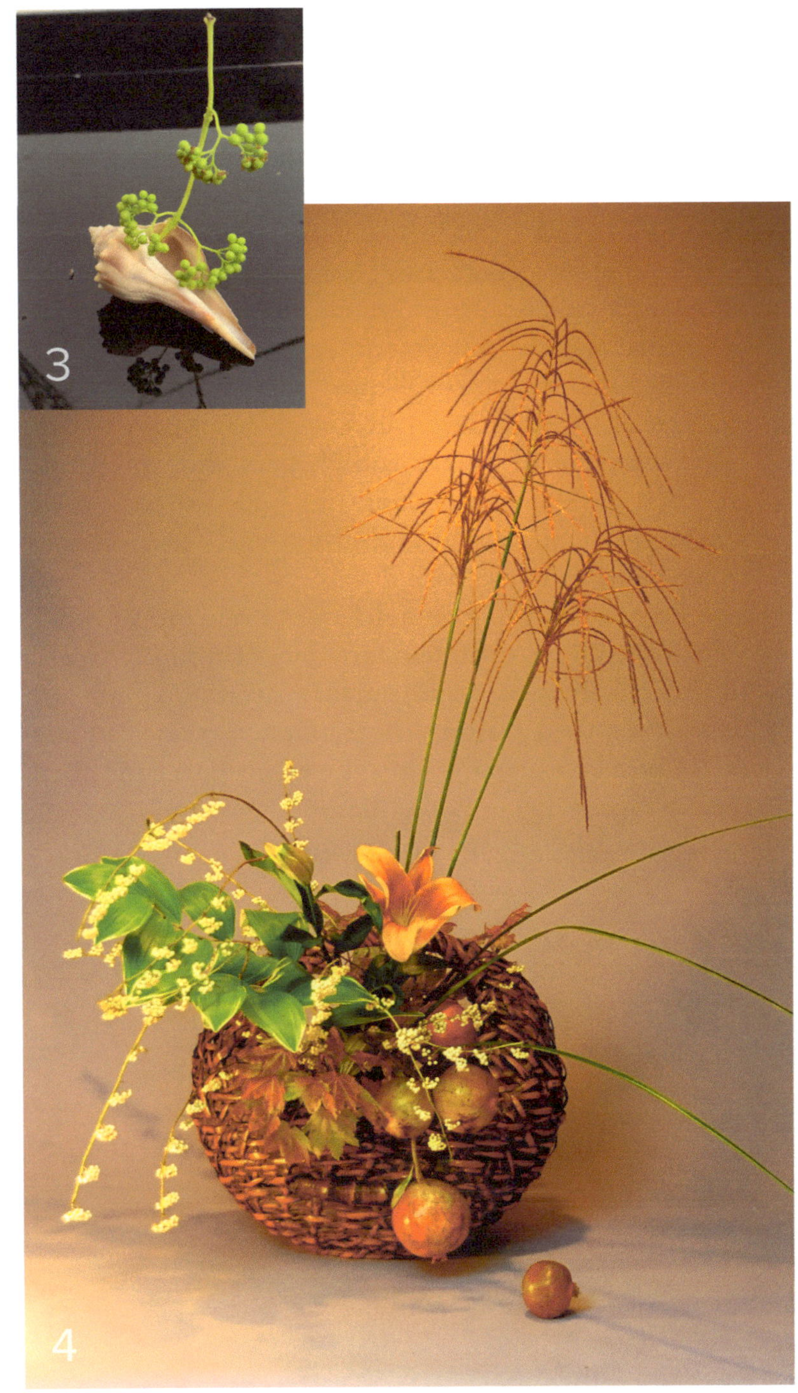

5

17

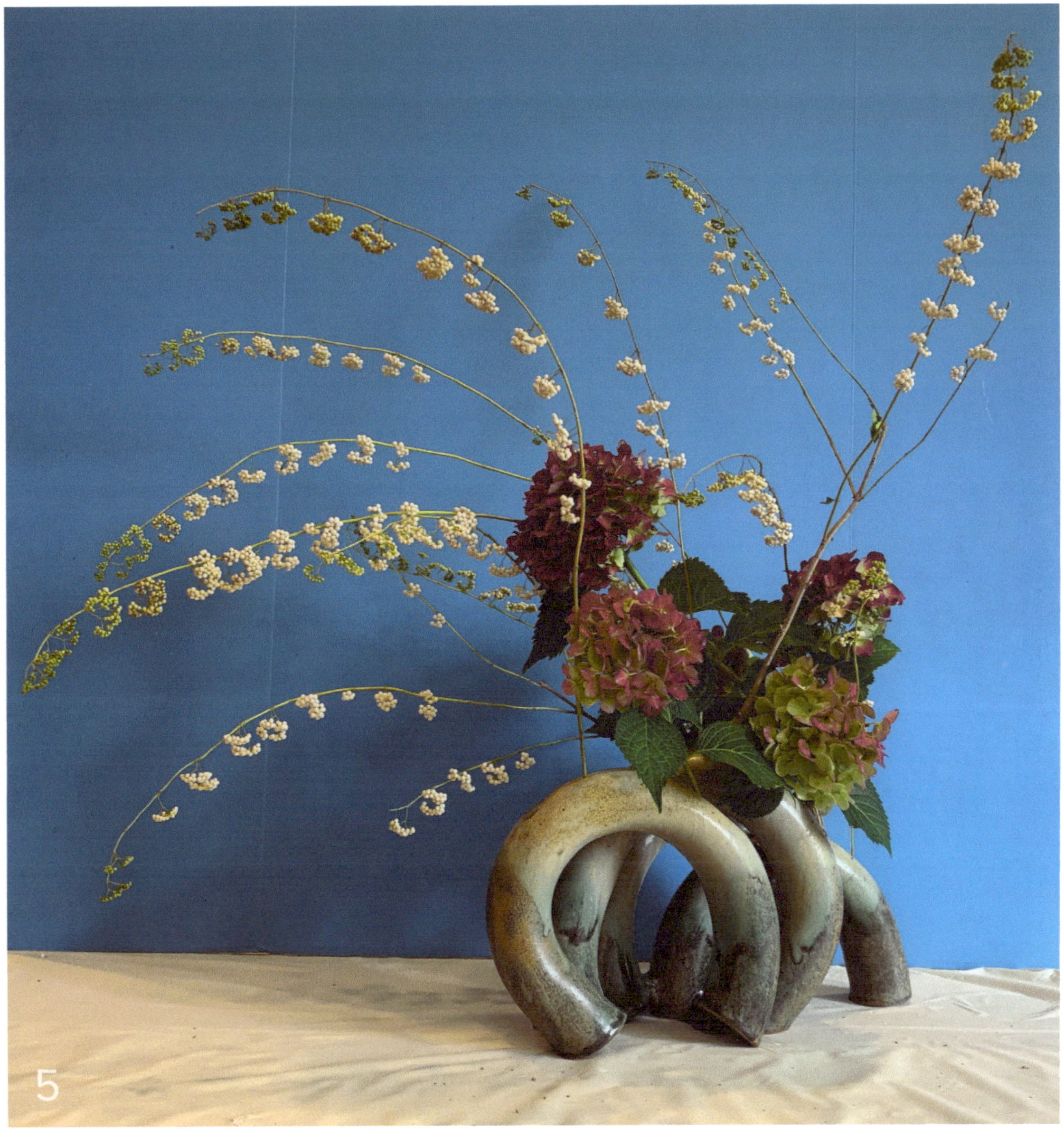

Cherry, Kwanzan   *Prunus serrulata 'Kwanzan'*

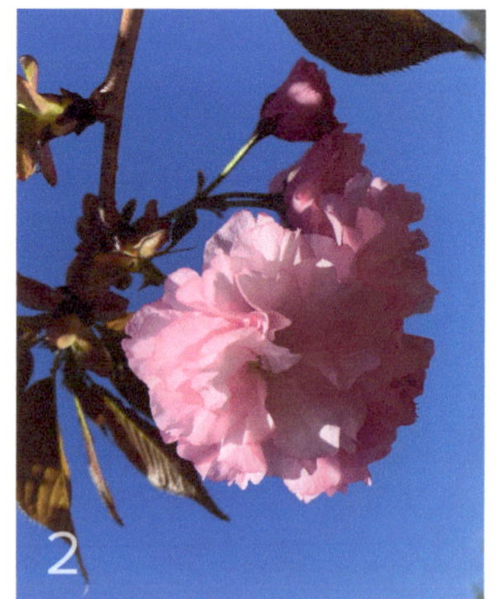

1   When a maple tree on our street died, the town kindly planted our choice of a Kwanzan cherry. Most cherry trees bloom briefly and the petals float to the ground. This tree holds its gorgeous blooms longer. The Flower Show in Boston occurs in March, when these blossoms are available in the flower market.

2   A single blossom - full of petals

3   The tree is attractive, even after the blooms have fallen.

4   Long branches of cherry complement this euonymus woody vine. Hanging amaranthus spills from the pink hydrangea, while green anthurium and ferns emerge from the water at the base.

5   This graceful budding branch carves a space to show off some calla lilies. Australian fern dances around them.

6   In this flower show arrangement featuring a giant cypress knee, the Kwanzan cherry branch creates a mass of blossoms contrasting with the empty space outlined by the cypress knee. Calla lilies, peonies, and leaves of aspidistra complete the arrangement.

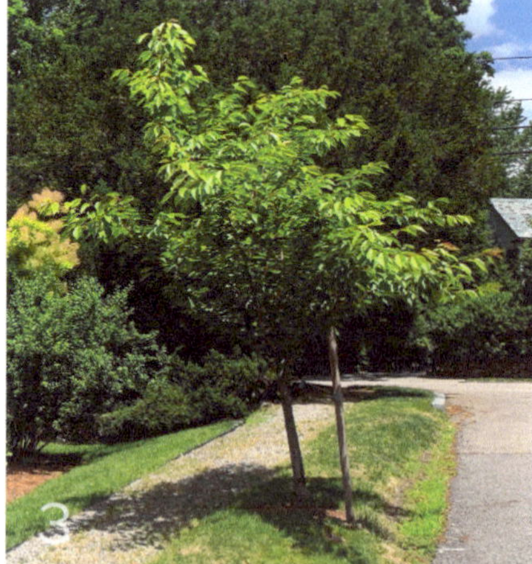

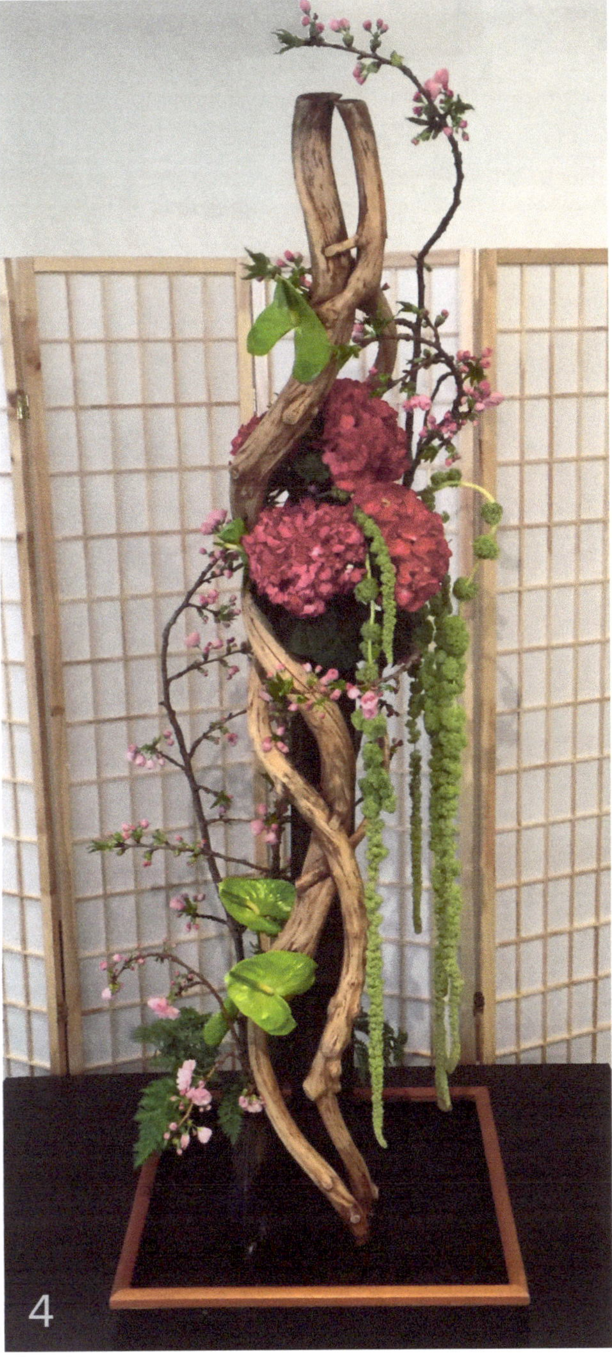

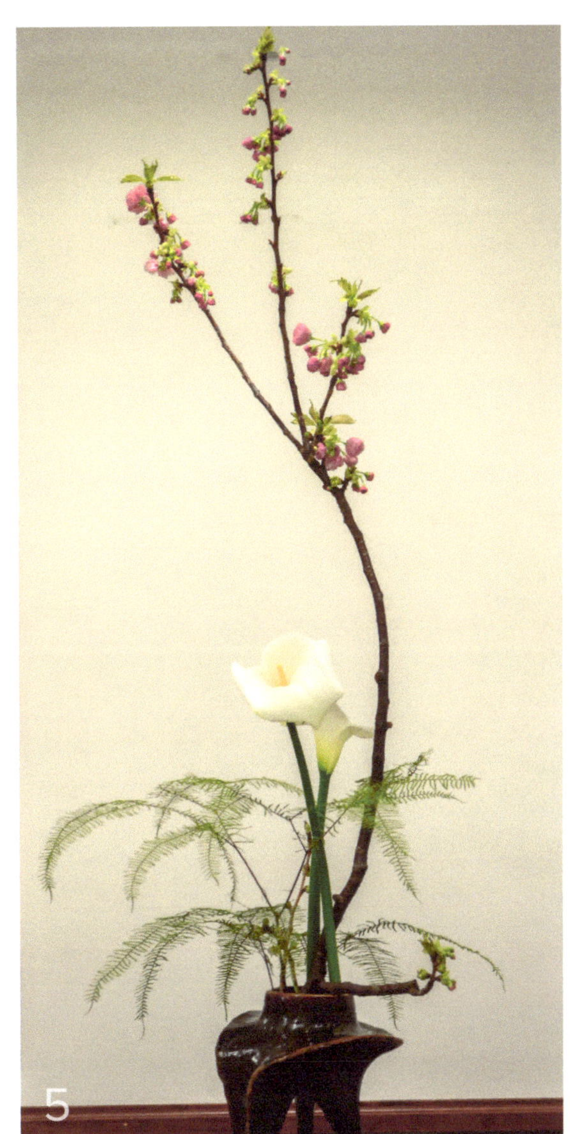

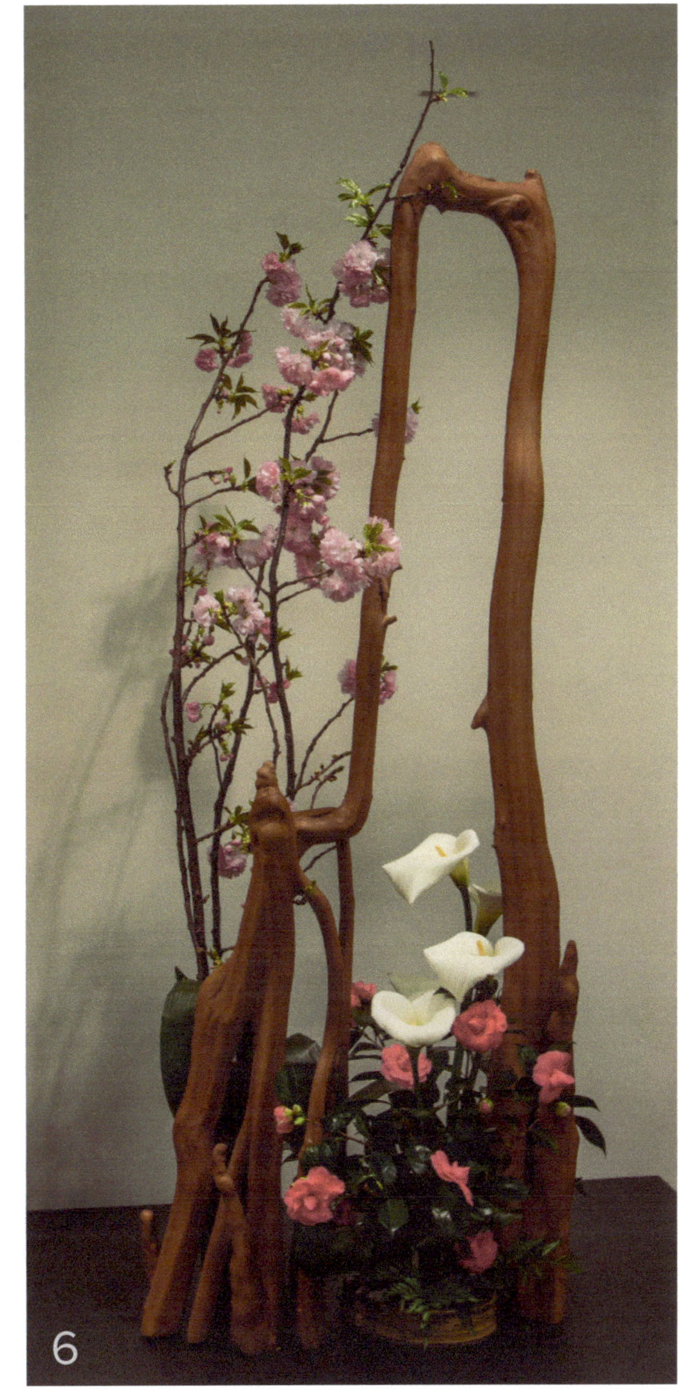

Cotoneaster

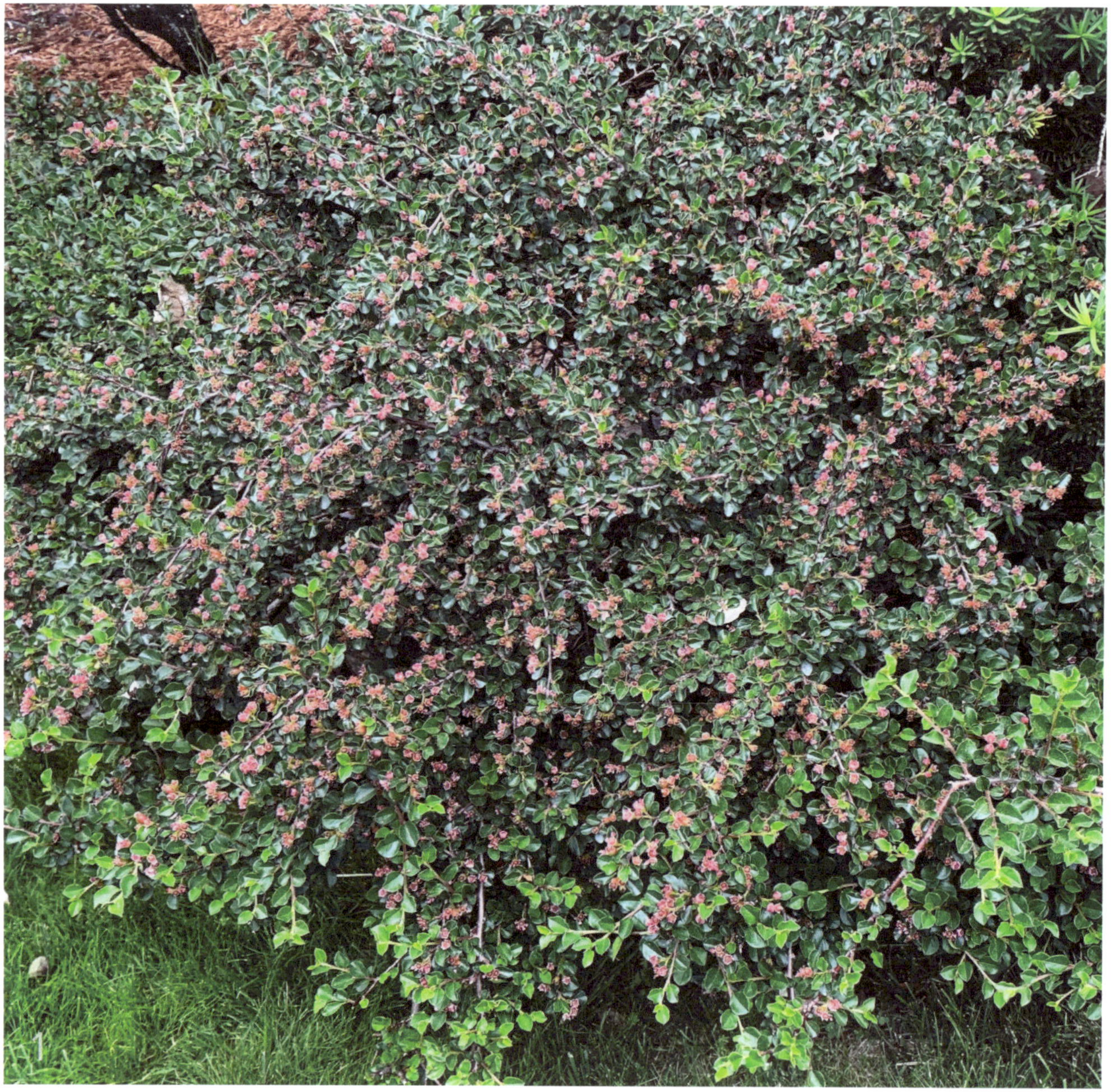

1. This low shrub can be used as a ground cover. Here you see the tiny pink blossoms in spring. Rabbits in our garden nibble on these low branches.
2. The closeup shows the red berries that develop from the blossoms.
3. This nageire is composed of one kind of material, cotoneaster. The dead branches reveal the unique branching form and contrast with the living branches. The opposing forces of yin and yang are represented here by the dead and the living branches.
4. The small leaves work well with the azalea and mountain laurel blossoms.
5. The cotoneaster branch showcases the peony bud in the basket.

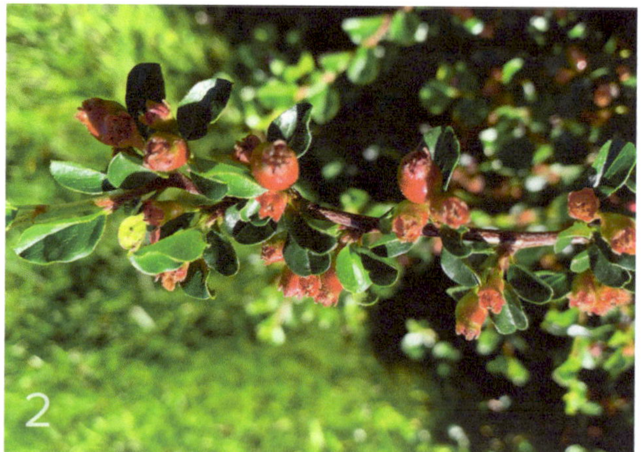

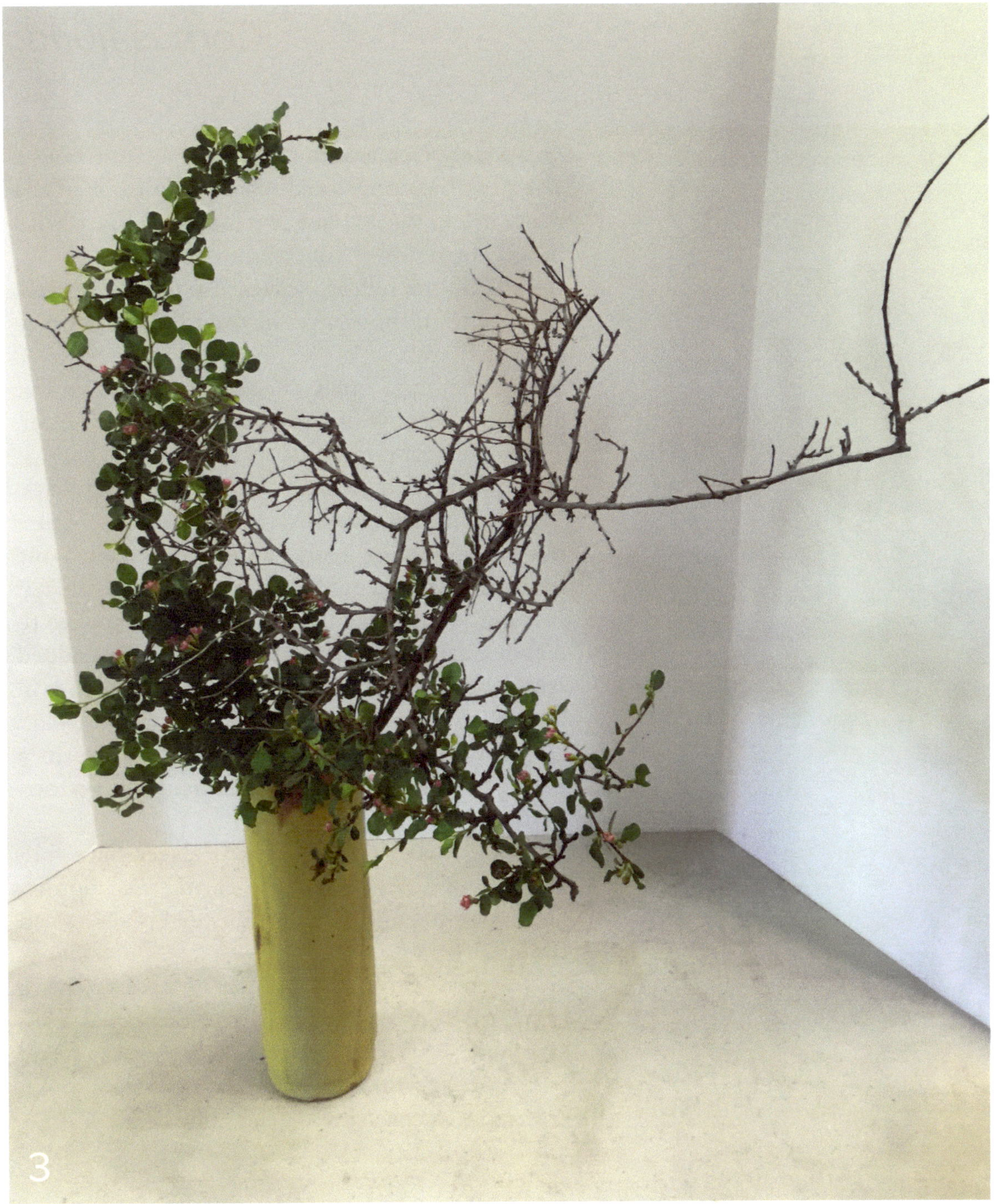

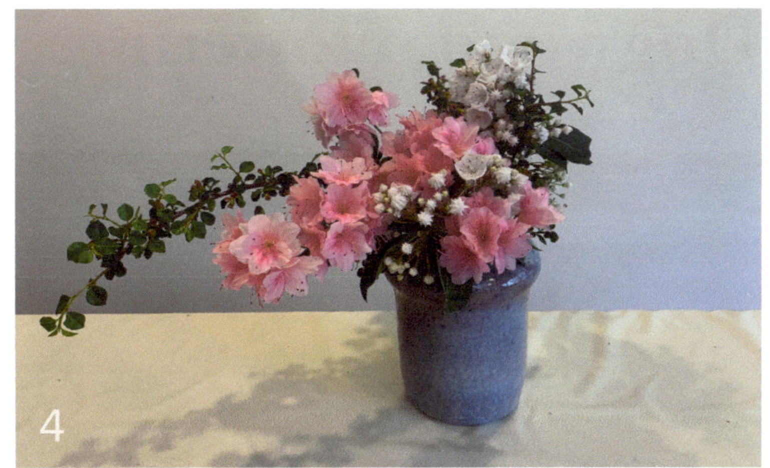

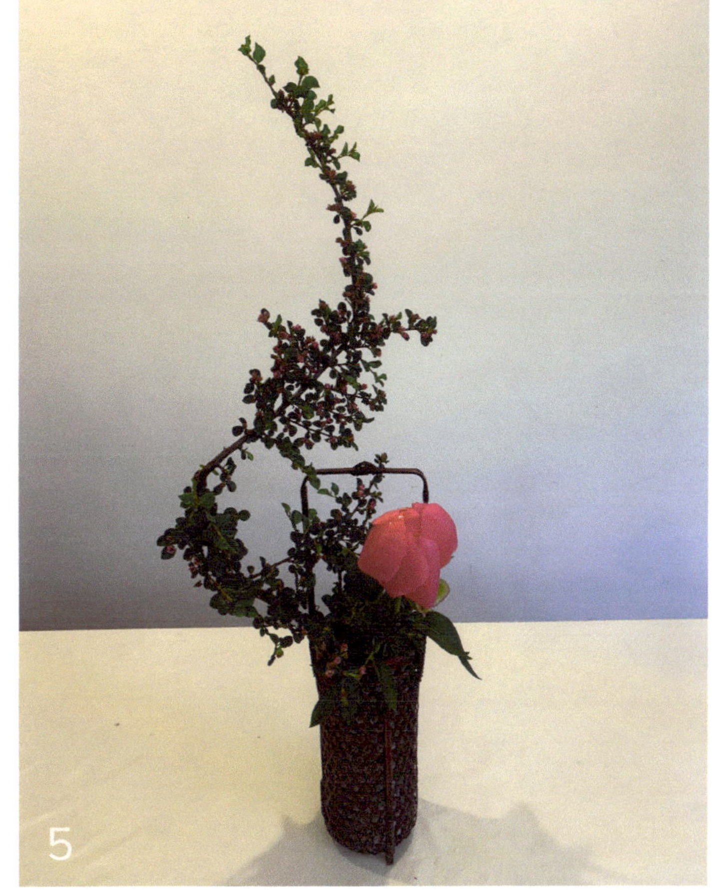

Dogwood, Flowering *Cornus florida*

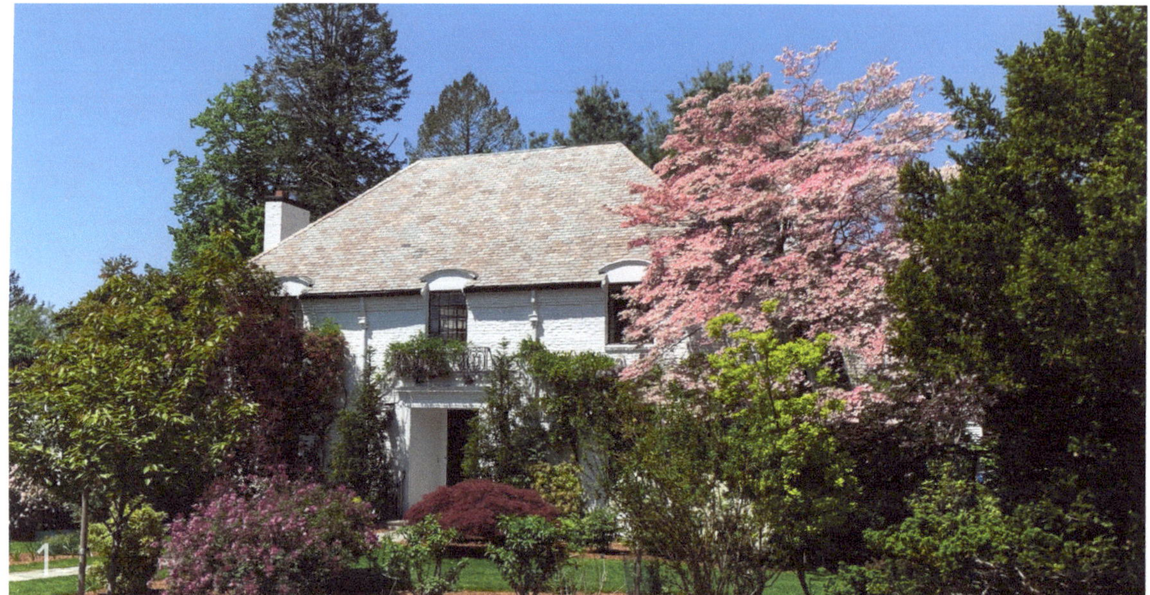

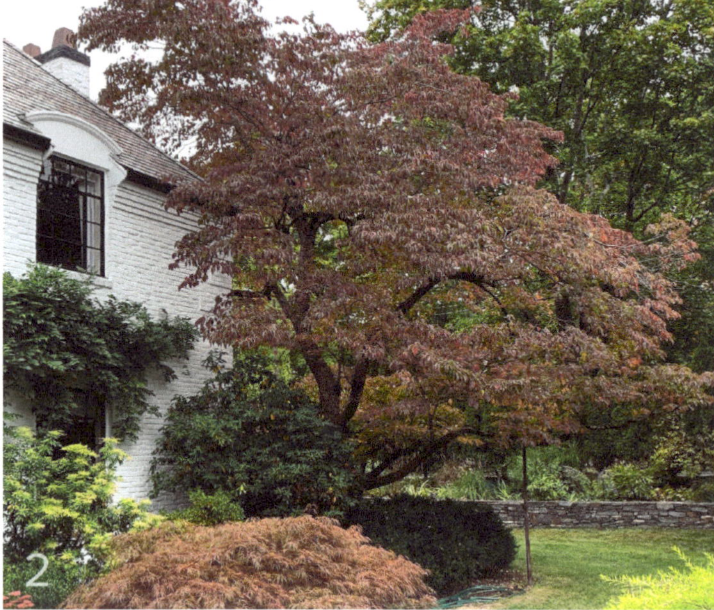

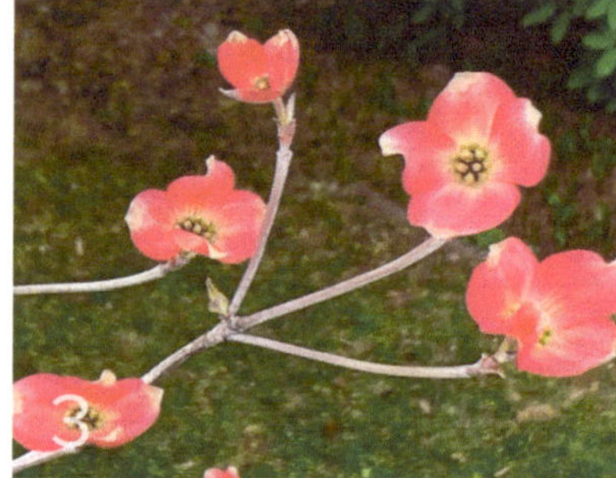

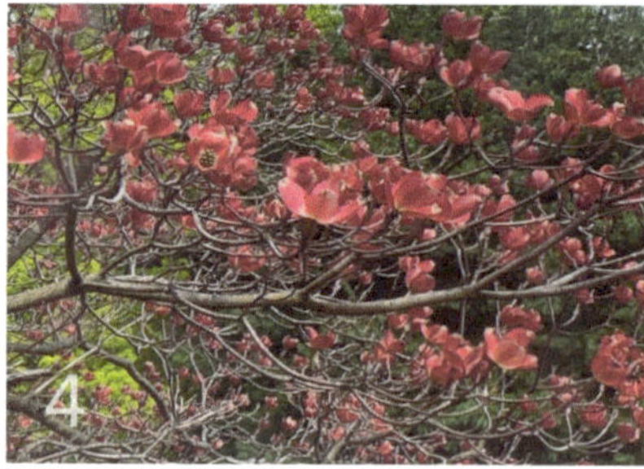

1. This lovely tree graces the corner of our house. The pink blossoms look beautiful in front of the white brick. We do have to treat it every year with fungicide to prevent anthracnose.

2. In the fall, the reddish leaves also provide a great contrast to the house. We have added a support to a heavy branch.

3. When they first open, the four bracts are a hot pink and the tiny flowers' buds are in the center. The flowers emerge before the leaves.

4. They form a rich pink cloud in early spring.

5. This floor arrangement has a metal structure that is supporting a large woody euonymus vine that my husband removed from the tree that it surrounded. We took our dogwood branches to North Carolina for this exhibition. I have added coral charm peonies and enkianthus branches in bloom.

6. Dogwood branches provide graceful lines in a basic slanting ikebana arrangement with peony buds.

7. The dogwood branches whose leaves have fallen are interconnected to form a sculpture. Spray-painted allium and milkweed pods rest on the limbs.

8. A flowering dogwood branch contrasts with a branch cut last winter that still has dried buds attached. Peonies balance the design. Yin and yang appear in many Asian arrangements, often referred to as two sides of the same coin.

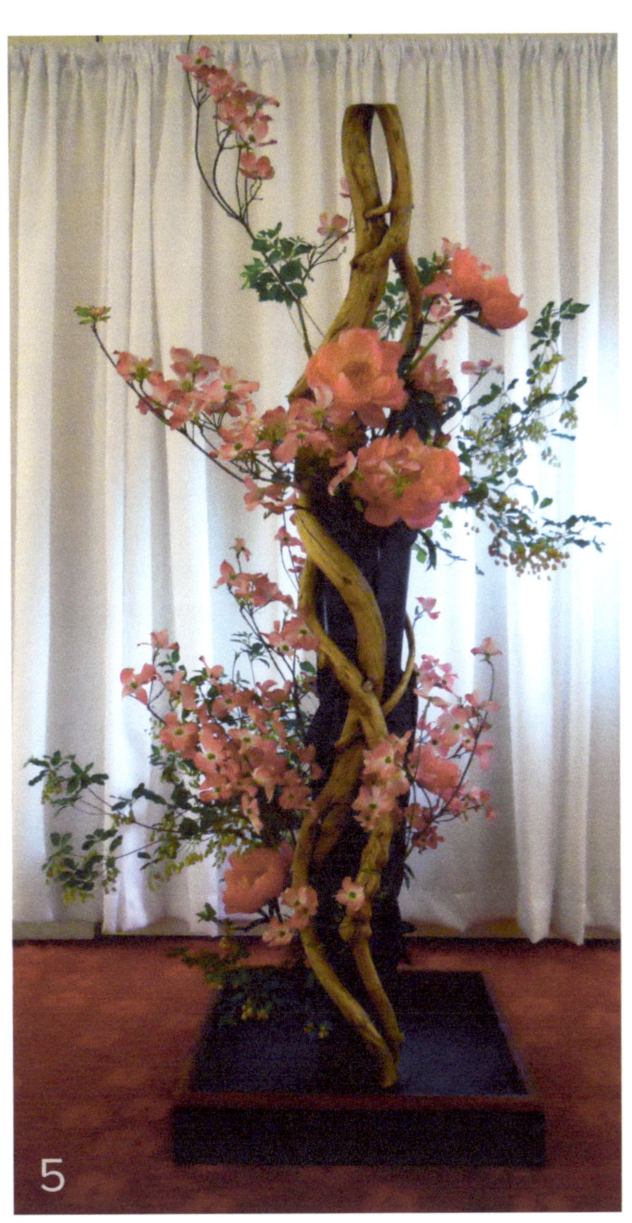

5

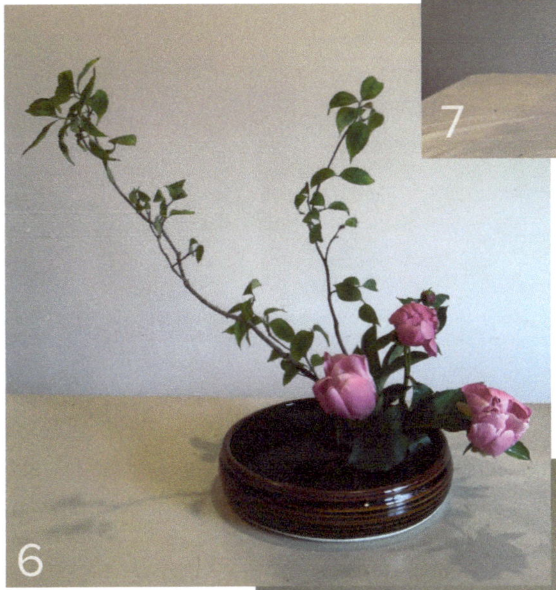

6

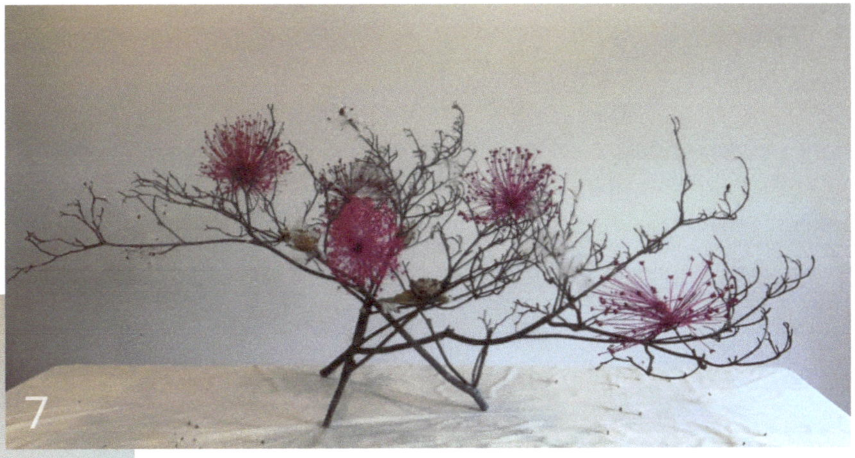

7

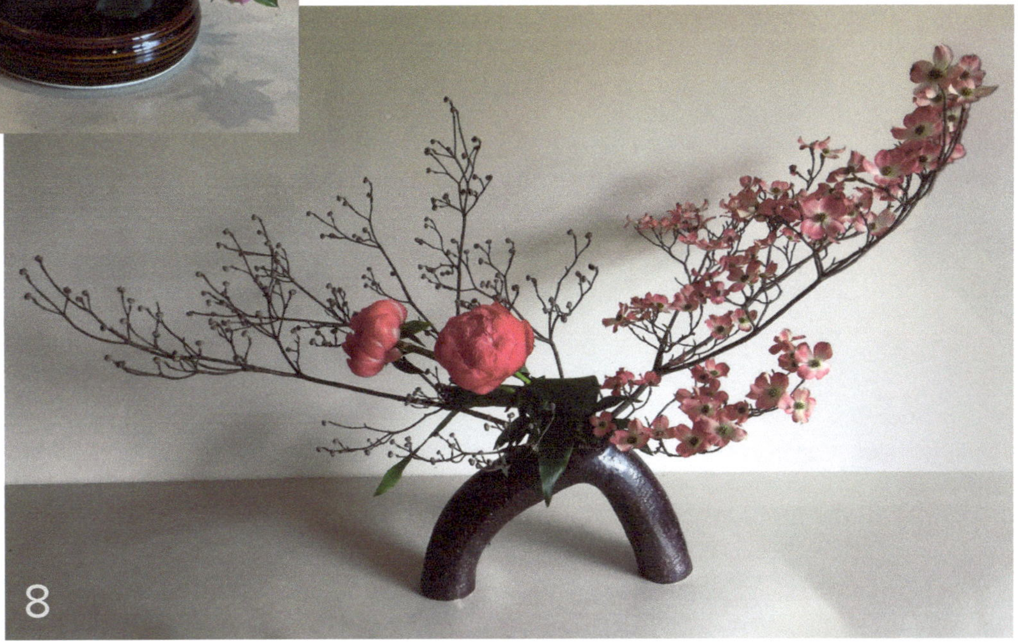

8

Dogwood, Kousa   *Cornus kousa*

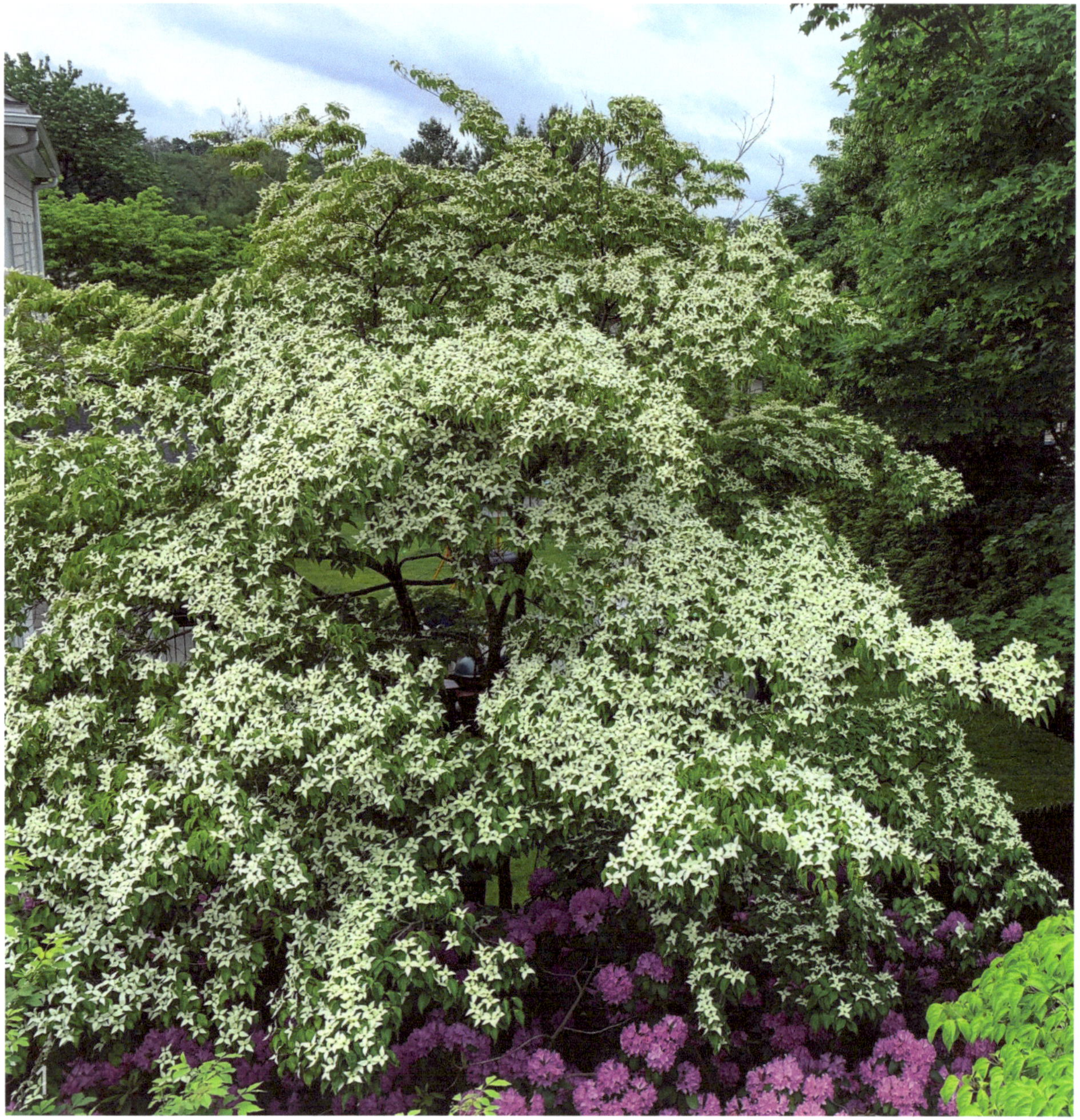

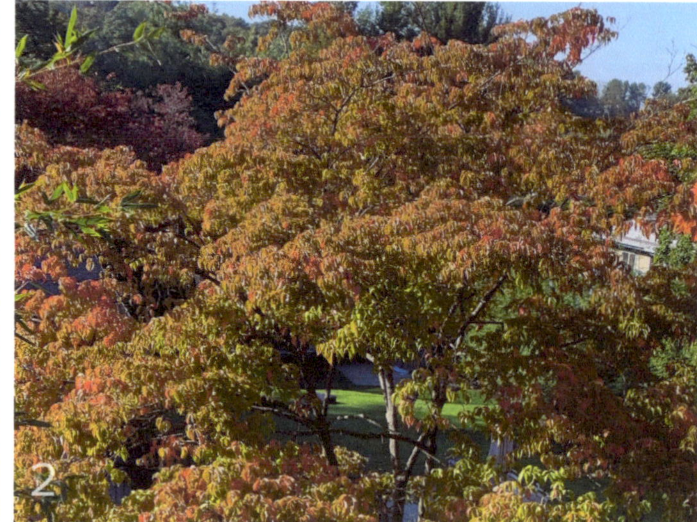

1   This dogwood blooms later than the *florida* species and after the leaves have opened; it usually blooms in June for us. The pointed bracts differentiate it from the rounded bracts of *C. florida*.
2   The leaves turn a lovely hue in the fall and the red balls of fruit hang, tempting the squirrels.
3   I noticed the orange and white swirls in this Iwata glass container designed by Akane Teshigahara, the headmaster of the Sogetsu School. I used my kousa dogwood and some orange roses to build a design that complimented the container.
4   Here, smoketree and peony are added to the dogwood to give a rich timeless look in the Japanese lacquer and gold containers.
5   A gorgeous branch showcases the large allium in this tall container.

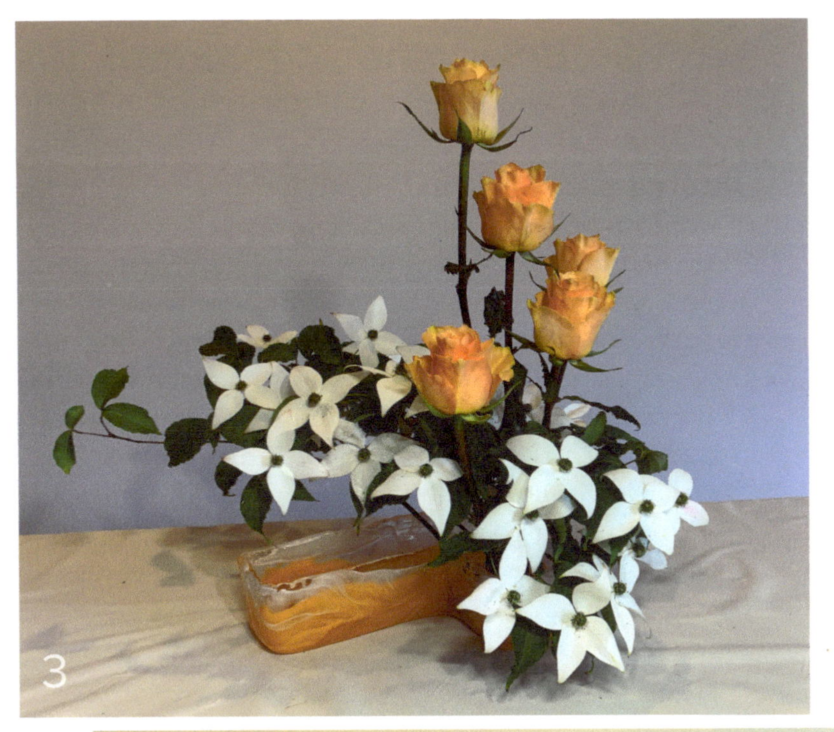

3

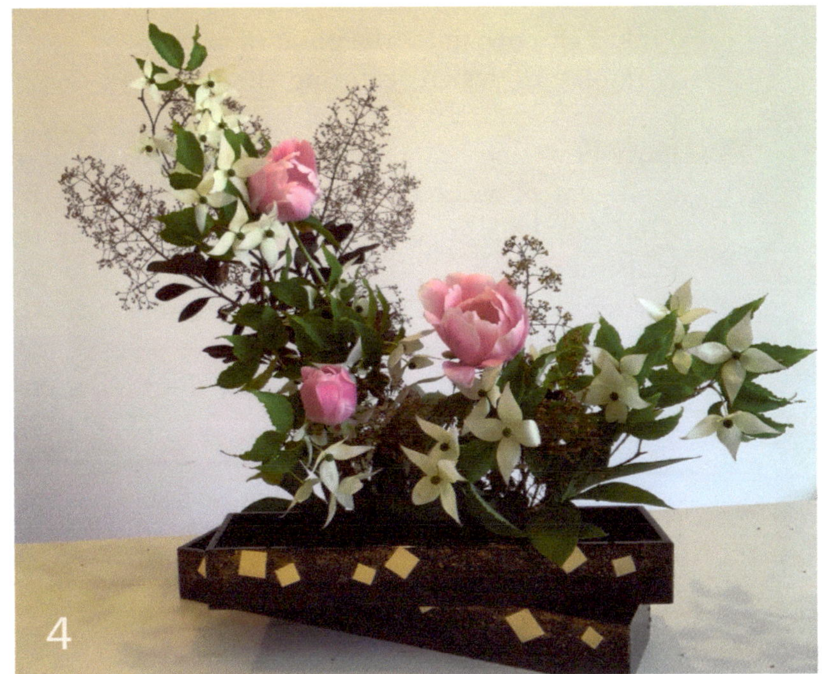

4

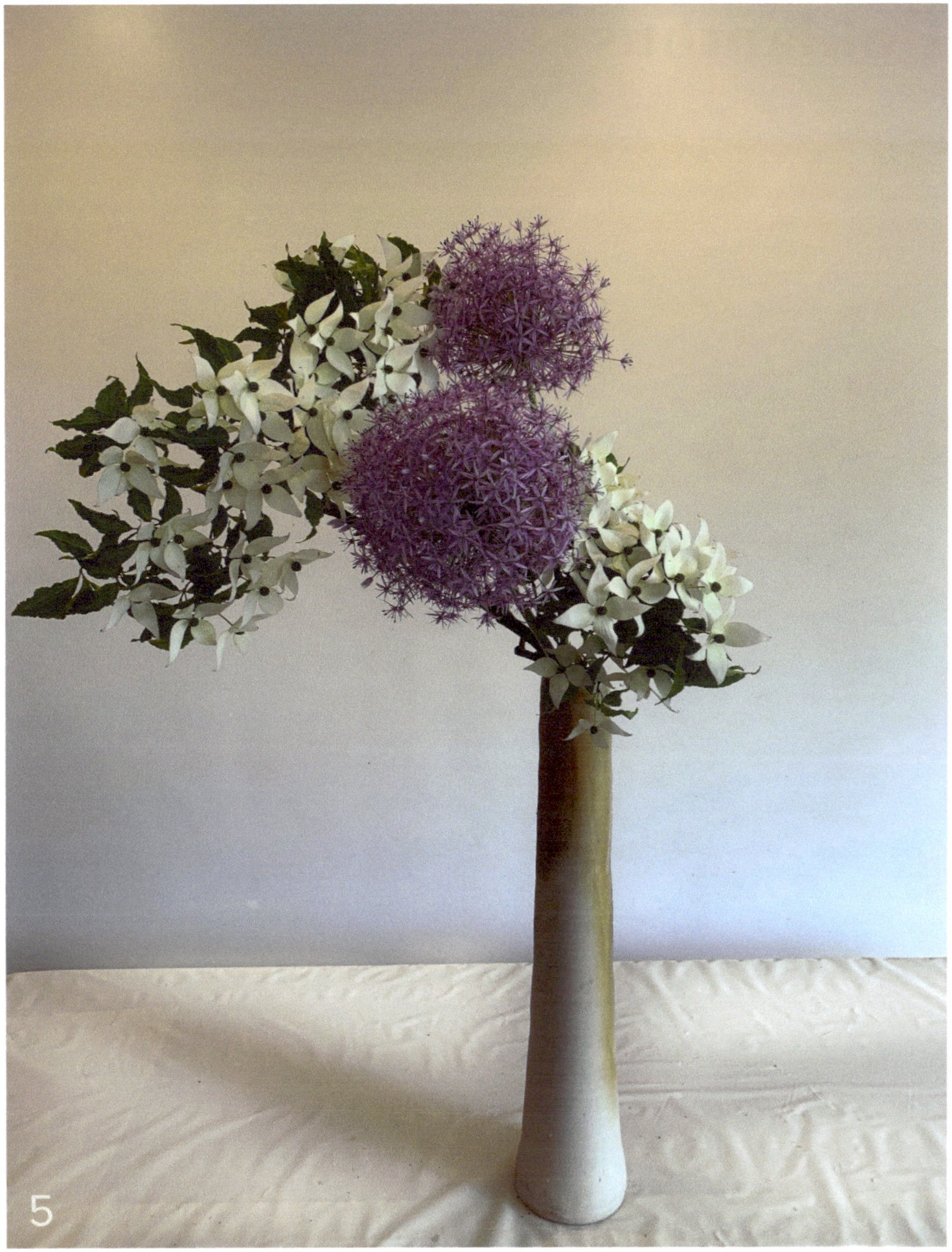

5

Enkianthus

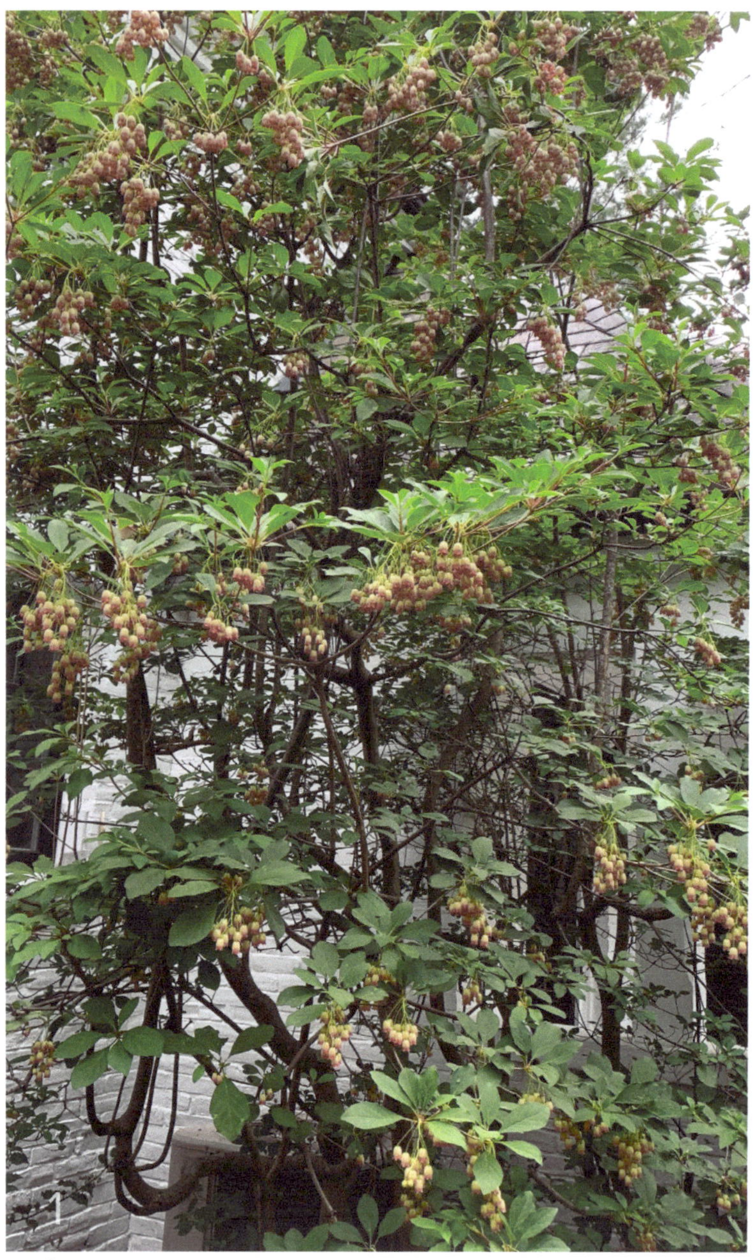

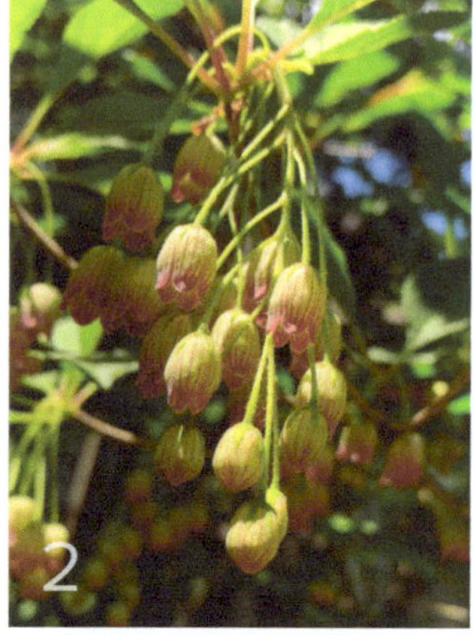

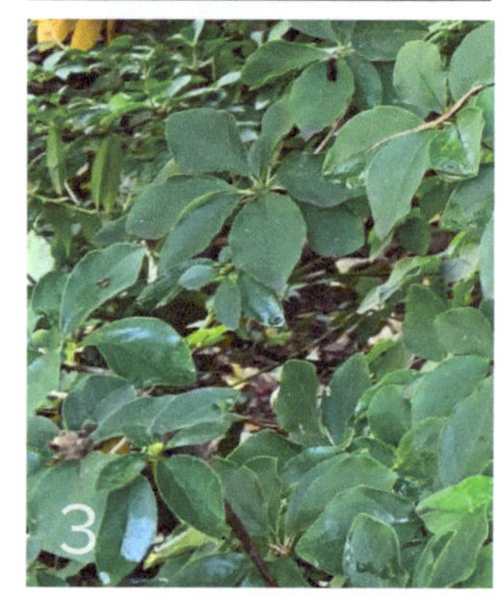

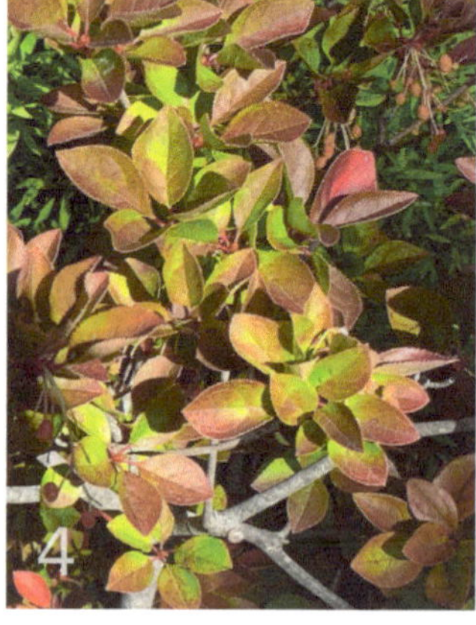

1. One of my enkianthus shrubs grows just outside my kitchen window. In the spring I watch, to my delight, the tiny cream and pink bells open with a whirl of leaves above them. I need to cut and arrange them soon because they are very sweet-smelling and, I suspect, sweet-tasting too. The squirrels and chipmunks climb up and feast on them if I don't get to them first. I was introduced to this plant in Japan when the Headmaster of the Sogetsu School created a large autumn floor arrangement. The fall color can be outstanding. The architecture of the plant is quite unusual, with radiating swirls of branches and leaves.
2. The tiny bells have a pink fringe on the edge.
3. The whirl of leaflets.
4. Fall colors on the leaves.
5. The angles of the branches echo the angular container. Pink azalea decorates the point of origin.
6. A miniature design featuring the bells and one azalea blossom.
7. Early flowering branches form a tripod to stand in this arrangement without a kenzan.
8. Abundant bells are balanced by a peony in a freestyle arrangement.
9. I created this design in an ikebana demonstration at the Museum of Fine Arts, Boston, using peonies and the graceful enkianthus branches after their blossoms had fallen.

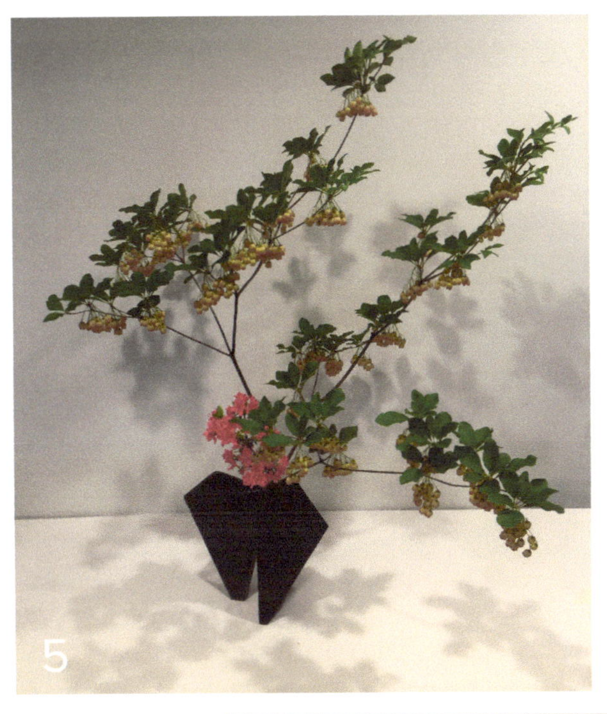
5

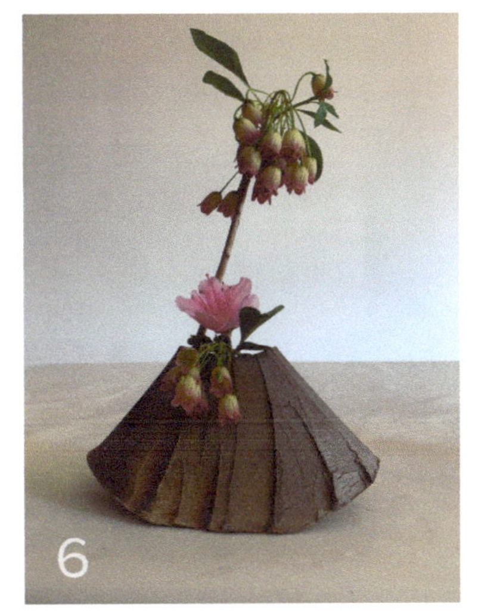
6

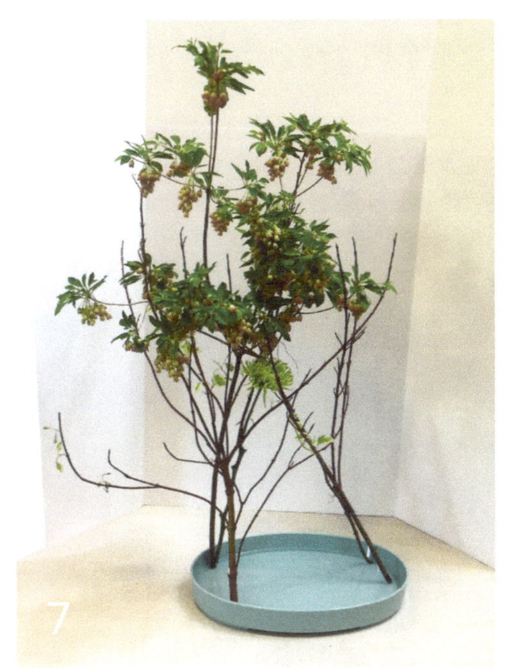
7

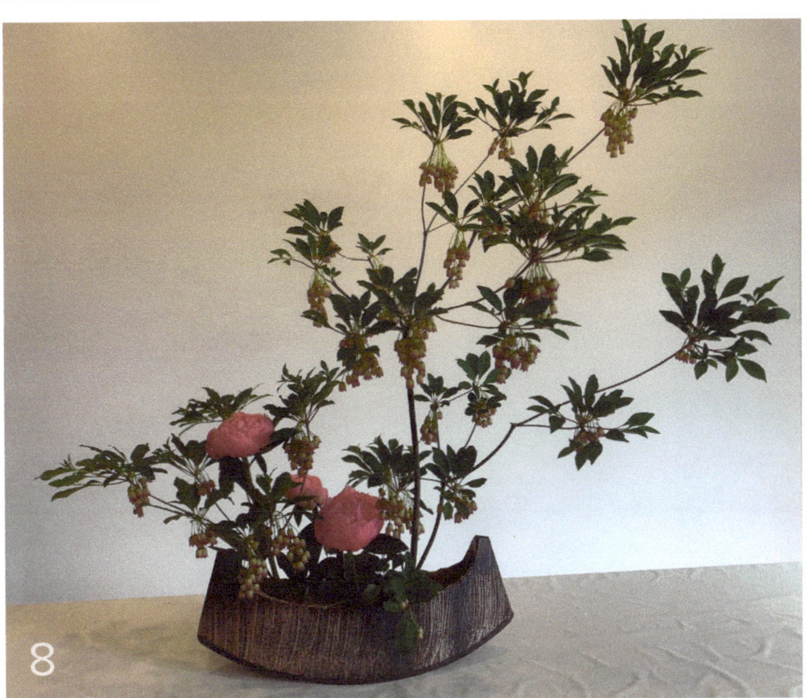
8

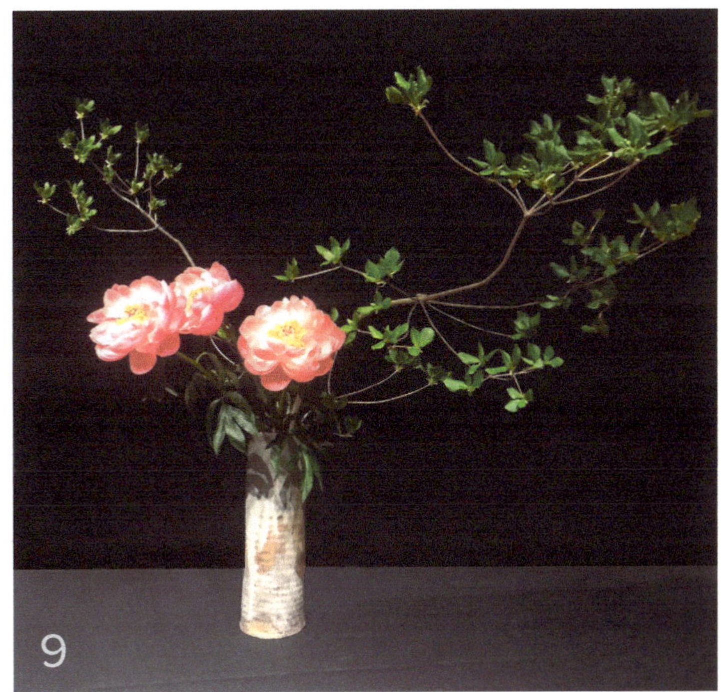
9

Forsythia, Show Off

1   This is a very common shrub. I found ours in a garden center; it stood out as having brighter and denser flowers. It has proved a vigorous grower. It is planted in the sun, but forsythias can bloom even in partial shade. I like it because I can use it all year. The branches are straight or curved and sometimes an interesting combination. The stems are a bit hollow and they work well in oasis and kenzans. Forsythia grows rapidly so I never mind trimming it for use in arrangements. I have never had problems with insects or disease. In the spring the yellow flowers last for almost a month; during the summer the green leaves outline the branches. In the fall, the color can change to mahogany; in January and February, I can force branches after a warm spell and if I cut them, bring them into the house and put them in water. In a few weeks, the flowers will burst into bloom.

2   A singular blossom.

3   Fall color tints the leaves.

4   Forsythia with allium, whose round shapes echo the holes in the container.

5   Fall color in forsythia can be beautiful. Here I have combined it with peegee hydrangea and dried orange maple leaves in an orange container.

6   This Japanese basket holds forsythia, green chrysanthemums, iris, aster and Boston fern. Notice how the lavender paper parasol accessory balances the purple iris on the other side of the arrangement.

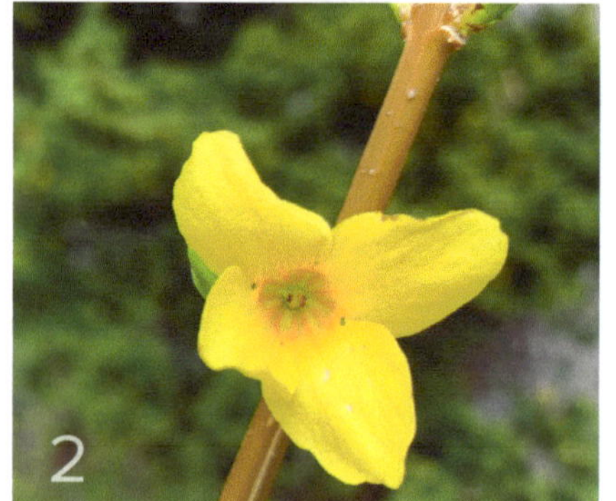

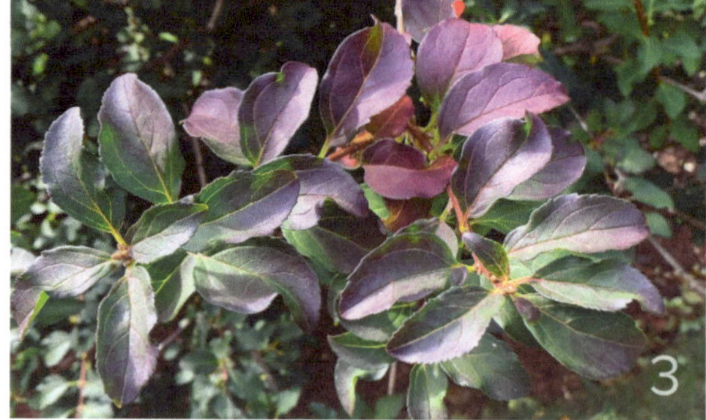

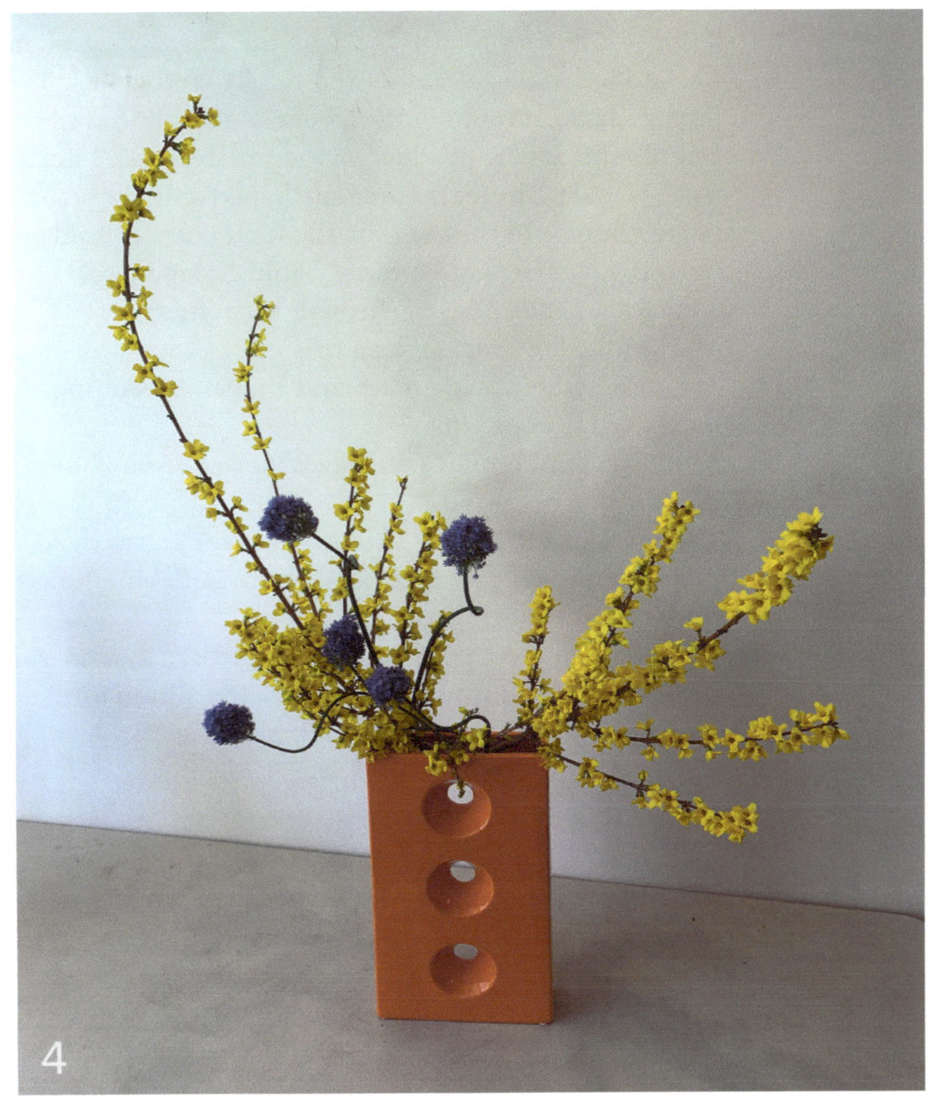

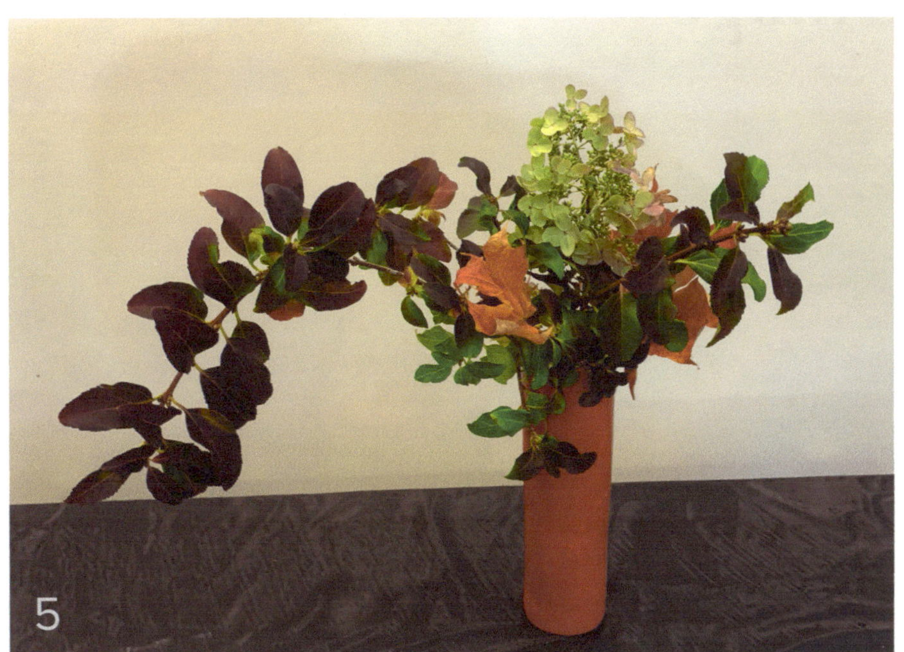

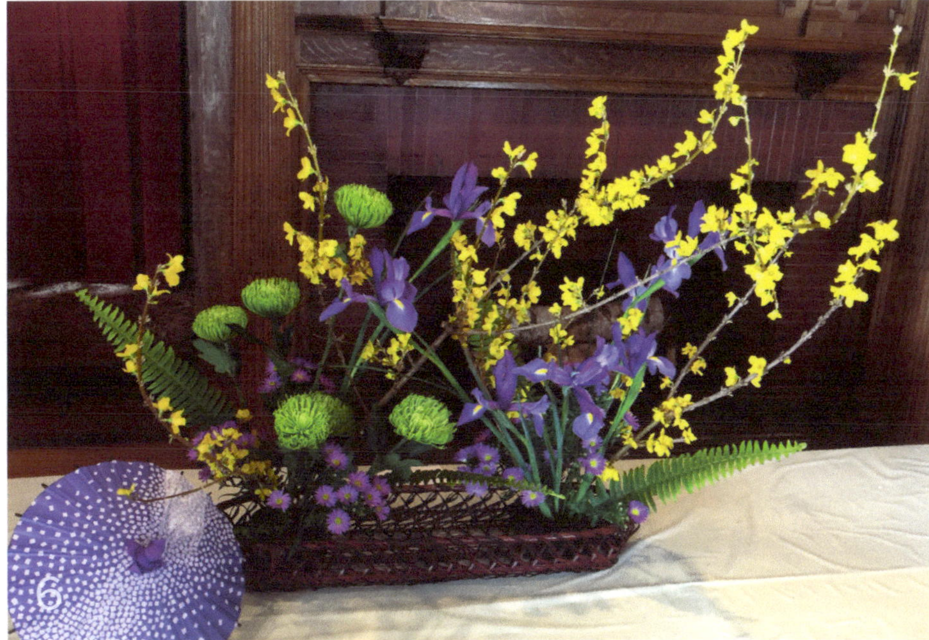

Ginkgo

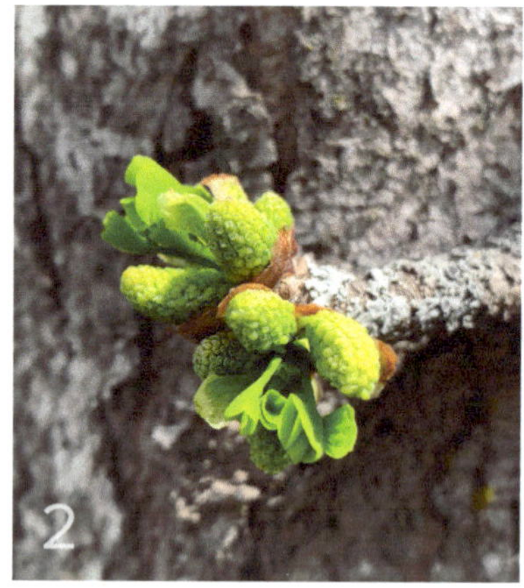

1 Ginkgo biloba is considered a living fossil. It evolved before flowering plants and it is the only living member of its division, class, order, family, and genus. Two hundred and seventy million-year-old fossils have been found. The female produces large smelly fruits. Luckily, mine is male. The leaves are fan-shaped and the branches are knobby. In the autumn, the leaves turn to gold and fall quickly. The name means "bank" in Japanese.

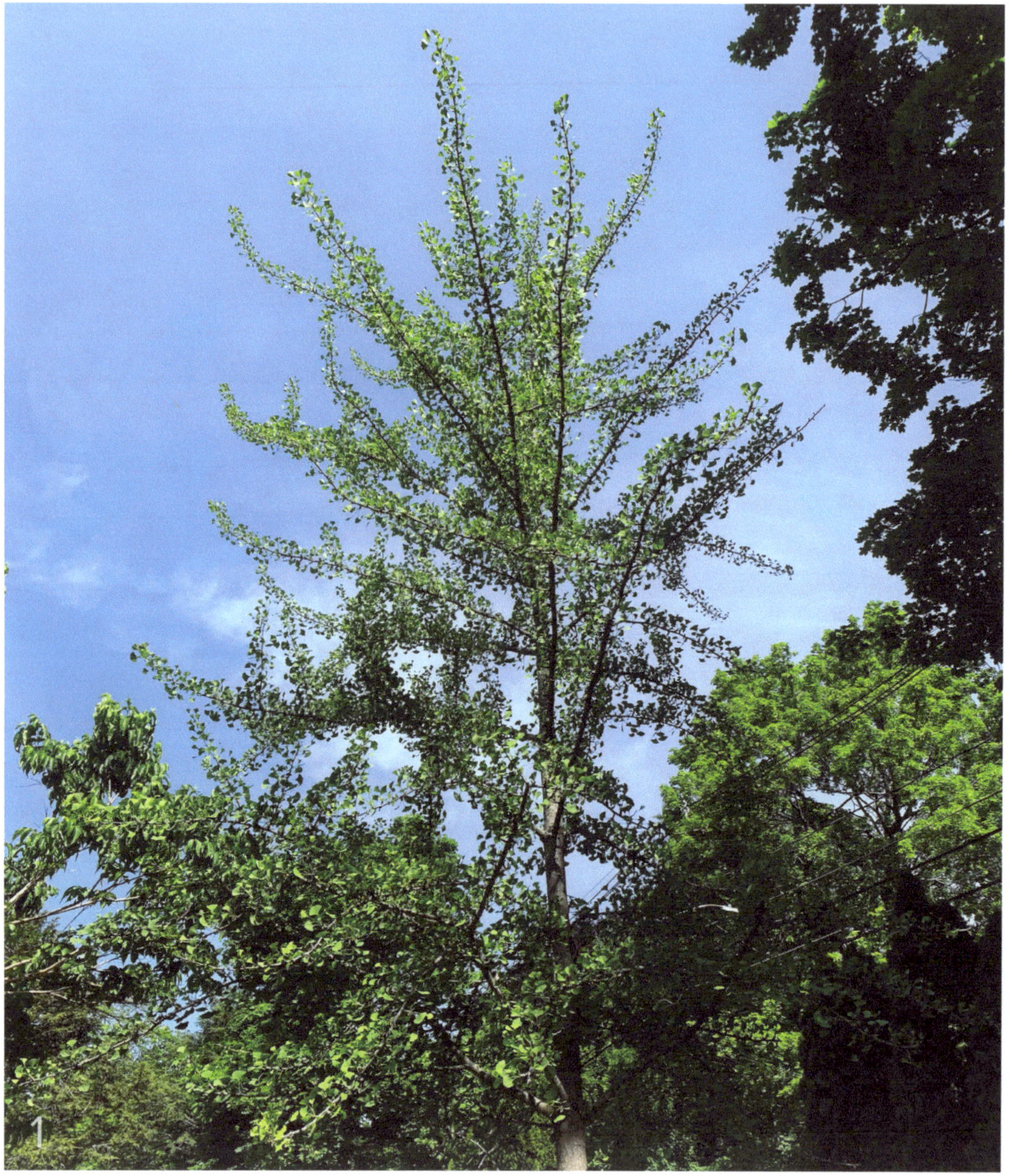

2 Tiny leaves and cones of the male tree emerge.

3 The unique fan shape of a leaf.

4 An arrangement with roses and branches echoing the rhythm of the container.

5 A miniature design of tiny leaves viewed from above. A kiwi vine surrounds it.

6 The branches with tiny sprouting leaves are wedged in this many-holed container along with hellebore flowers from the early spring garden.

7 The leaves dance along the graceful branches in this variation two slanting style nageire. The allium form exclamation points in the center of interest.

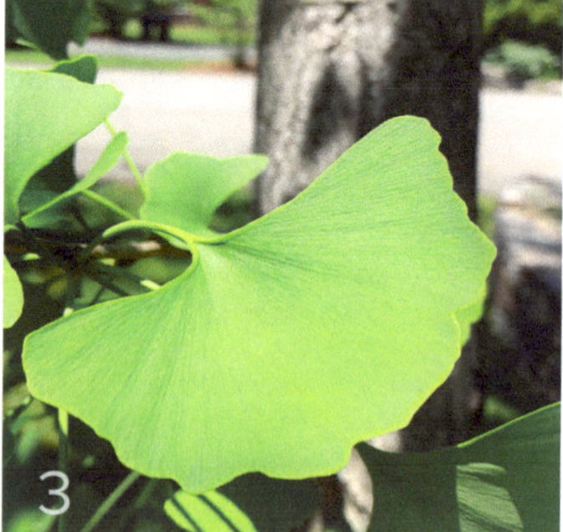

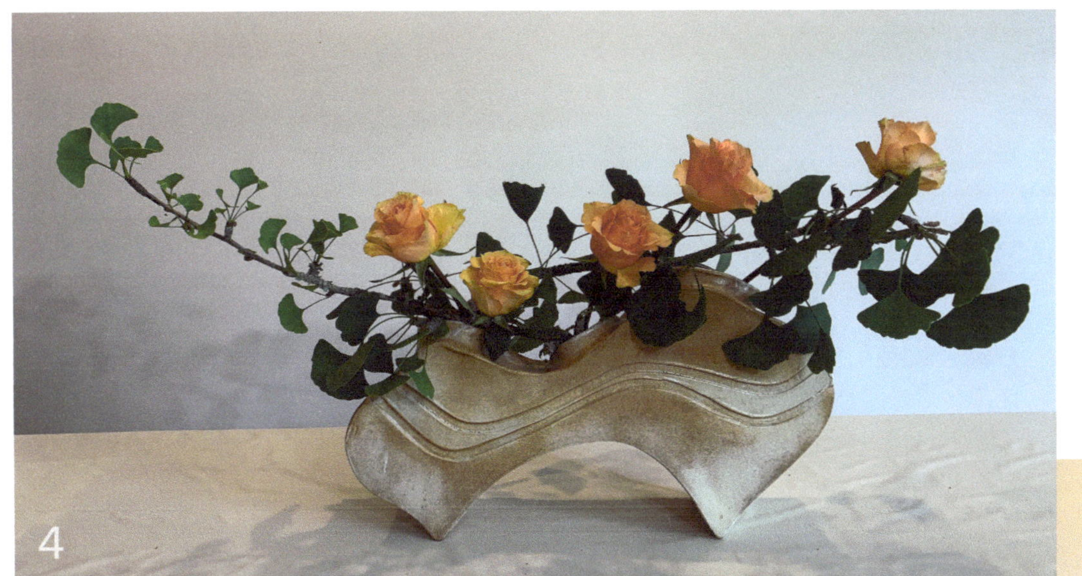

4

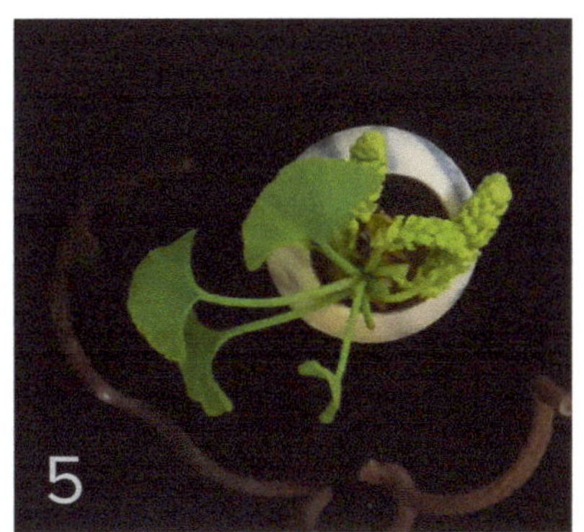

5

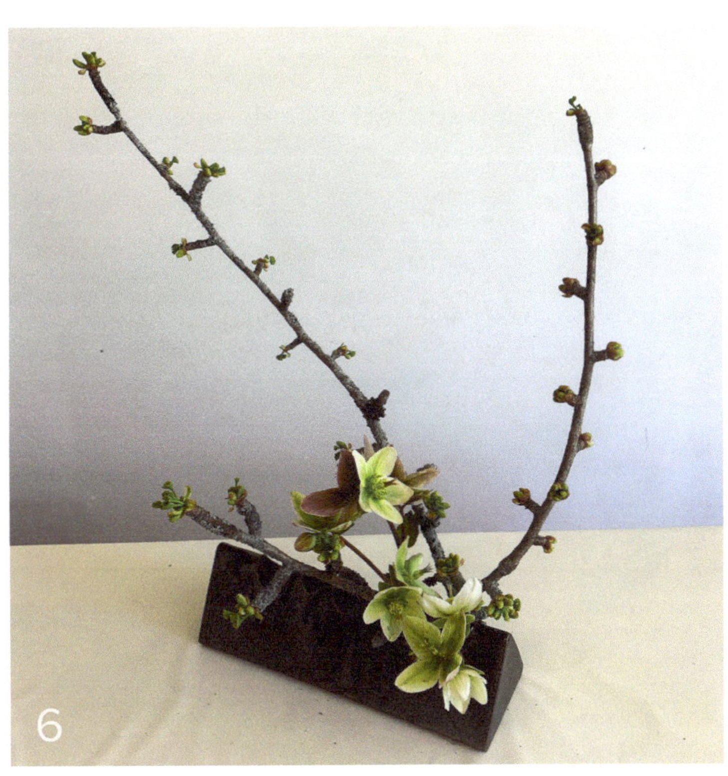

6

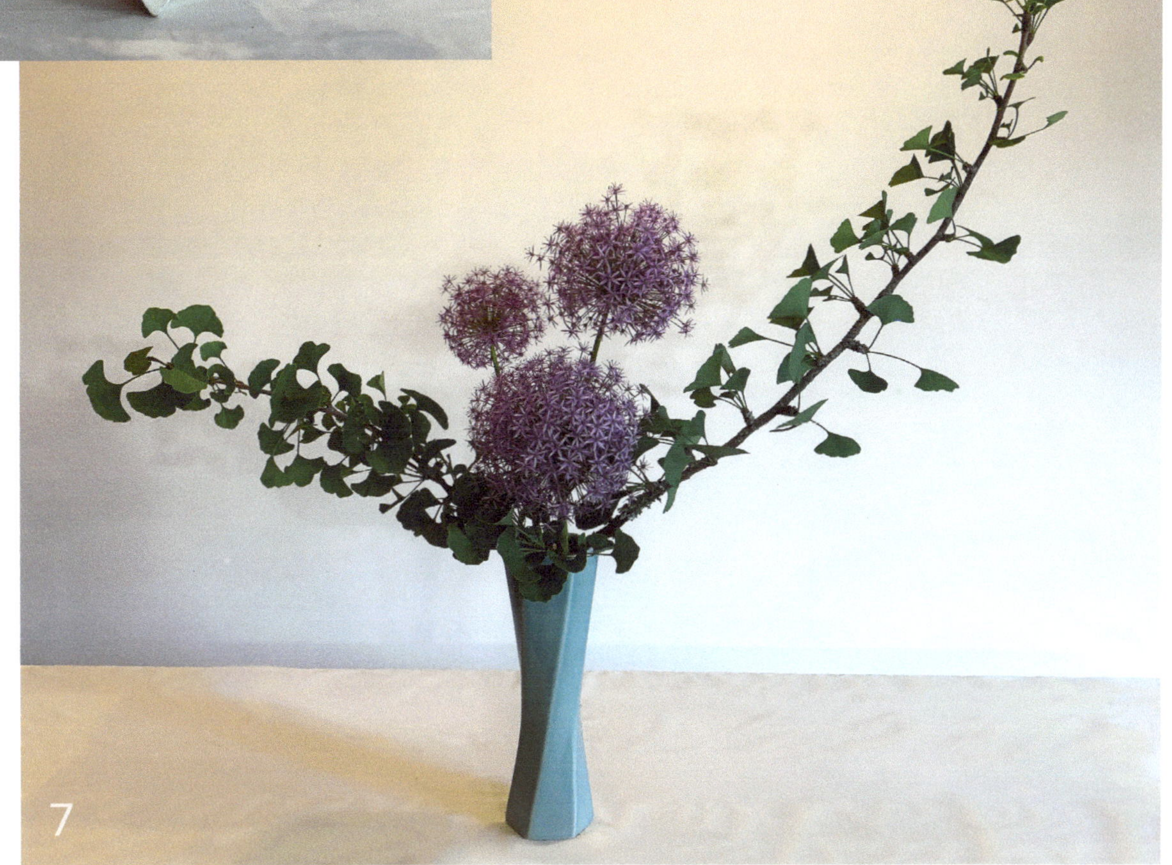

7

Grass, Miscanthus

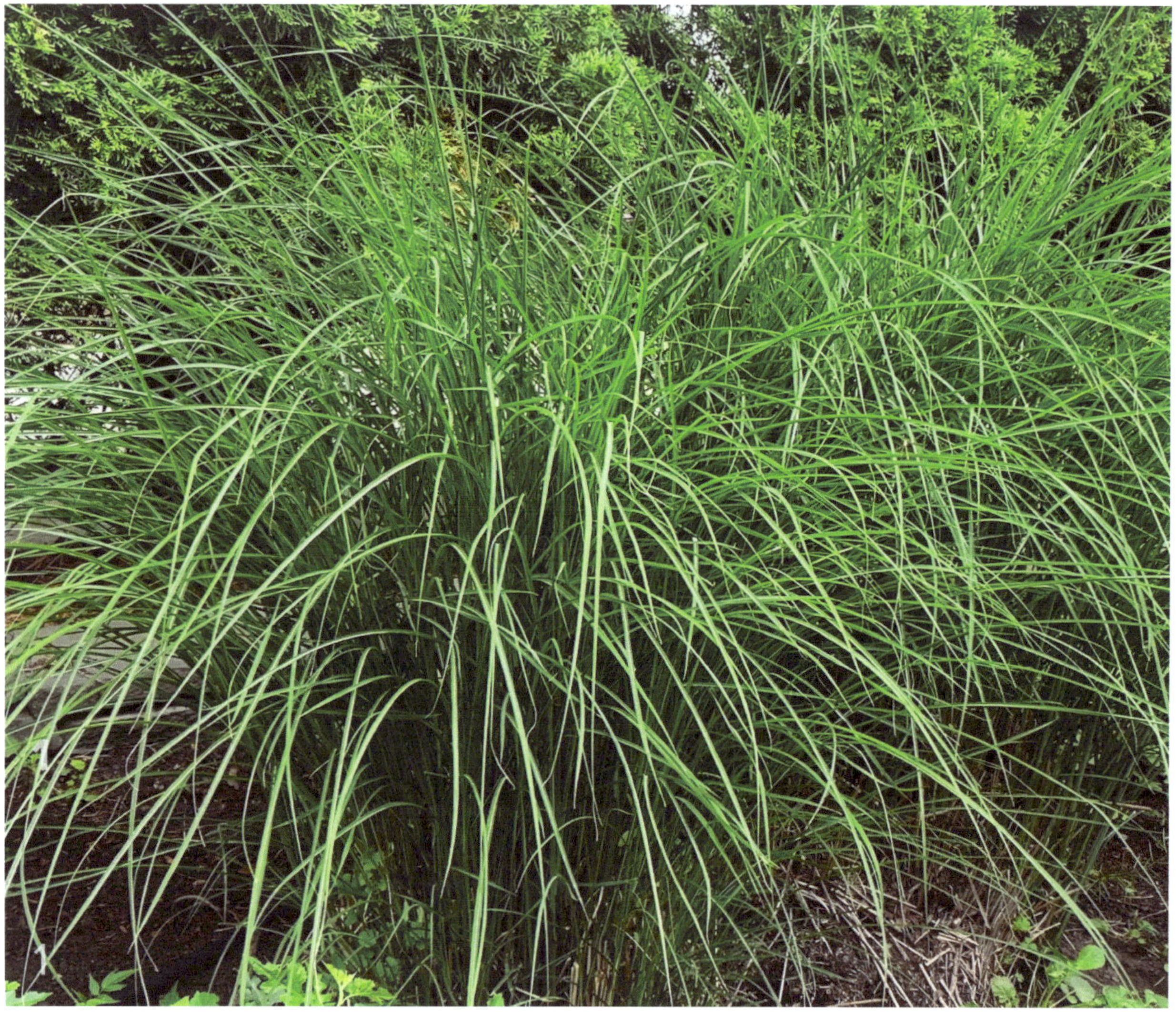

1. This lovely grass blooms later than many other miscanthus. The graceful leaves are a beautiful green presence all summer long.
2. In the fall it produces plumes.
3. This is an arrangement I did for a Sogetsu exhibition in Texas with borrowed miscanthus, on-site-purchased red containers, and yellow fuji mums. Bleached palm fronds complete the design.
4. These graceful tall blooming grasses emphasize height in this vertical arrangement of chrysanthemums, azaleas, and red berries.
5. Grass groupings strengthened with coxcomb flowers and rosehips. Notice the grouping on the right is stronger than the one on the left, creating asymmetric balance.

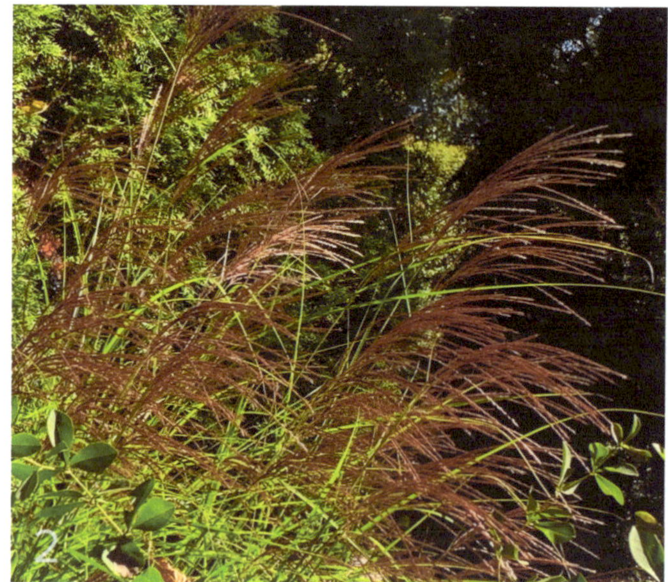

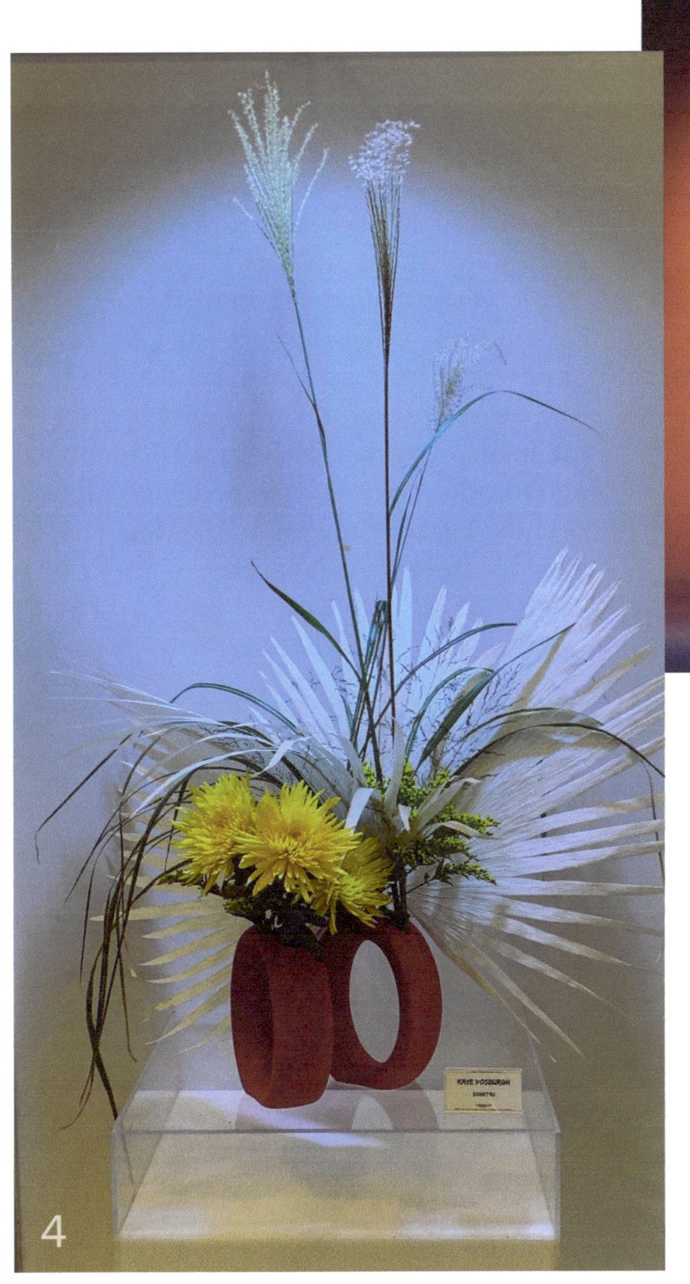

4

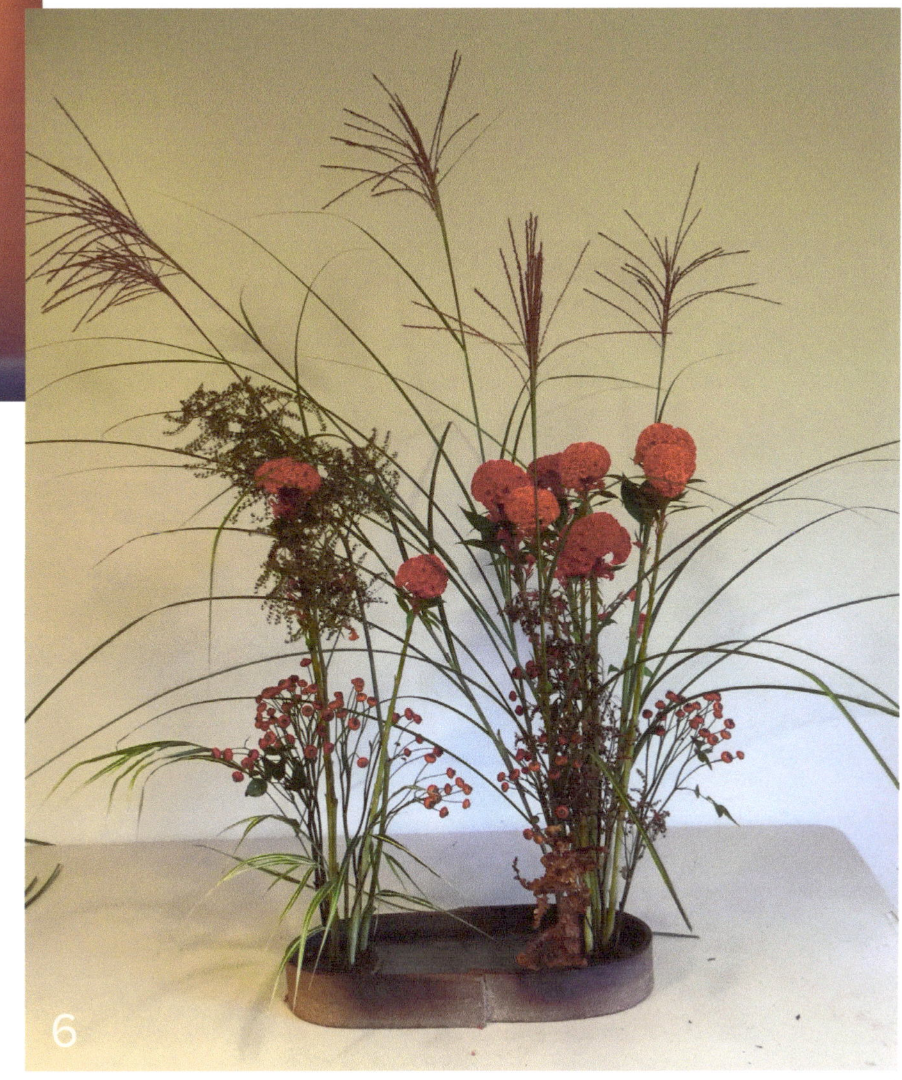

5

6

Grass, Zebra

Miscanthus sinensis 'Zebrinus'

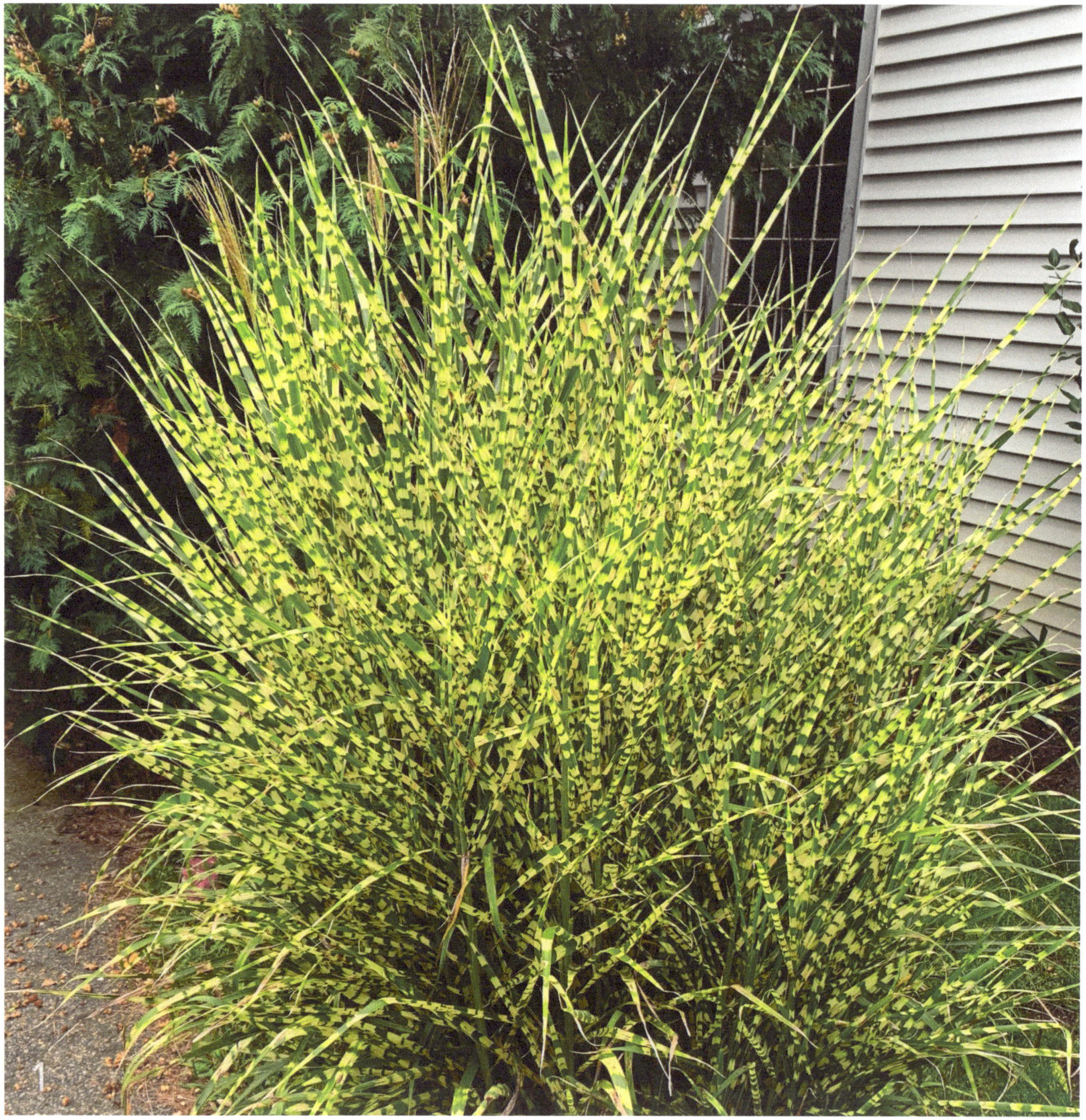

1 Zebra grass is an exciting addition to any garden. The light spots on the leaves give it its name. As it reaches maturity, it will produce many flower panicles.
2 The leaves and plumes in more detail.
3 An autumn celebration with maple leaves, grass leaves and tassels, and sunflowers.
4 The leaves of grass unify this mixed arrangement including day lilies, foxtail lily, smoke, and meadow rue. An arrangement with five or more types of materials, like this one, is called *maze-zashi* in Japanese.

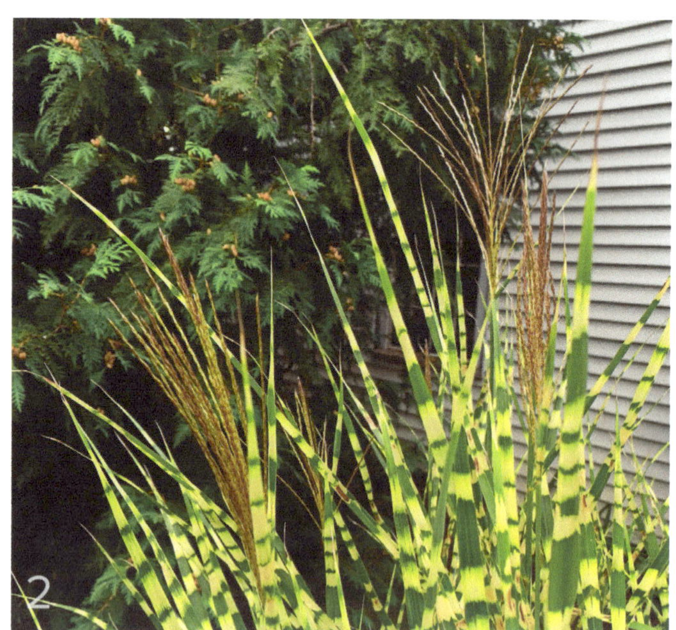

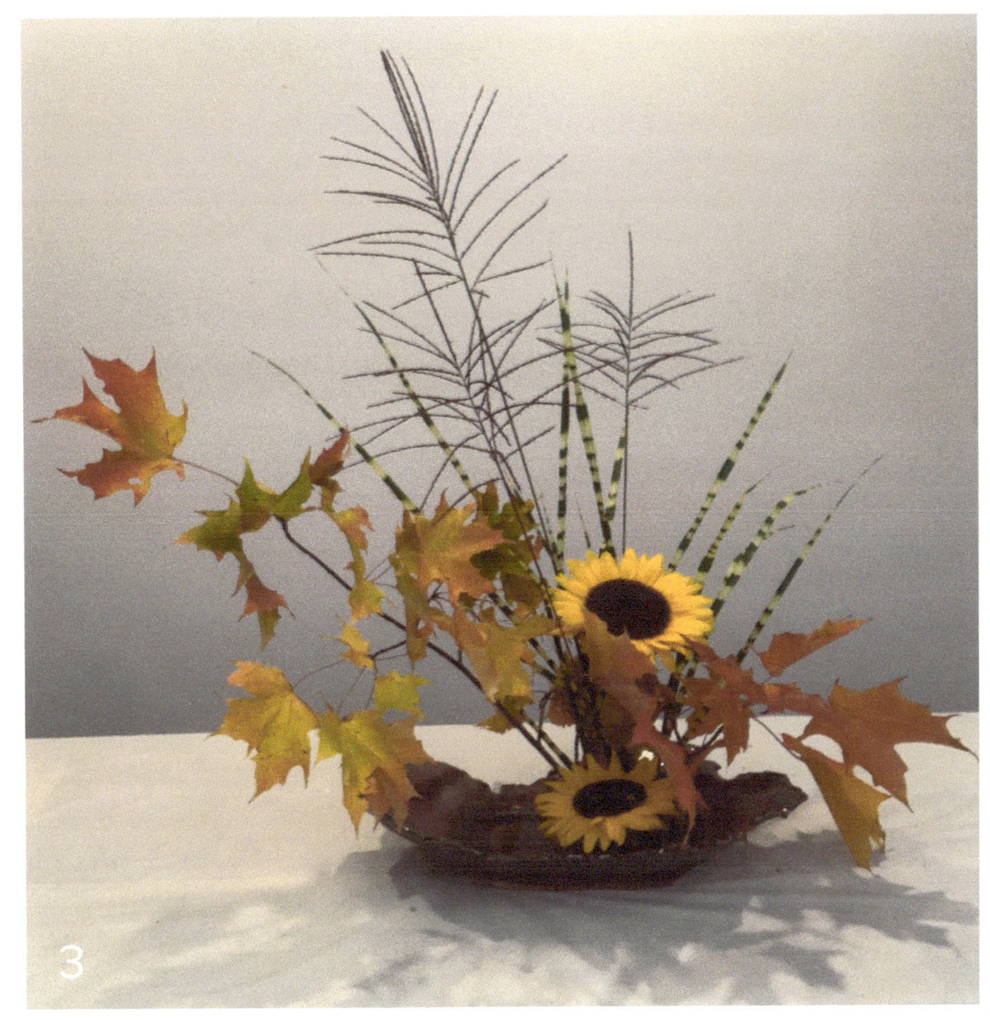

3

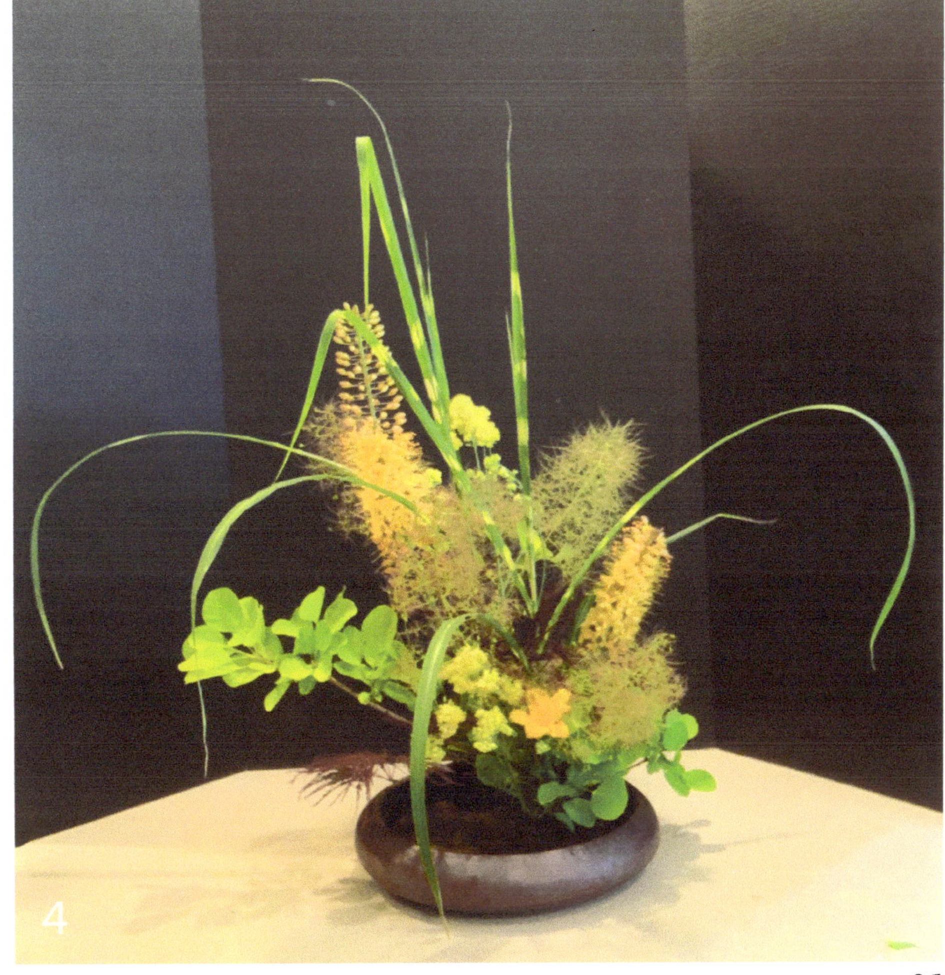

4

Holly

Ilex sp.

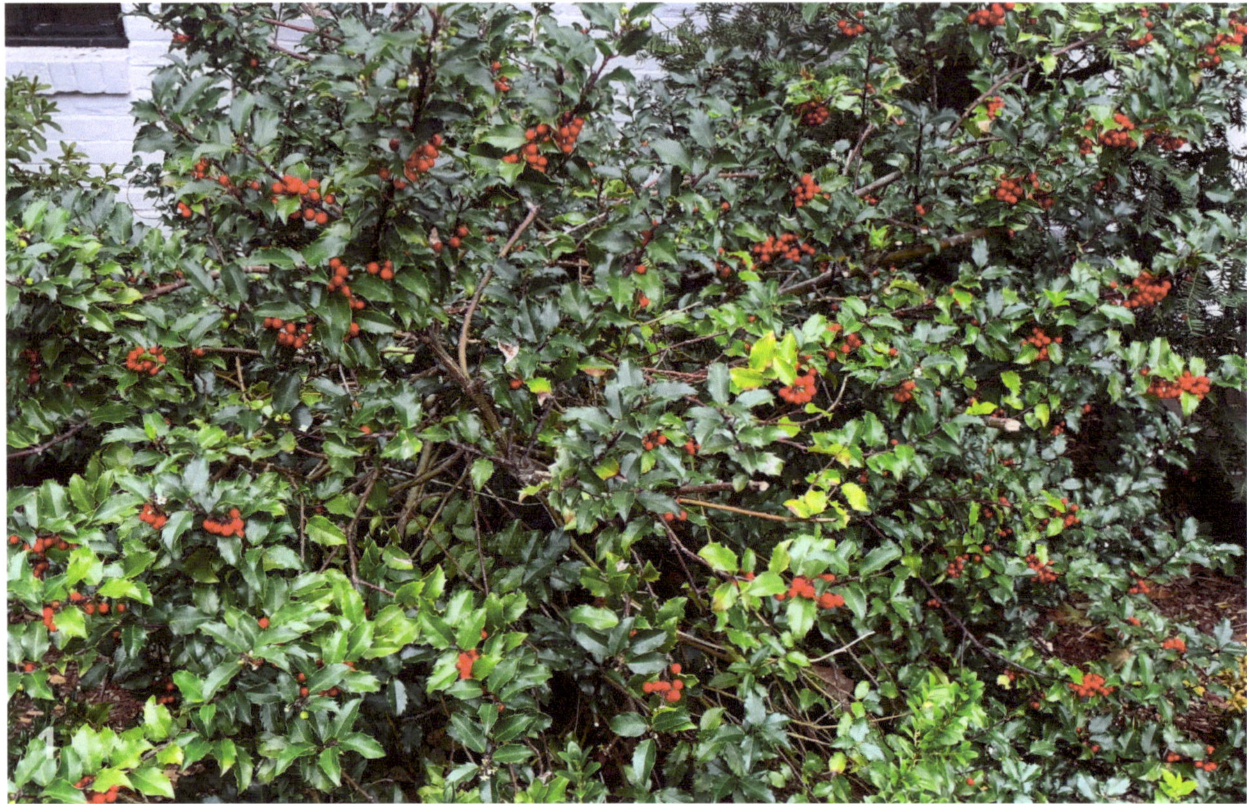

1 English holly, *Ilex aquifolium*, has been crossed with another ilex to form this shrub with lovely glossy leaves. This one came with the house so I don't know its name, but it might be 'Blue Prince and Princess'. They managed to create one plant that has both male and female parts, even though they are usually two separate plants. There is an American holly which grows into a tree; its leaves are matte. In my new garden, I just planted a deciduous holly, *Ilex verticillata*, that is grown for its bountiful berries. Hollies grow well in full sun and produce more berries there.

2 Detail showing some blossoms and leaves with sharp points.

3 The red berries.

4 Holiday freestyle arrangement with bleached privet root and gold *mizuhiki*, a Japanese paper string used for festive occasions. Two red containers are used. The strong rhythm of the *mizuhiki* unifies the arrangement.

5 Here is an arrangement of one kind of material, holly. It shows the interesting branching, the beautiful leaves and bunches of orange berries in early fall colors.

6 Holiday arrangement of white pine, silver-sprayed peegee hydrangea, and *mizuhiki*.

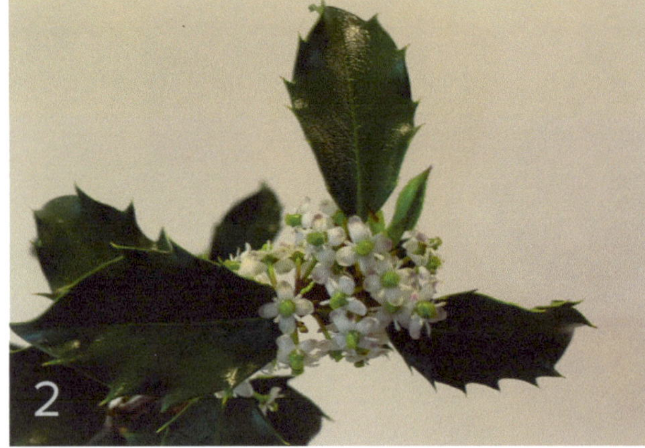

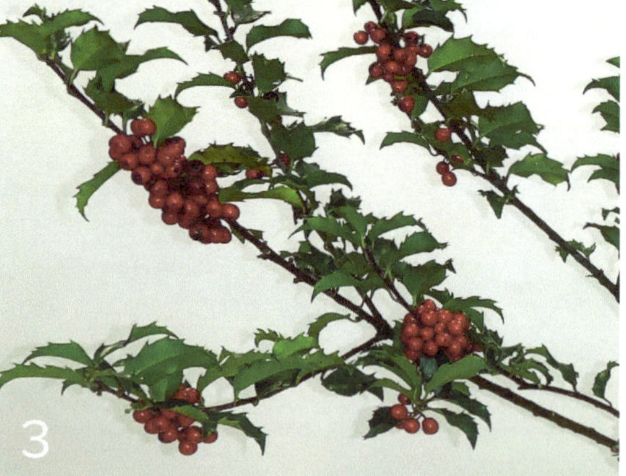

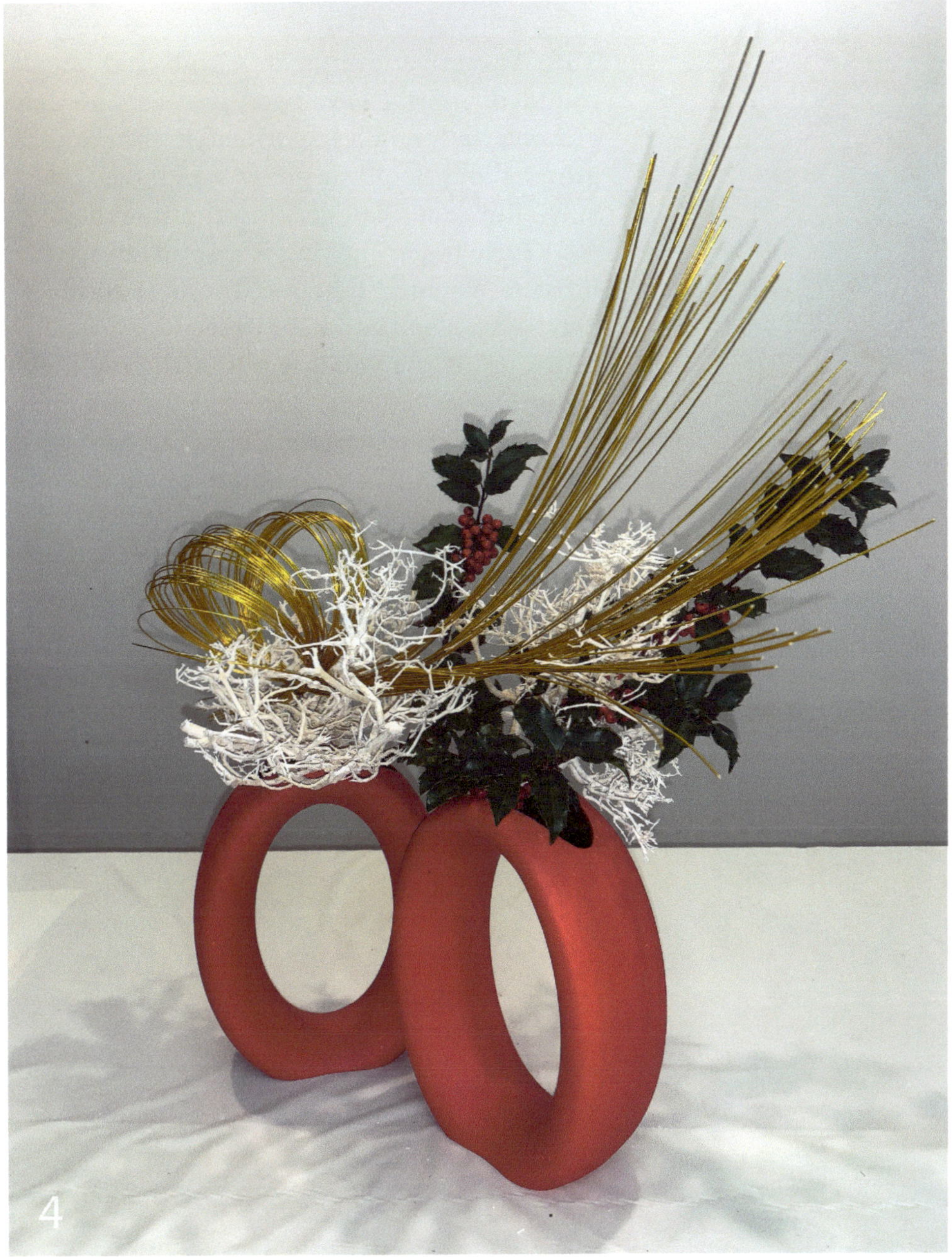

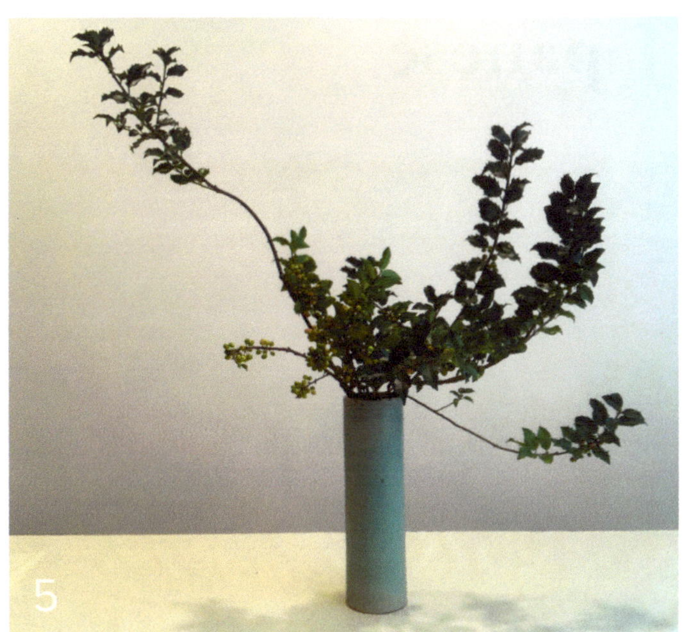

5

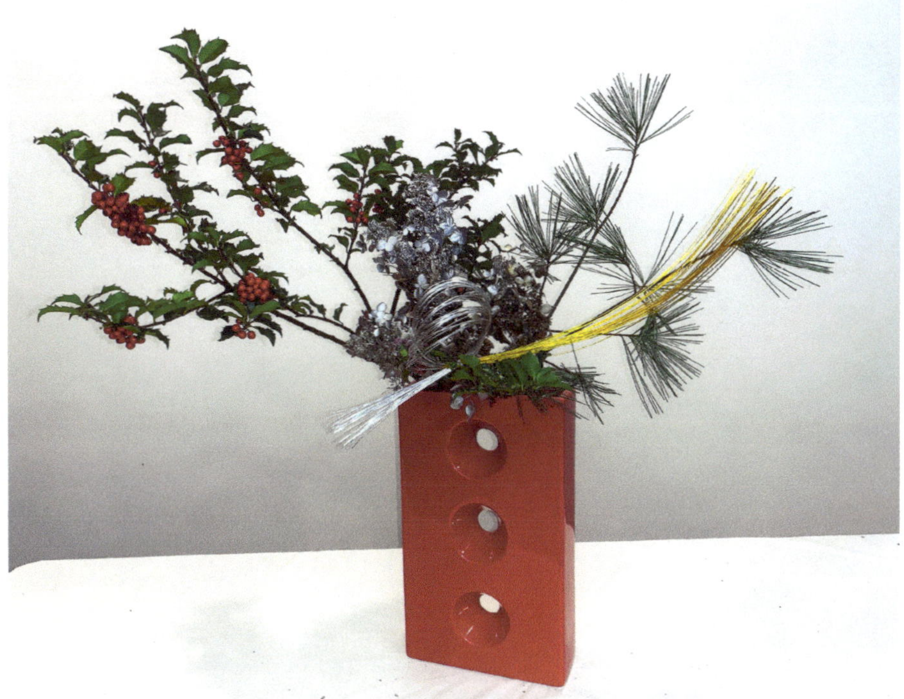

4

37

Holly, Japanese *Ilex crenata*

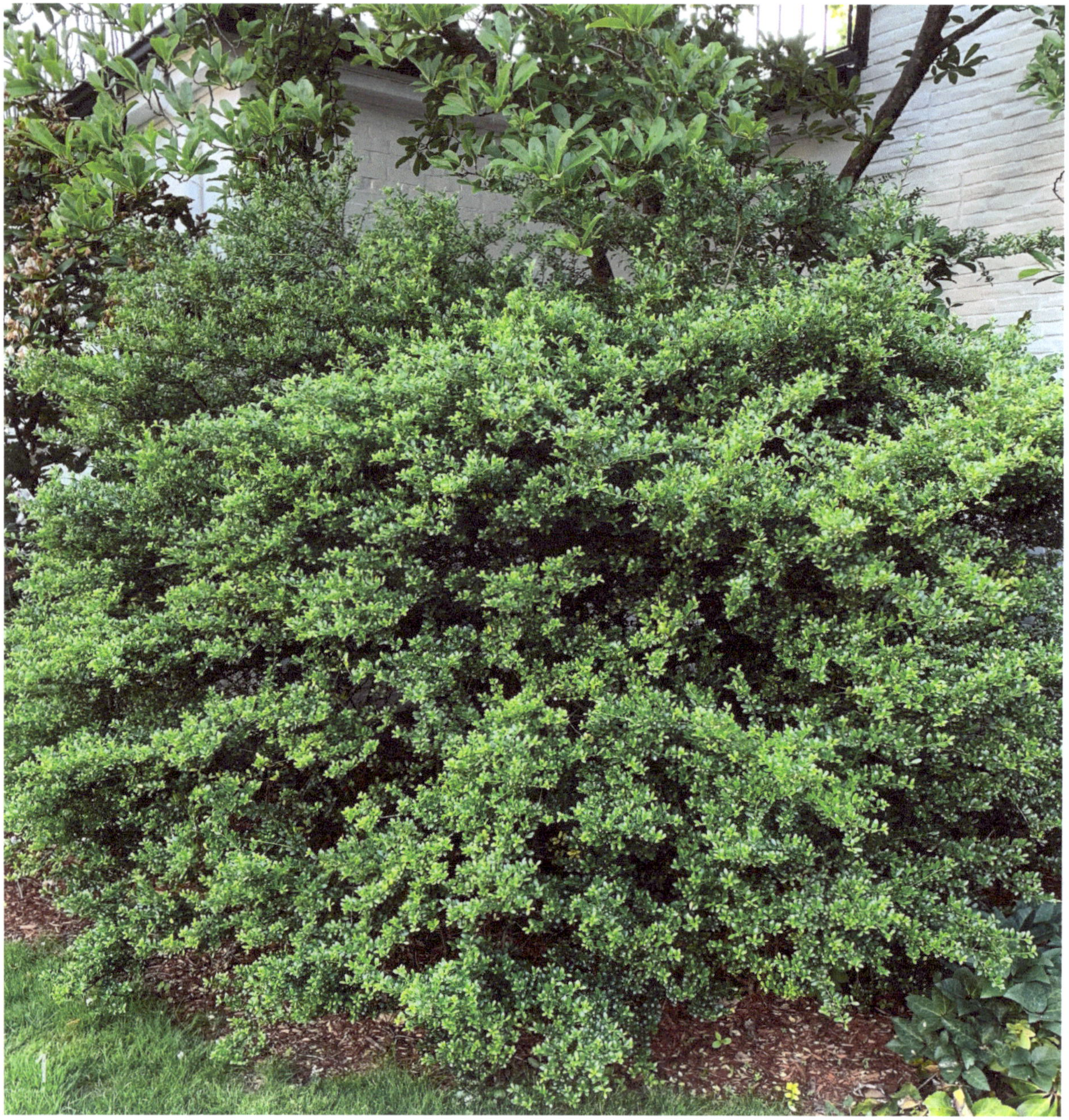

1. This attractive evergreen shrub has small rounded leaves. I have two varieties, one that grows 6' tall, and a larger-leafed variety that grows about 8' tall. It grows rapidly and reliably. The stems can grow to the thickness of your little finger making it a good source for ikebana nageire branches. The blue to black berries are small and hard to see.
2. Close up of the small leaves with tiny blossoms.
3. The larger-leaved variety.
4. This is a basic ikebana design in a nageire container with pale pink peonies.
5. The pattern on this round container is continued upwards with the ilex branch. Mature peonies follow the upward thrust.
6. The branches work well in traditional American designs, creating the framework which in this case is filled in with leucothoe, iris and peony from the garden.

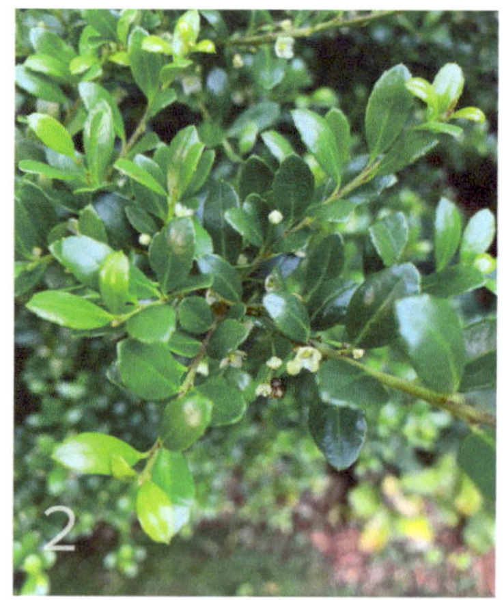

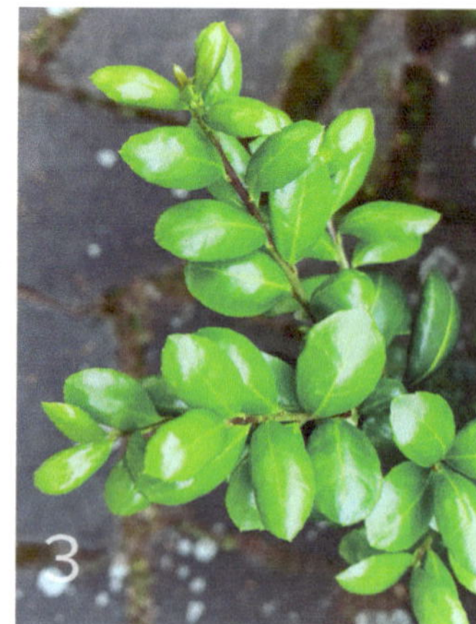

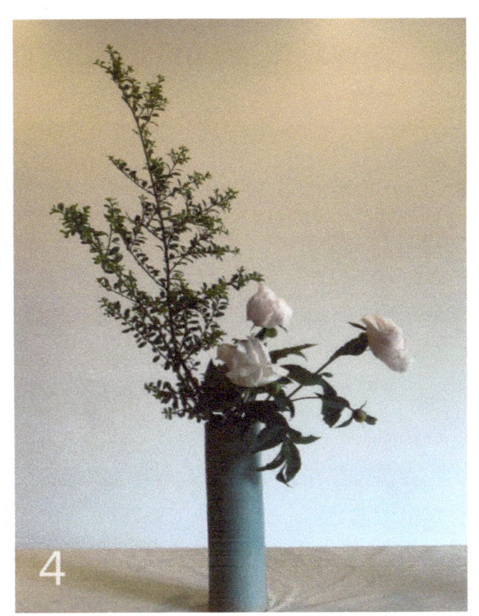

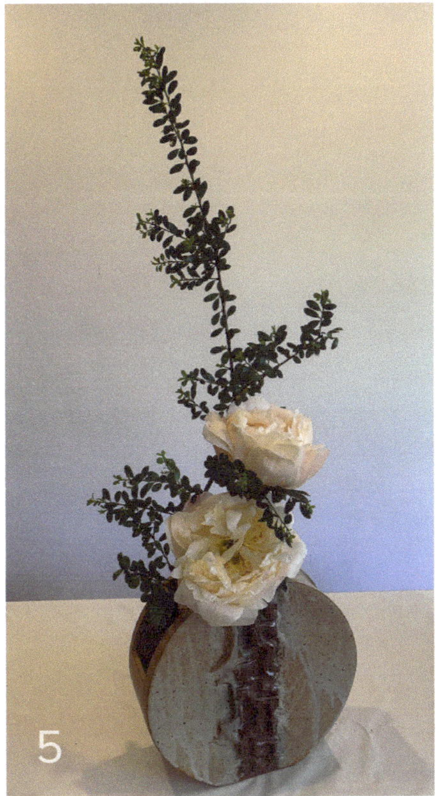

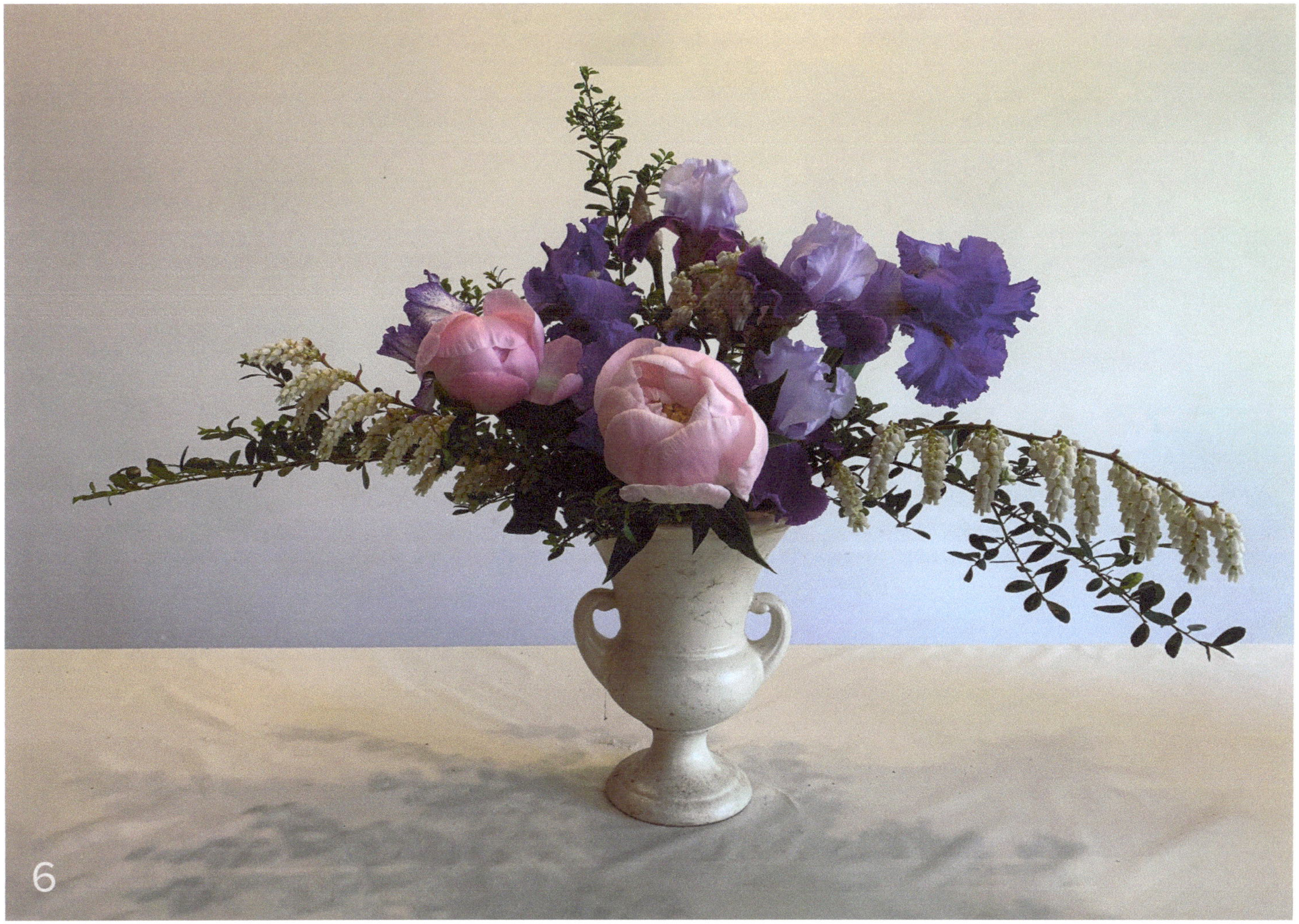

Honeysuckle

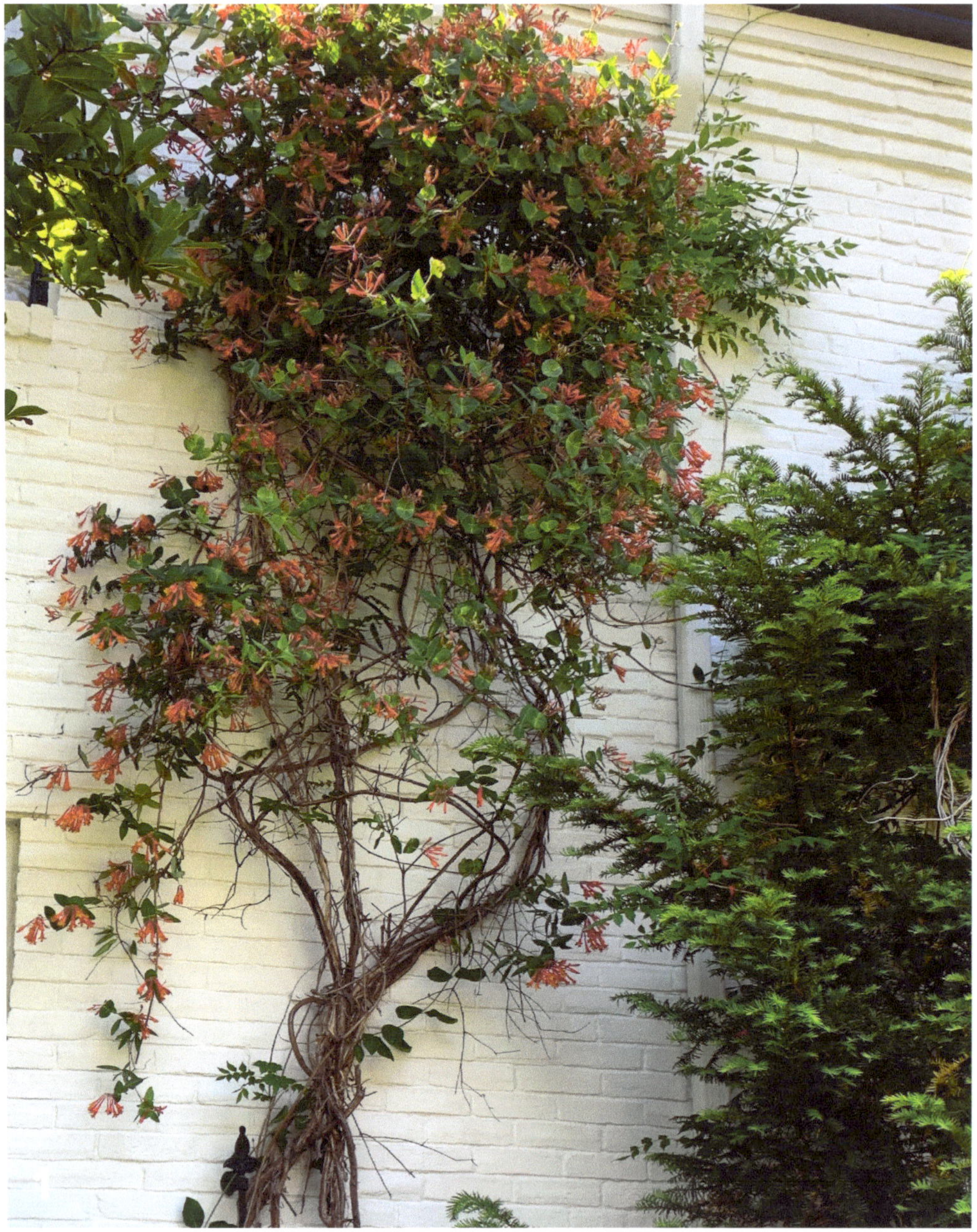

1. This vine grows well with a little support. We anchored some wires above for it to climb. Its full bloom only lasts a few weeks, but it continues most of the summer, blooming now and then. Some other varieties of honeysuckle vines and shrubs are considered invasive; this is not.
2. Detail of the beautiful blossoms and the leaves which surround the stem.
3. The vine sits comfortably in this yellow container with many slits. The graceful curves make the design.
4. This arrangement was made for a friend for her 90th birthday. The wispy smoke and allium give it an aged appearance, and the flowers represent her bright personality still coming through.
5. The Korean lilac arrangement is enhanced by the colors of the honeysuckle relating to the glass container.
6. The circular form of the container is repeated somewhat in the sinuous curve of the vine.

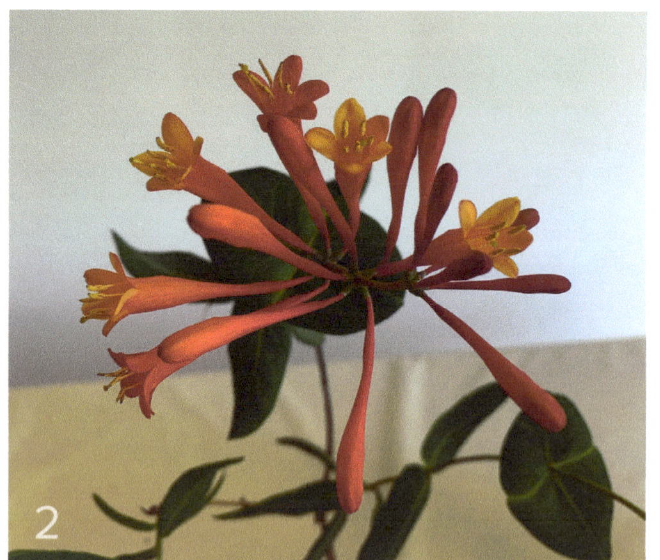

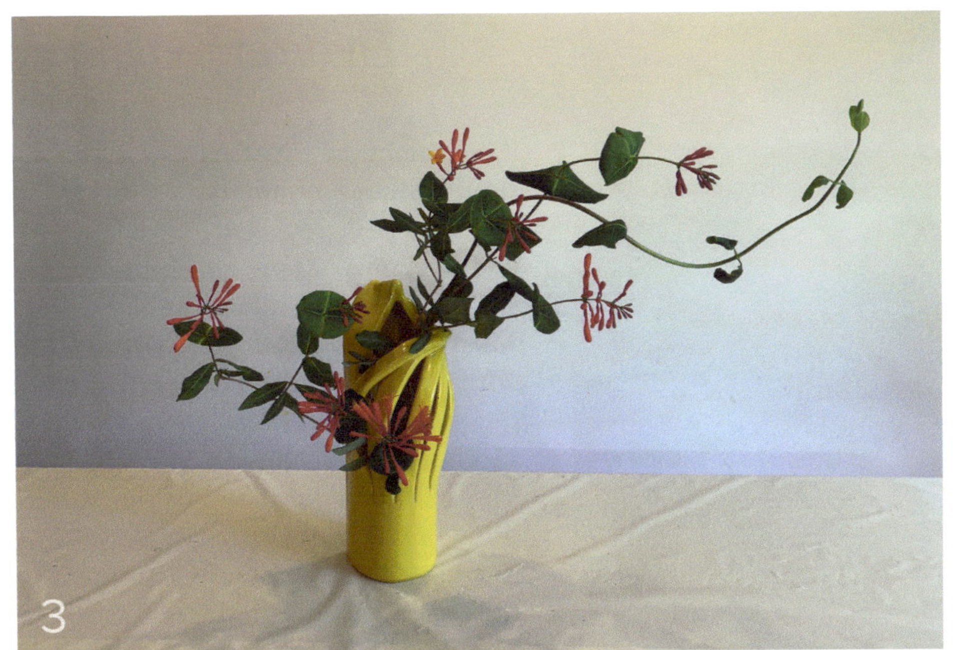

3

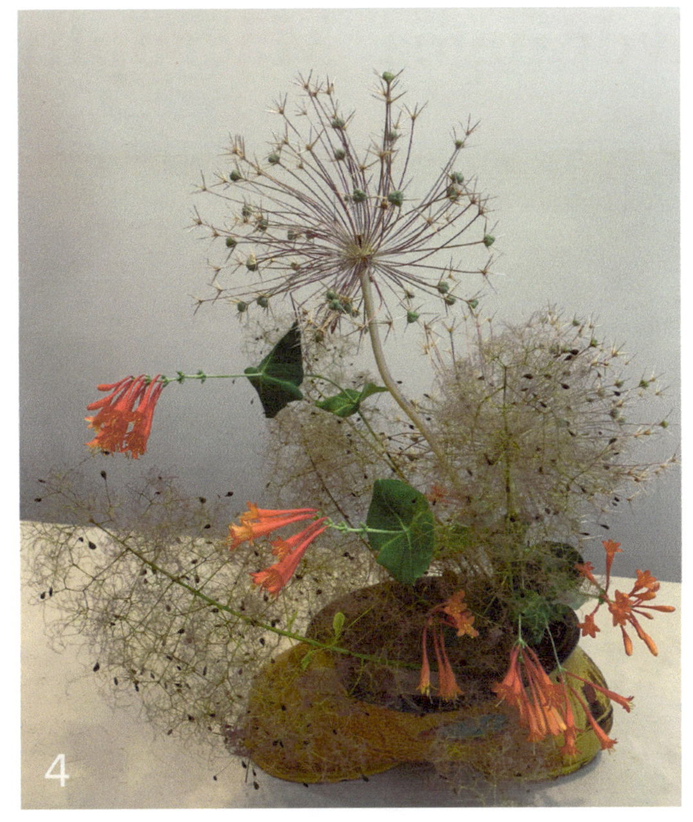

4

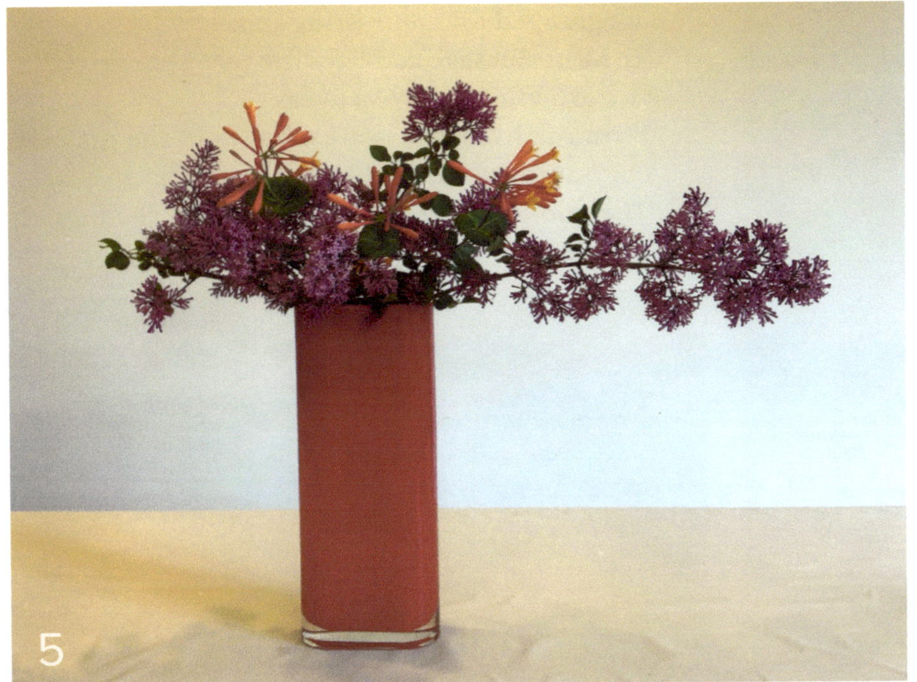

5

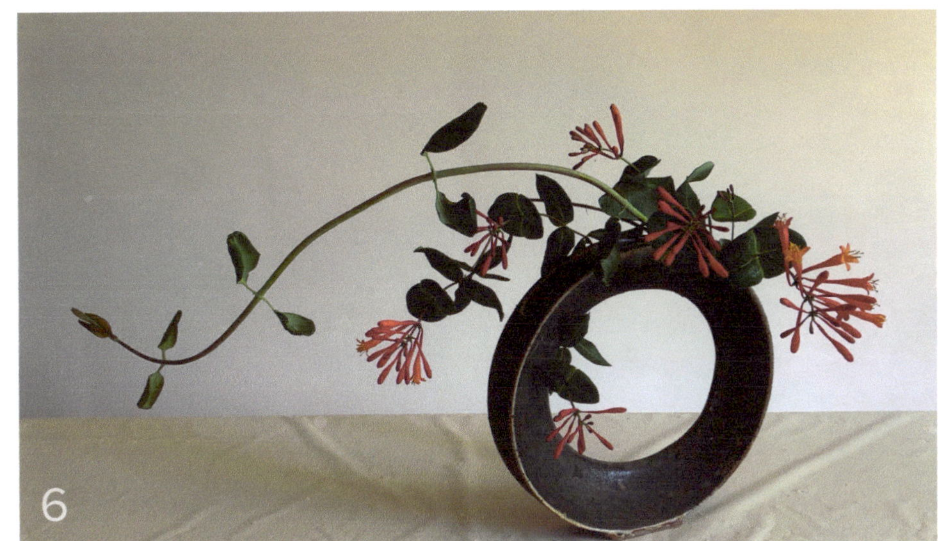

6

Hydrangea, Macrophylla

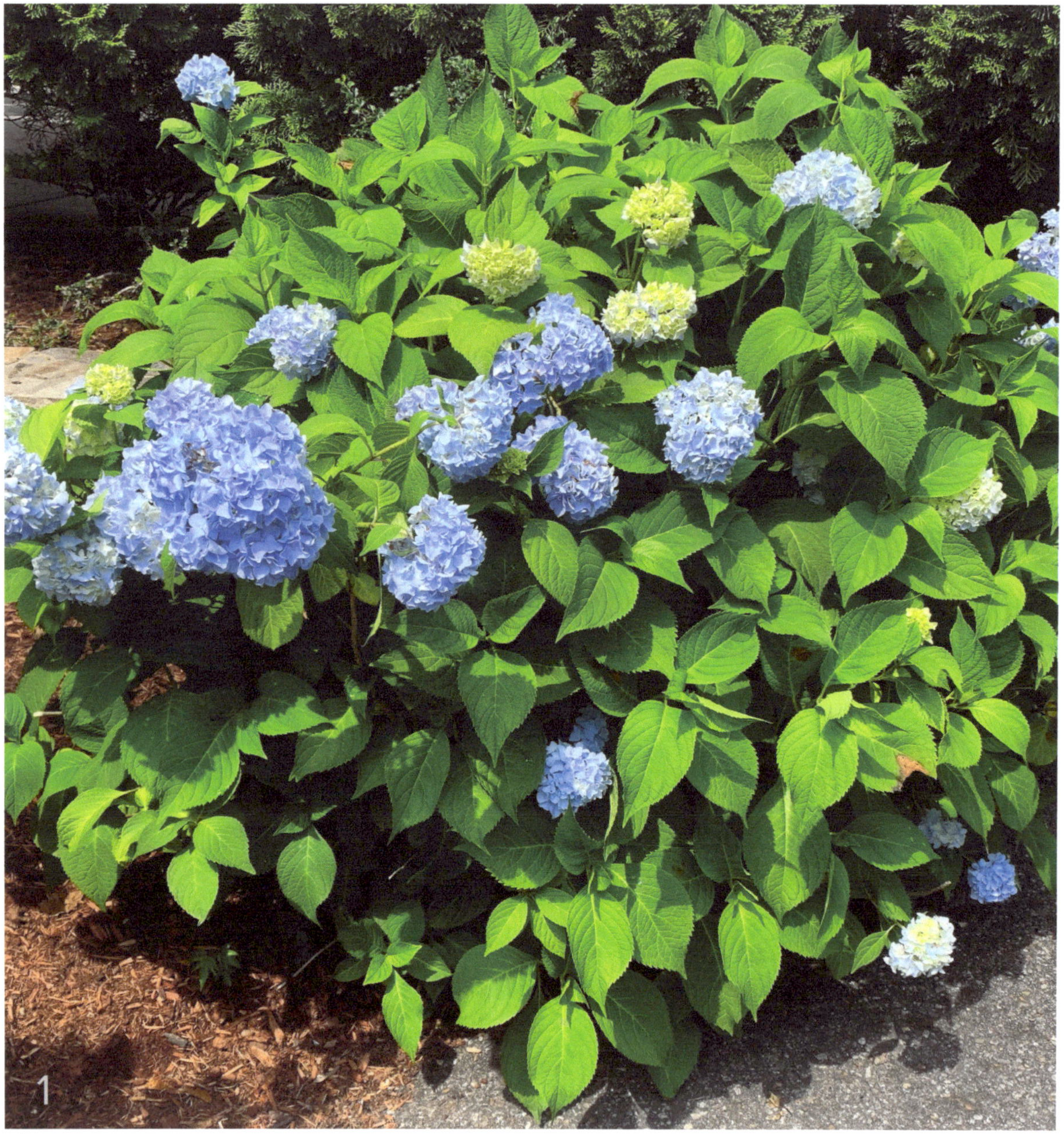

1. These plants are easy to grow in sun or shade and produce large numbers of flowers. Their leaves are beautiful, especially in fall when they may change color. Many of the flowers keep their shape and sometimes their color when they dry. Most plants have flowers whose colors change with maturity. We have many hydrangeas in our garden because my son gives them to me on Mother's Day each year.

2. I love the rich blue color of this variety from another of our bushes.

3. The blue hydrangea globes contrast in color with the red and yellow day lilies. The hydrangeas' solid sphere forms contrast with the allium's hollow sphere. The amsonia pods with leaves removed are grouped for contrasting spikes.

4. The Russian sage activates the space between the two groupings of hydrangeas.

5. Here the hydrangeas are what hold the grasses, chrysanthemums and spirea branches in place. The smoke inflorescence is resting on the tops of the blooms.

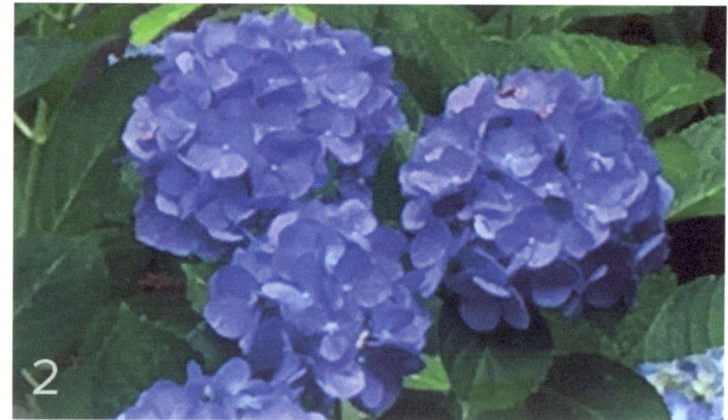

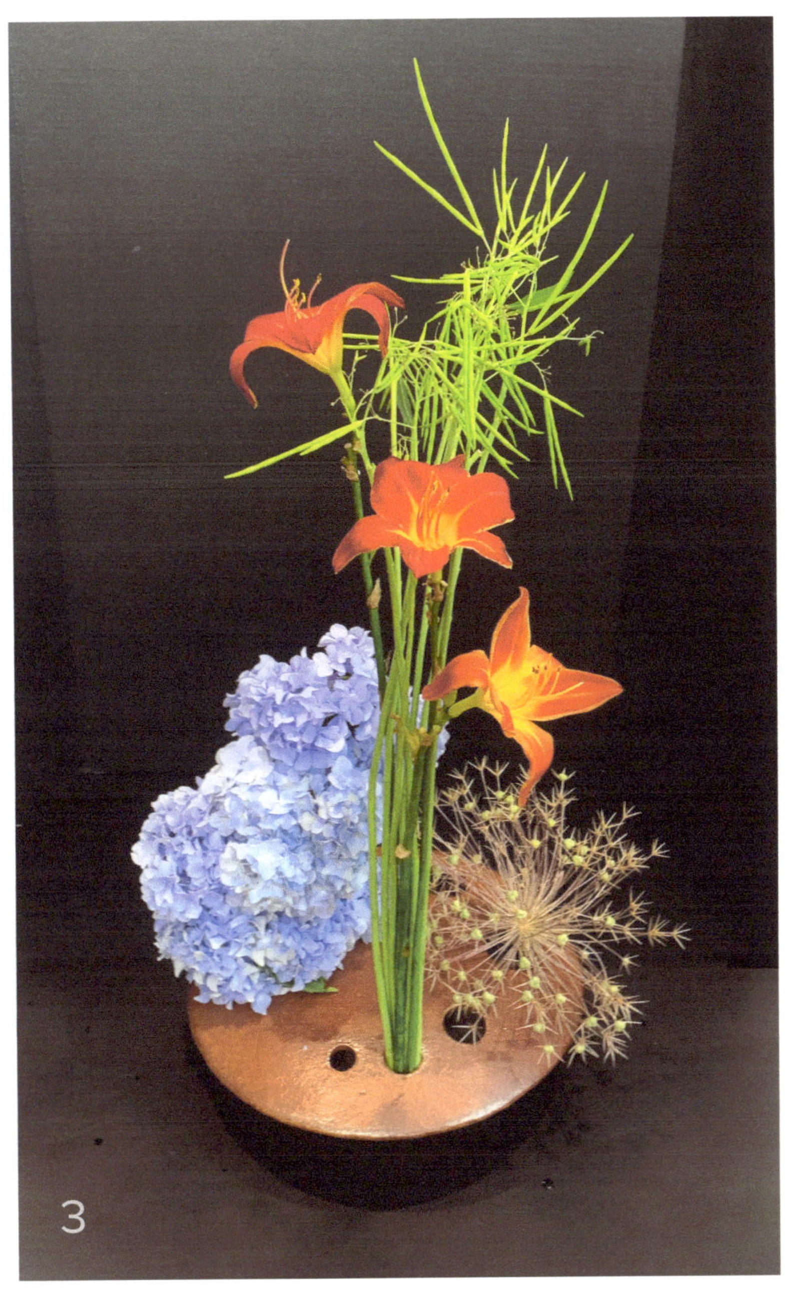

3

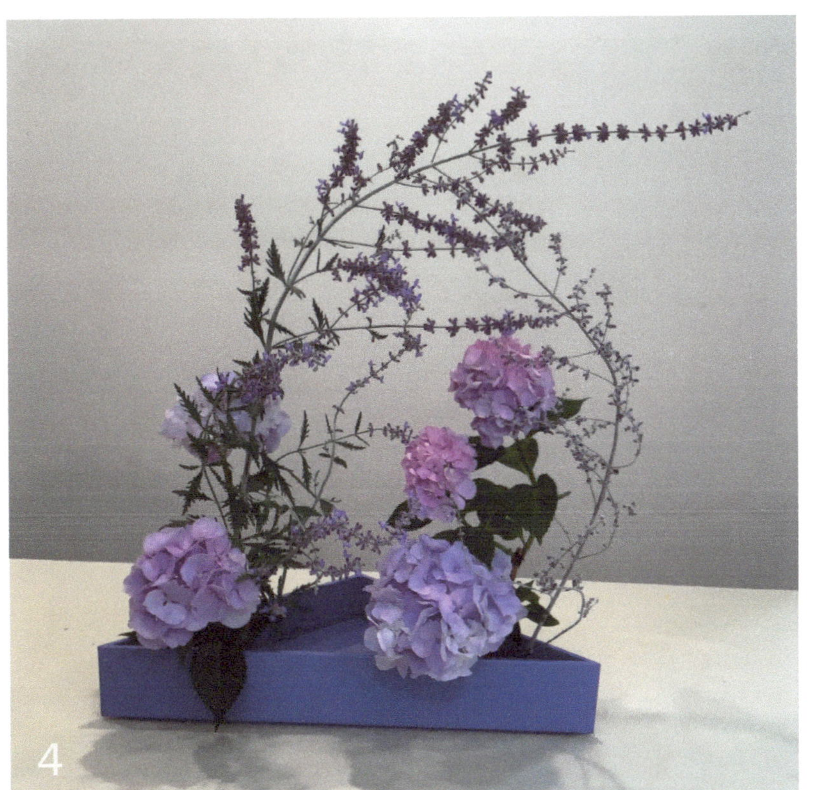

4

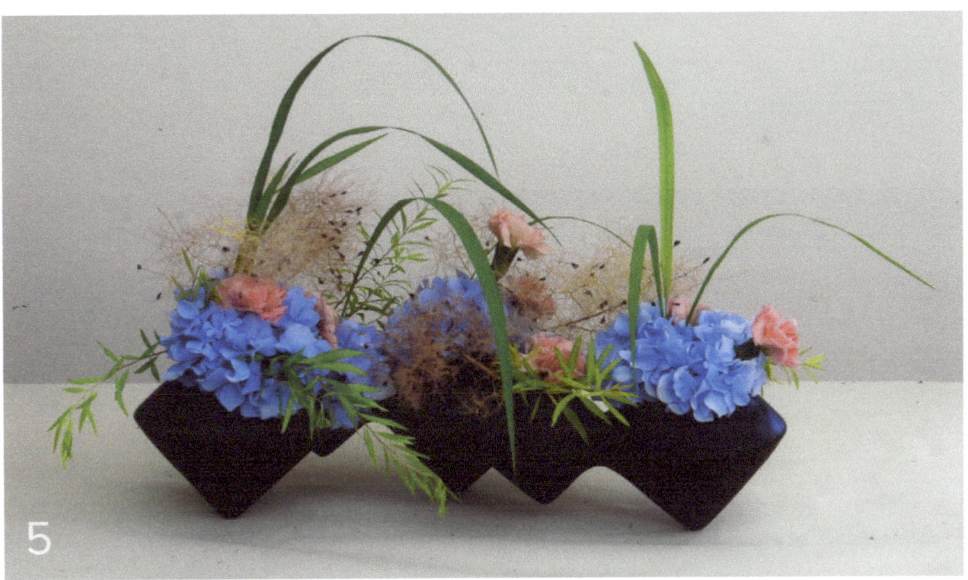

5

Hydrangea 'Princess Beatrix' Hydrangea macrophylla 'Princess Beatrix'

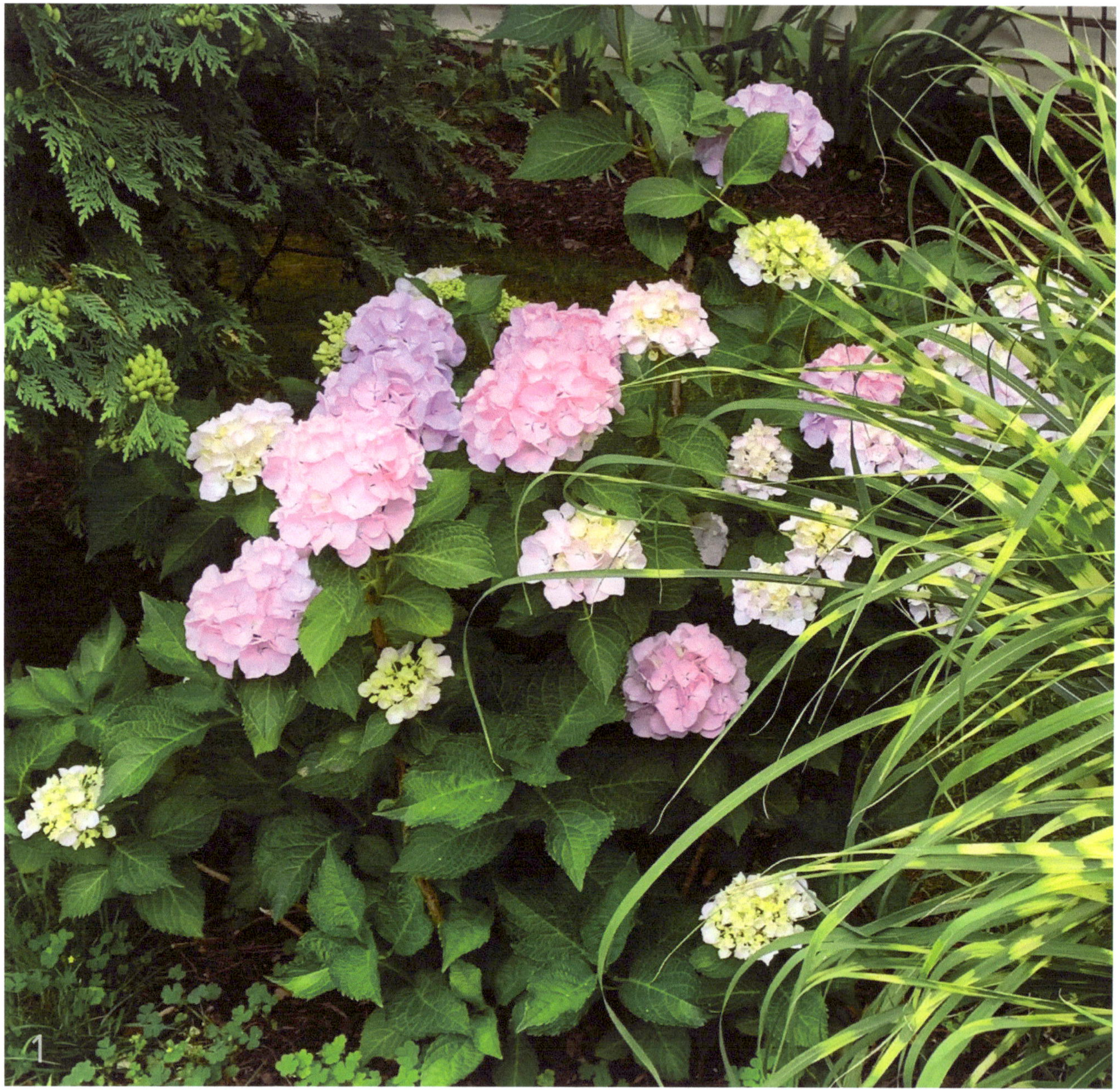

1 Many new varieties of Hydrangea macrophylla have been introduced by breeders in recent years with different characteristics like stronger color, or ability to dry with color and form intact. Beatrix stays pink, unlike the common hydrangea, which is blue in acid soil and pink in alkaline soil.

2 The fall color of these flowers is more intense.

3 Peeled wisteria vine surrounds hydrangeas in this curved container. The vine encloses space, which is a key element in most contemporary designs.

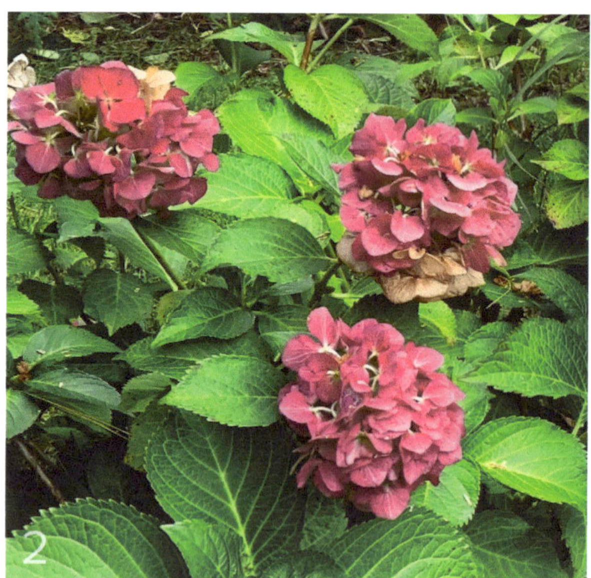

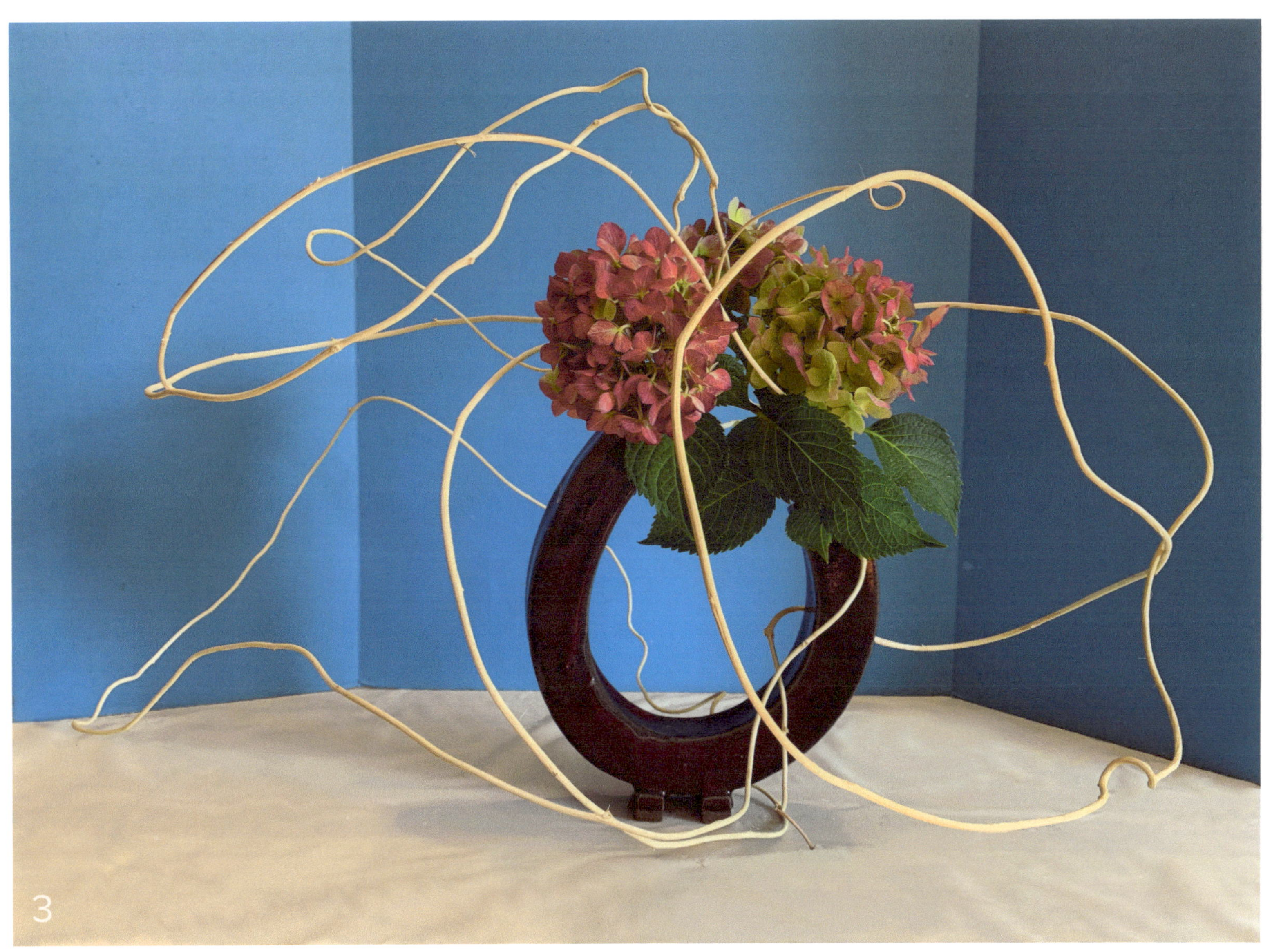

3

Hydrangea 'Limelight'

1. This panicled variety is green at first, maturing to white and then pink. Ours are giants, growing to more than six feet tall with large blossoms. We prune them in the fall.
2. Detail.
3. Wisteria vine swirls around these mature lime-colored blossoms, true to their name, 'Limelight'. Smoke from the smoketree is caught in the vine.
4. In the fall, the blossoms fade to pink. Here, gomphocarpus, spirea, and pennisetum grasses join the party in this freestyle arrangement.
5. New blossoms are white. In this arrangement, you can see the characteristic shape of the flower creating a vertical mass with milkweed pods.
6. Branches of hydrangea, pruned in the fall, were used to create a matrix design in this glass container with white lilies.

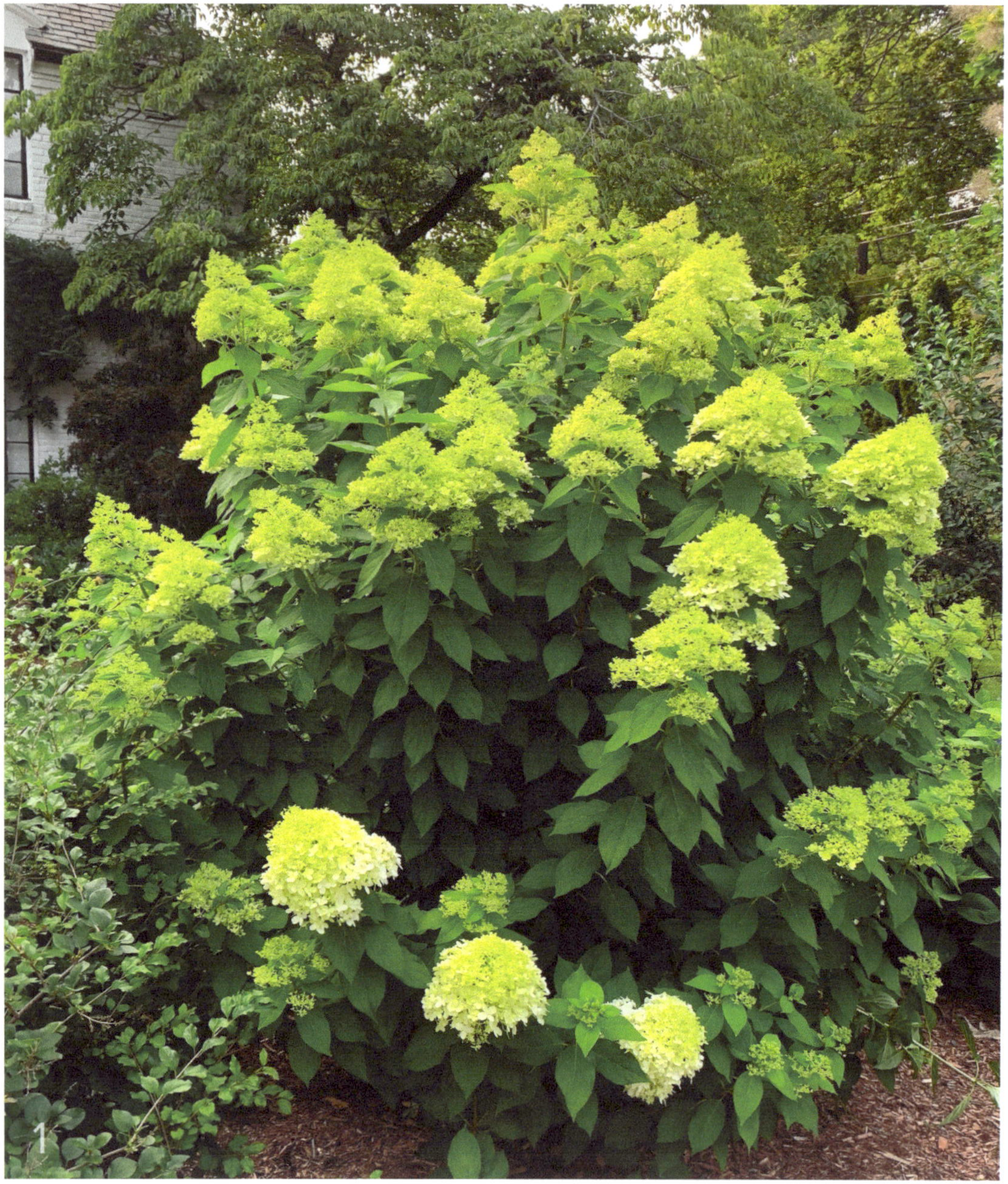

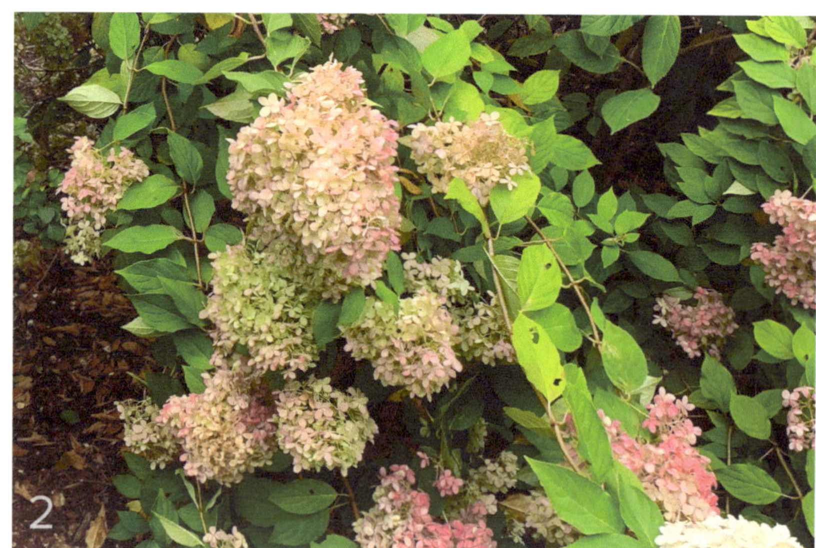

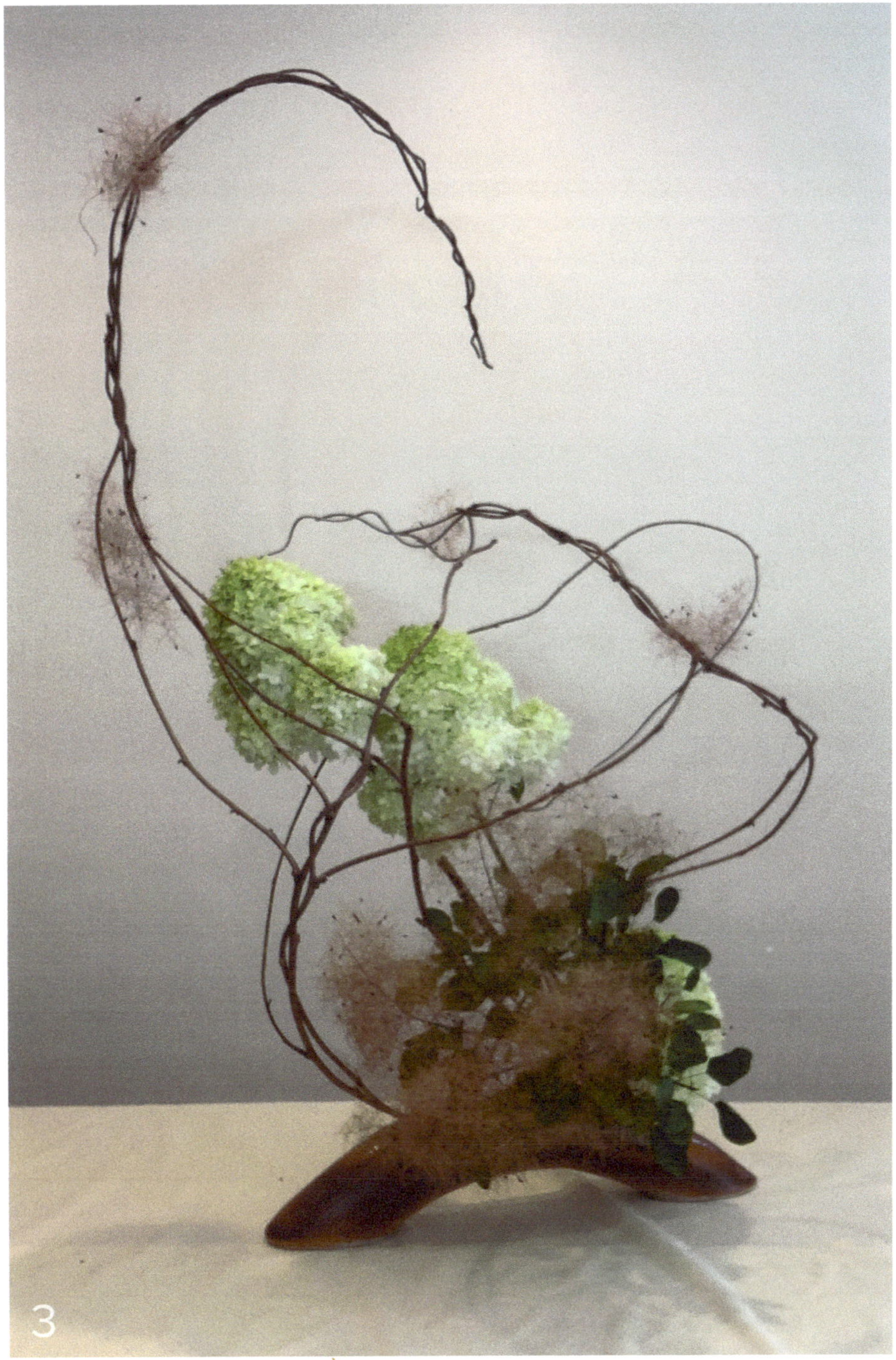

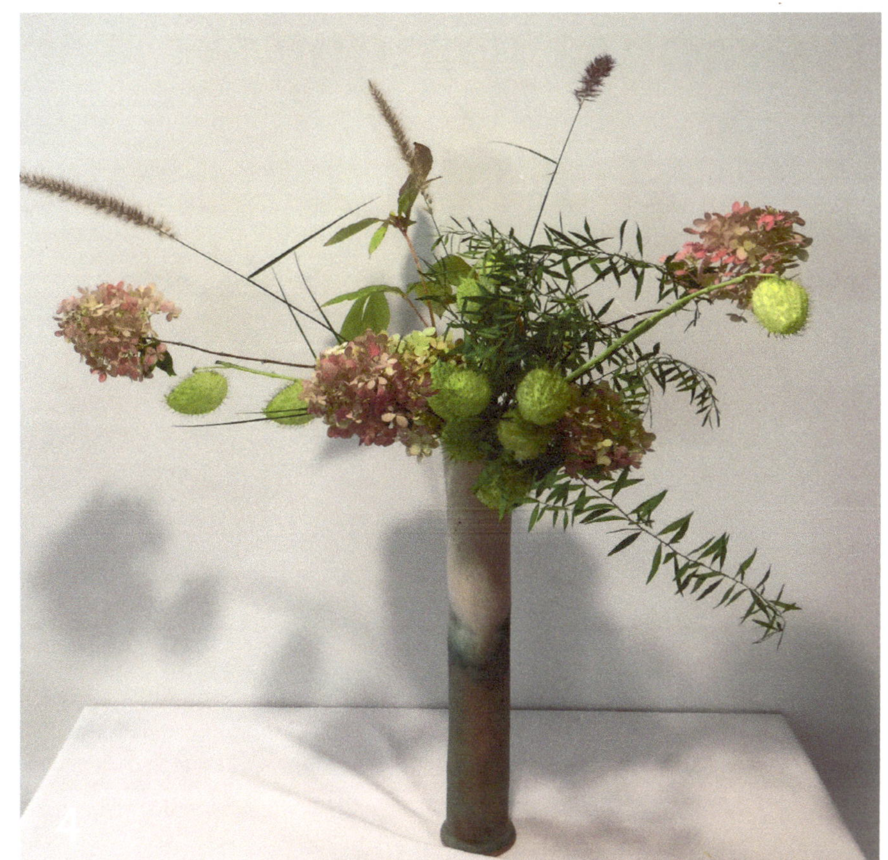

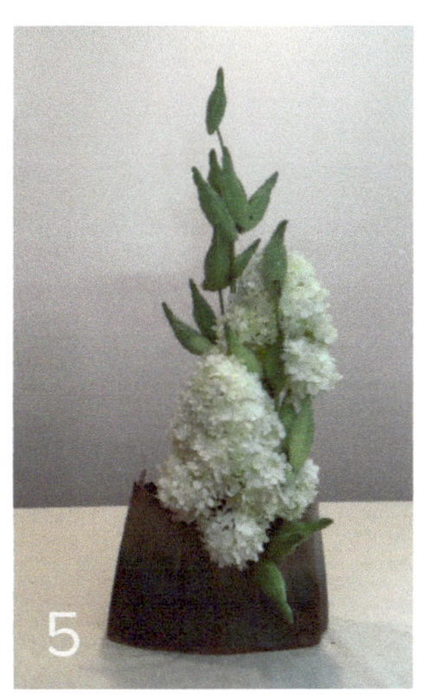

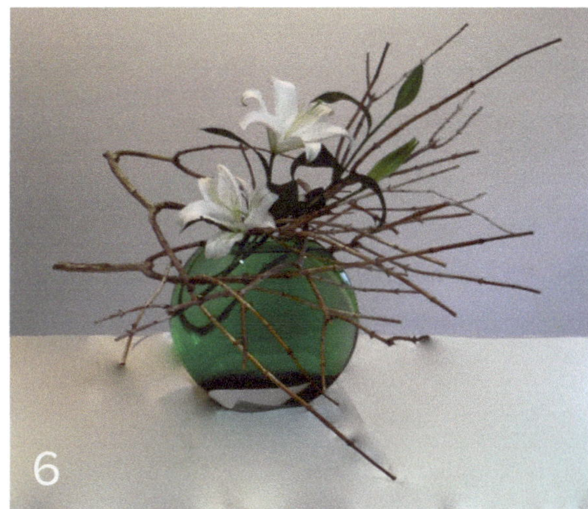

Hydrangea 'Unique'

Hydrangea paniculata 'Unique'

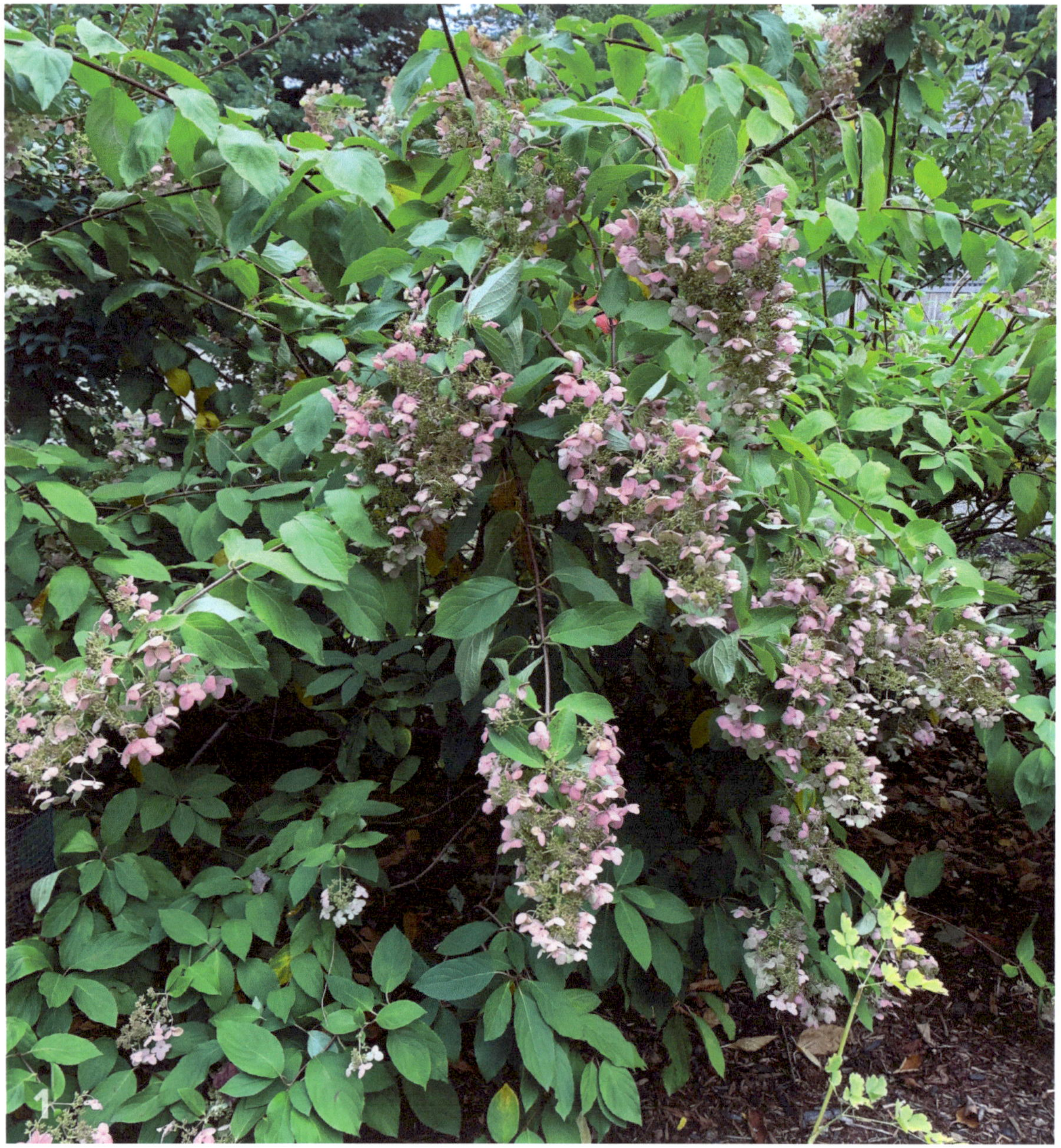

1 Panicled hydrangea varieties are often referred to as "peegees" (although that is the name of an old-fashioned variety). These flowers are different than limelight hydrangea. The new flowers are white, fading to pink as they mature, and then to green. Another variety with sterile and fertile flowers is the lace cap, a shrub with flat blossoms with fertile flowers in the middle and sterile petals surrounding them. We planted oak leaf hydrangea in our new garden, and in our last home we grew climbing hydrangea. Hydrangea are easy to grow, good for arranging, and attractive in the garden.

2 The tight, bud-like blossoms are fertile and the ones with petals are sterile. This makes them frilly.

3 This tall arrangement is meant to feature the stems later in the season when the flowers have turned green. Lavender chrysanthemums draw your eye to the pattern formed by the stems.

4 Summer is expressed in the white arrangement. The caladium and 'Unique' show smooth and fluffy contrasting textures.

5 Dogwood and purple smoketree provide color contrast with the hydrangea.

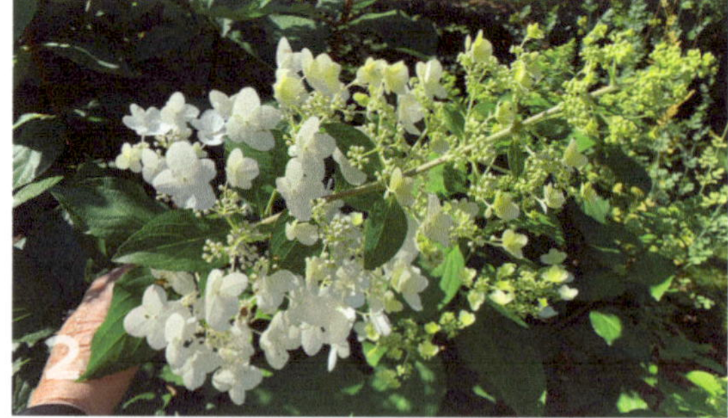

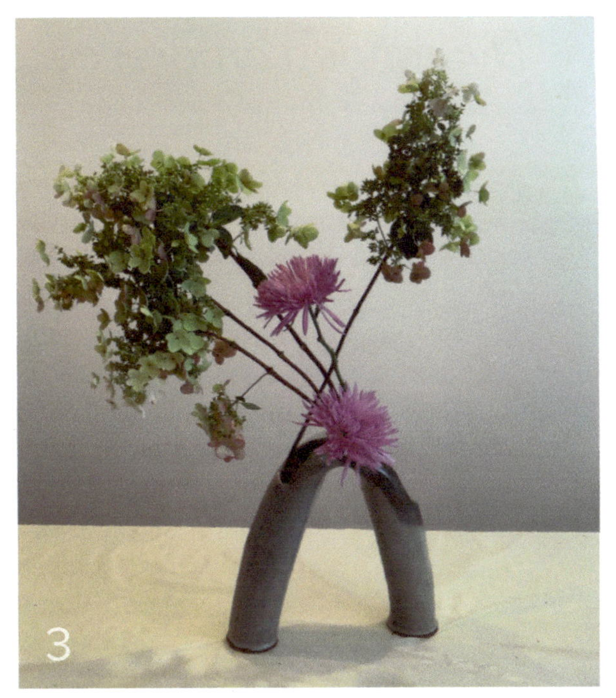

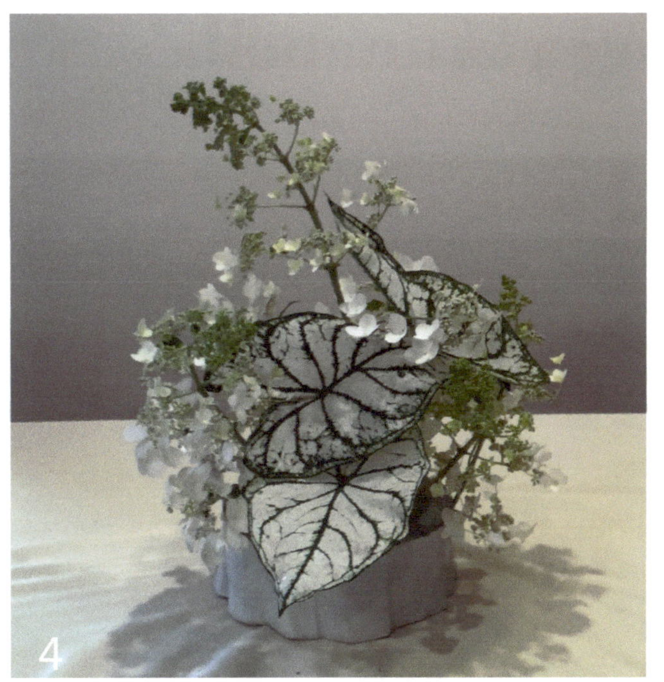

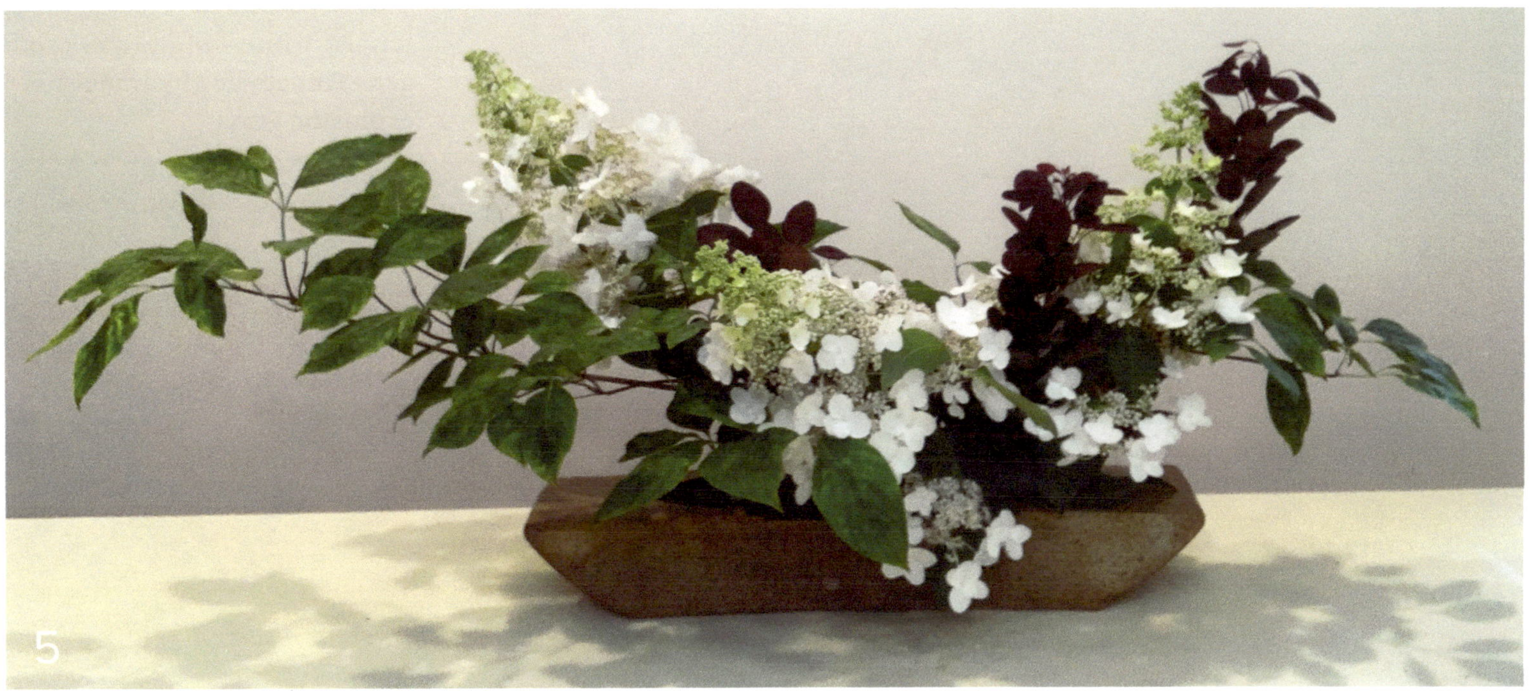

Hydrangea 'Annabelle'

Hydrangea arborescens 'Annabelle'

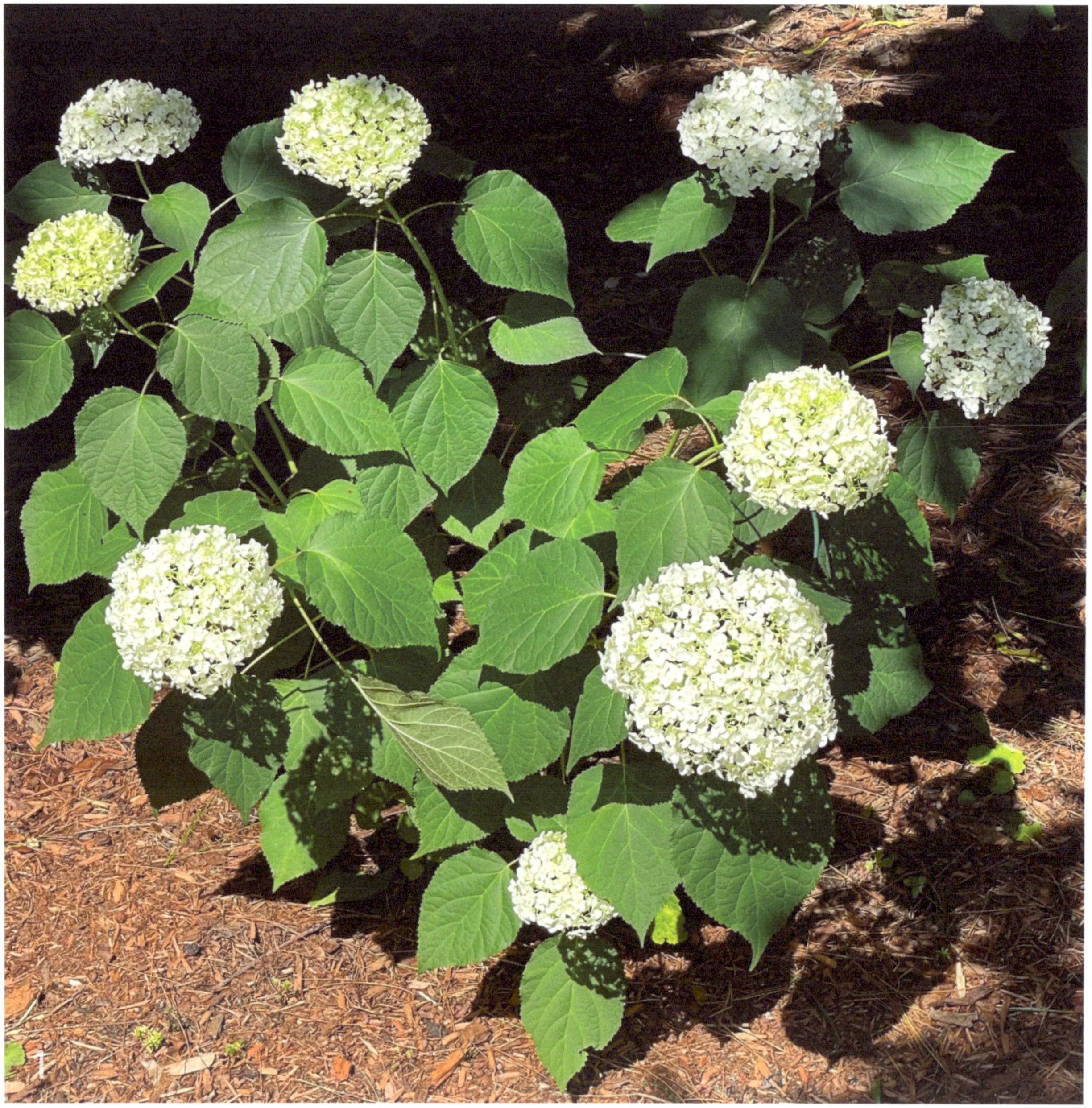

1   This *Hydrangea arborescens* is a different species from my other hydrangeas. The flower heads of 'Annabelle' are quite large when it matures. This plant likes semi-shade and lots of water.

2   The new buds are small, filling out to these enormous flower heads. I have found that cutting the blossoms of any hydrangea early in the season often results in it wilting. Later in the summer and fall, the fibers in the petals have strengthened and don't wilt as much. Treating a stem by dipping it in alum will also help condition the hydrangea.

3   This summer arrangement features 'Annabelles' and green and white caladium leaves.

4   This vertical mass arrangement has five materials: white cymbidium orchids, pink ginger, 'Annabelle' hydrangea, caladium, and explosion grass.

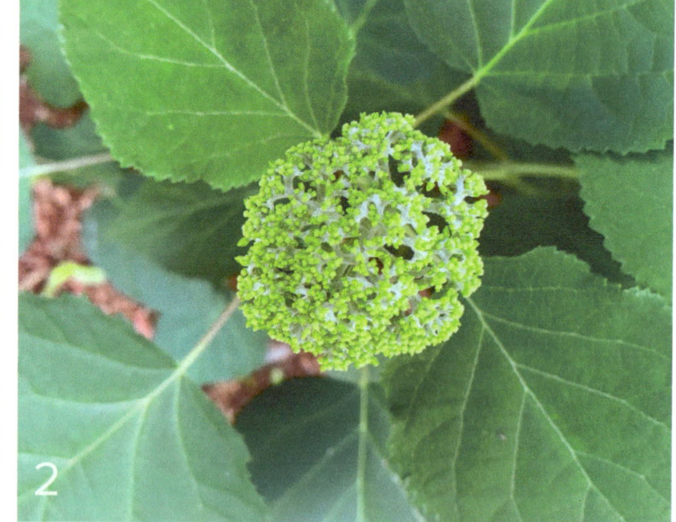

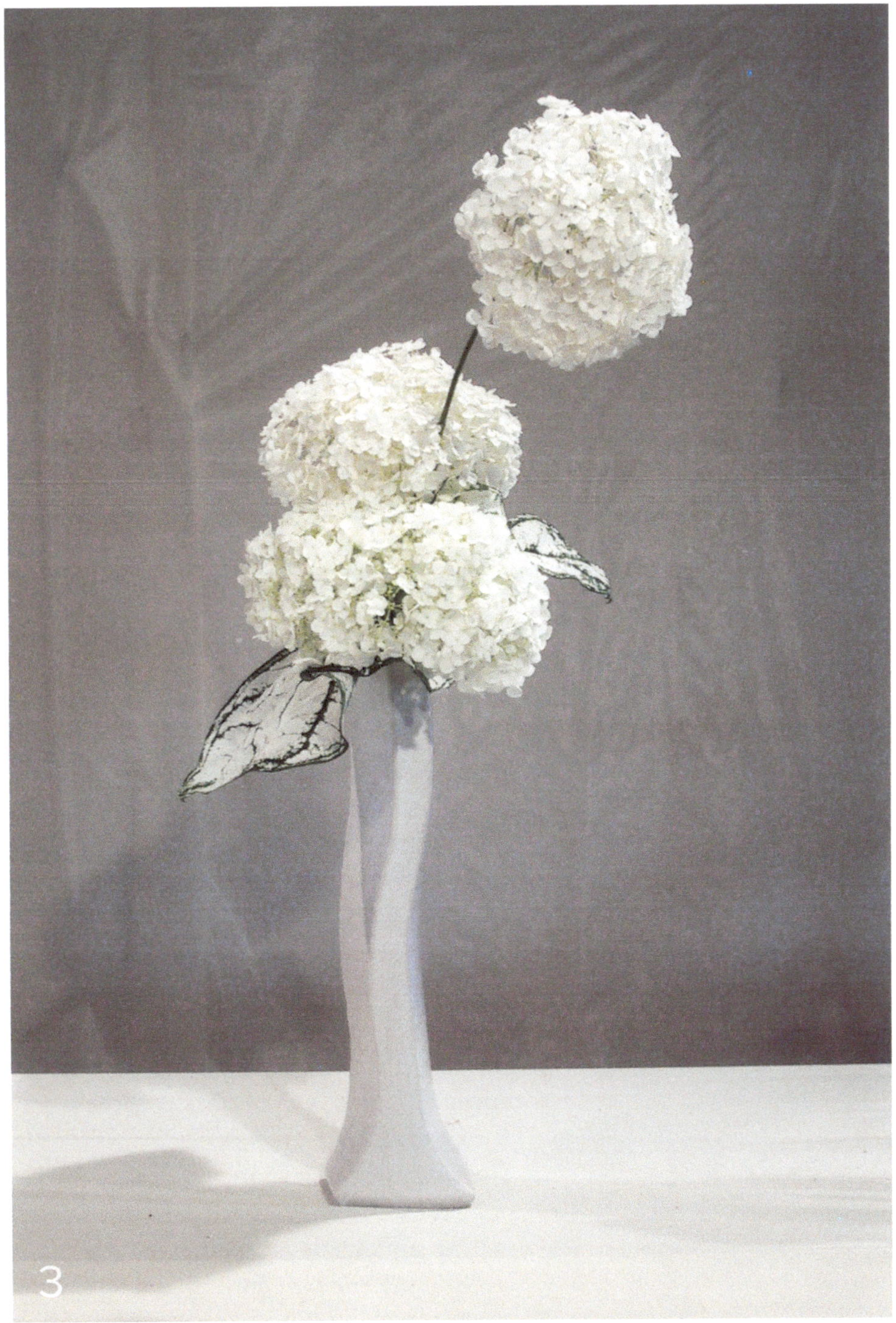

3

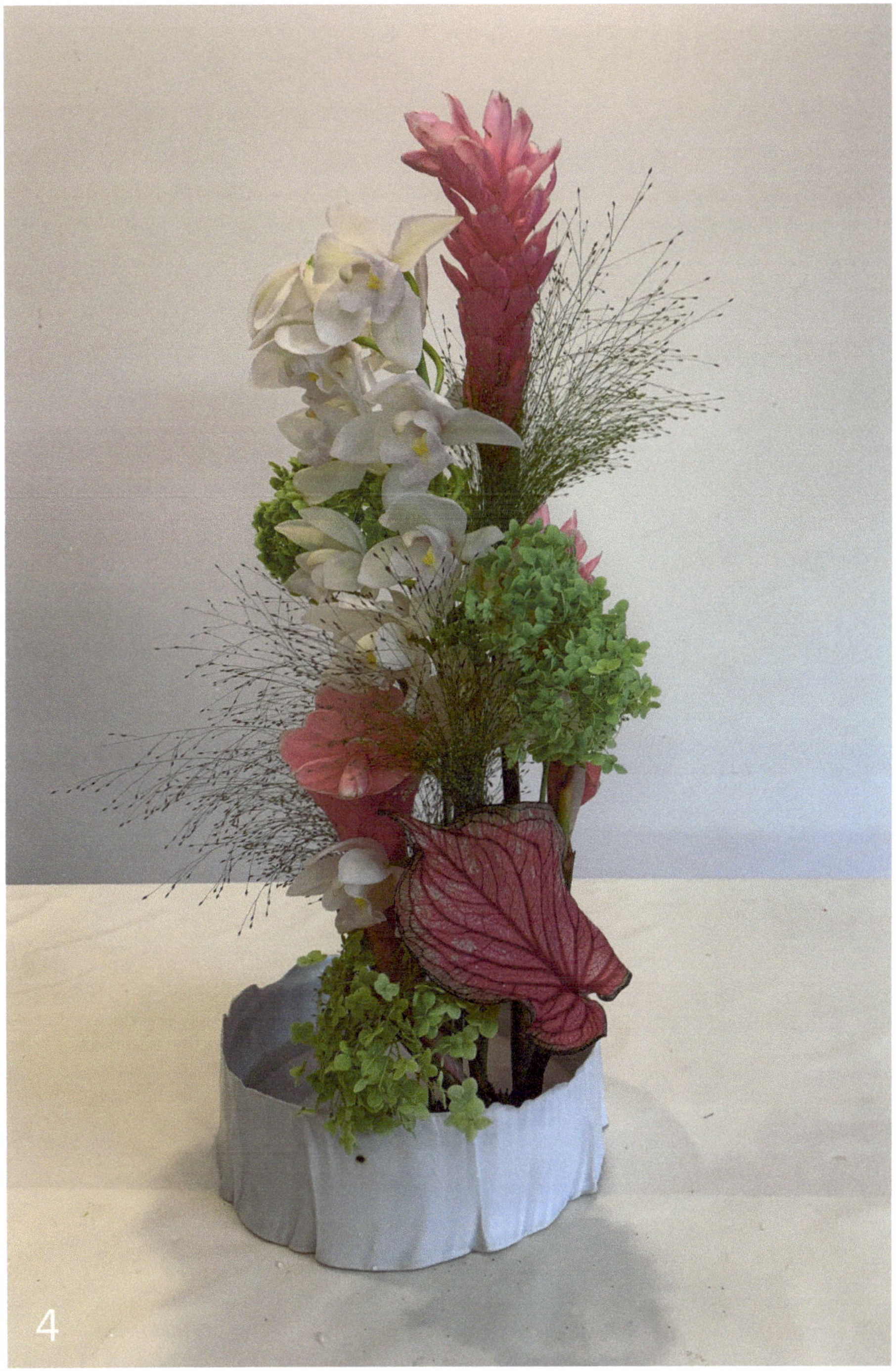

4

Leucothoe

Leucothoe fontanesiana

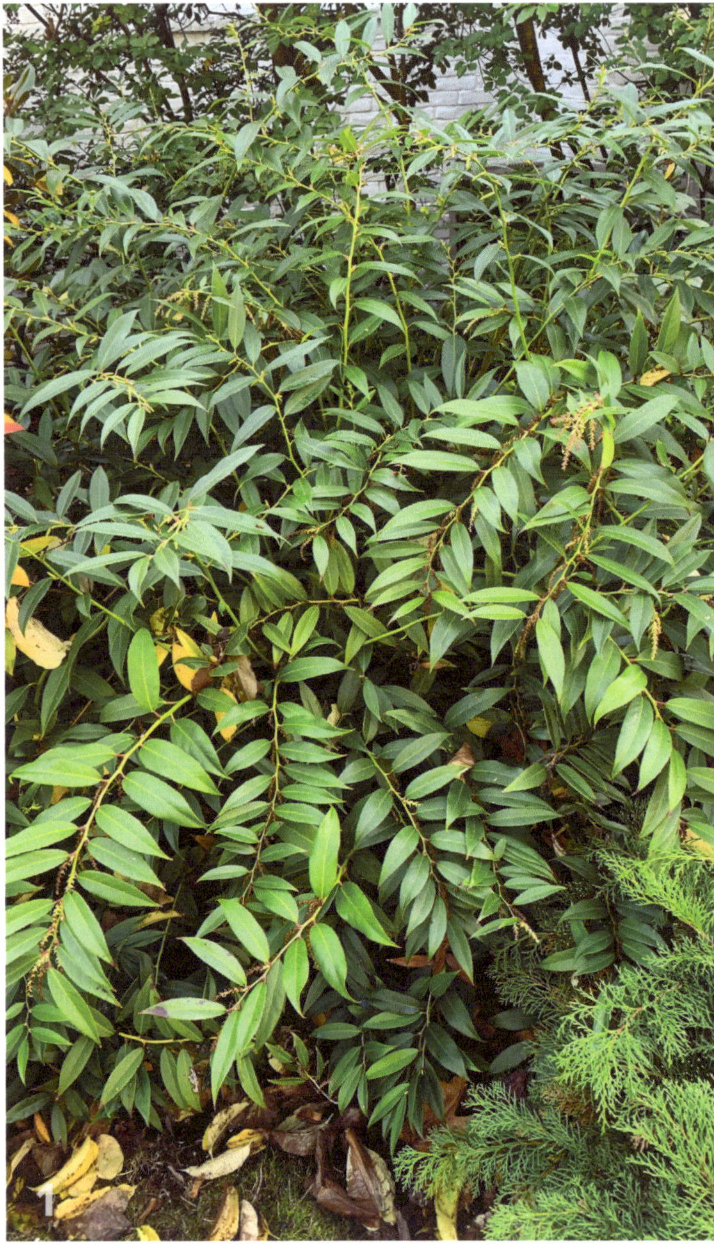

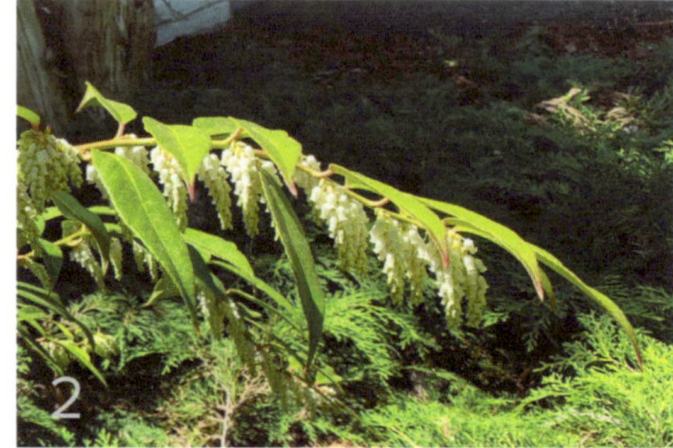

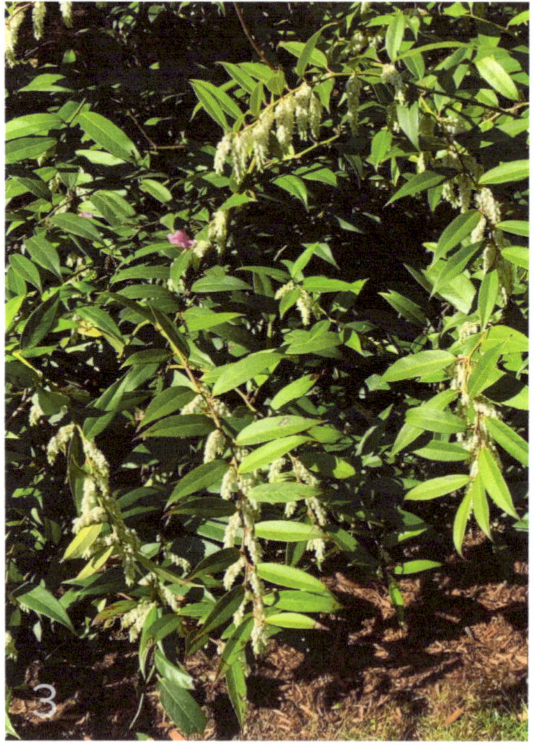

1 This evergreen plant grows with graceful hanging branches. Our leucothoe is green. In our new garden, we have planted the rainbow variety, which has pink and white variegation in the green leaves. When I want hanging branches, it is my go-to plant. The flowers are white and rather insignificant, but the seed heads are graceful. Freezing winter temperatures sometimes damage a few leaves, which require pruning in the spring.
2 Detail of blossoms.
3 The plant in bloom.
4 Leucothoe, delphinium and dendrobium orchids form a horizontal design in a glass vase.
5 This traditional design in an urn-shaped vase has graceful leucothoe branches with many of the leaves removed to reveal the tiny bells. Iris, mountain laurel and lilac fill out the design.
6 This traditional arrangement has a triangular form evinced by the leucothoe branches. The lily is the center of interest and the carnations, goldenrod, and viburnum leaves and berries complete the arrangement.
7 The form of the arching containers is repeated by the curving leucothoe branches. The pink azaleas create a colored path connecting the two containers.

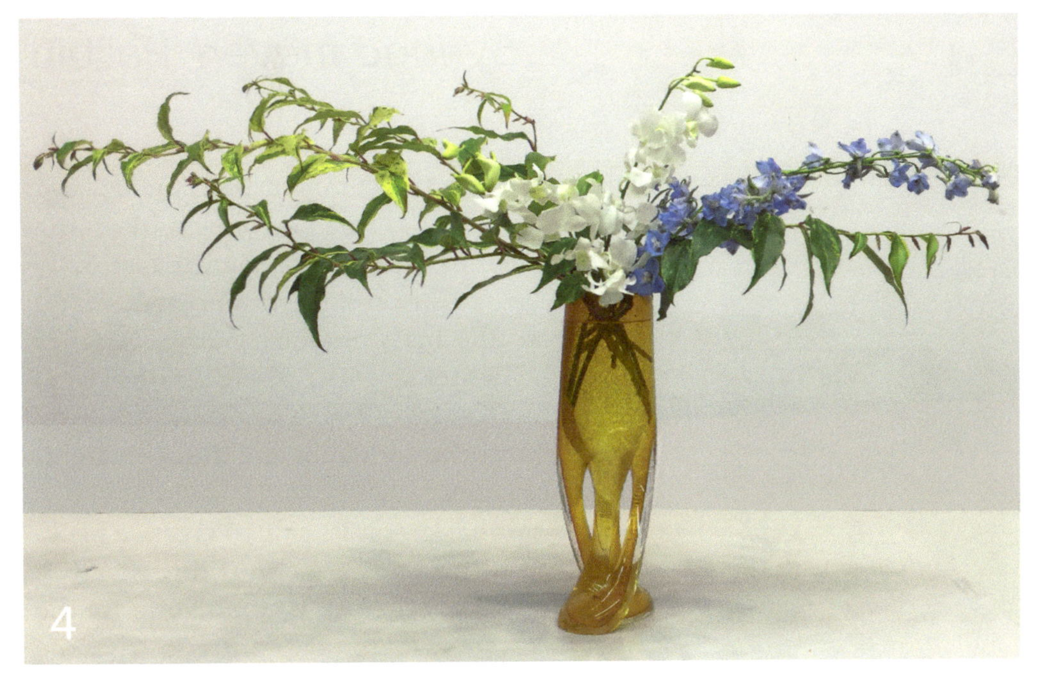

4

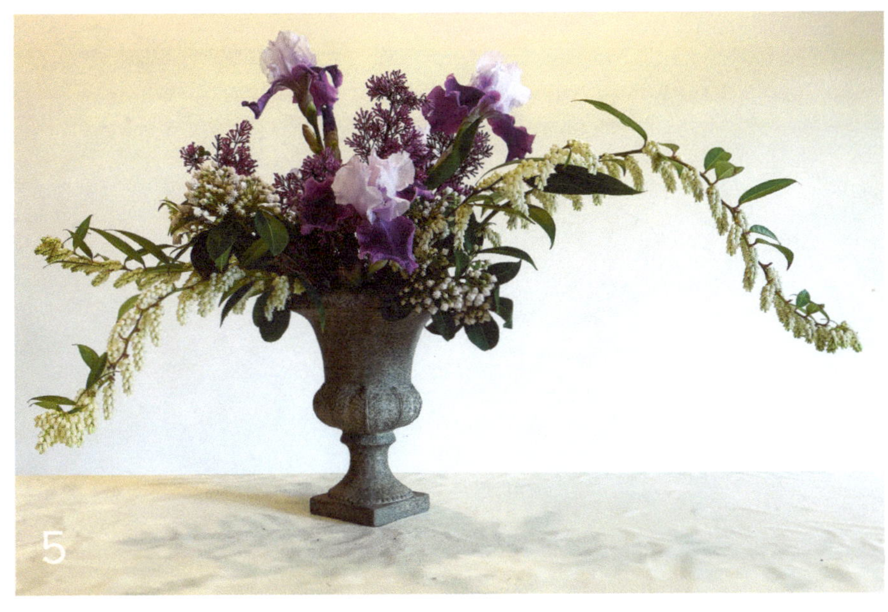

5

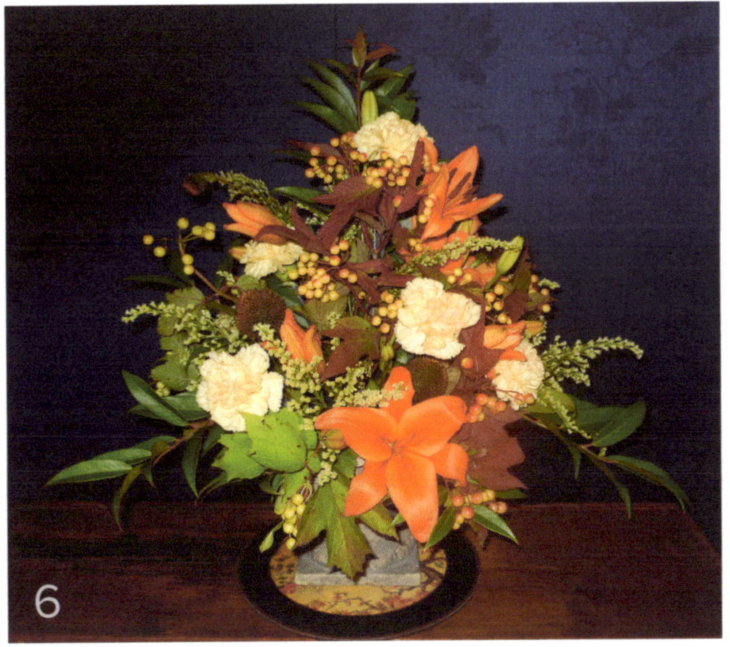

6

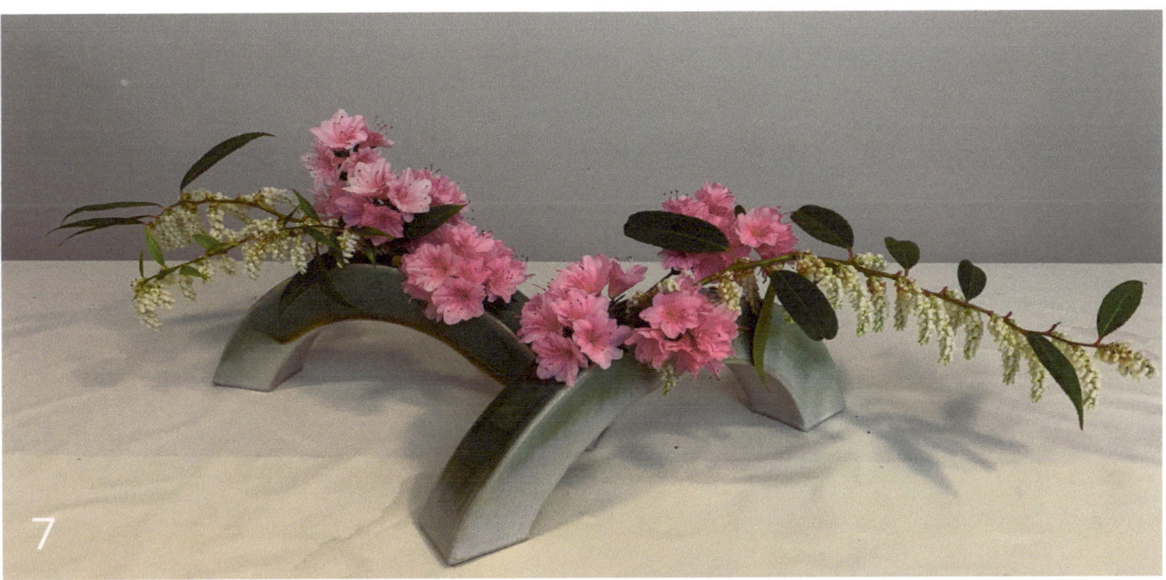

7

Lilac, Korean

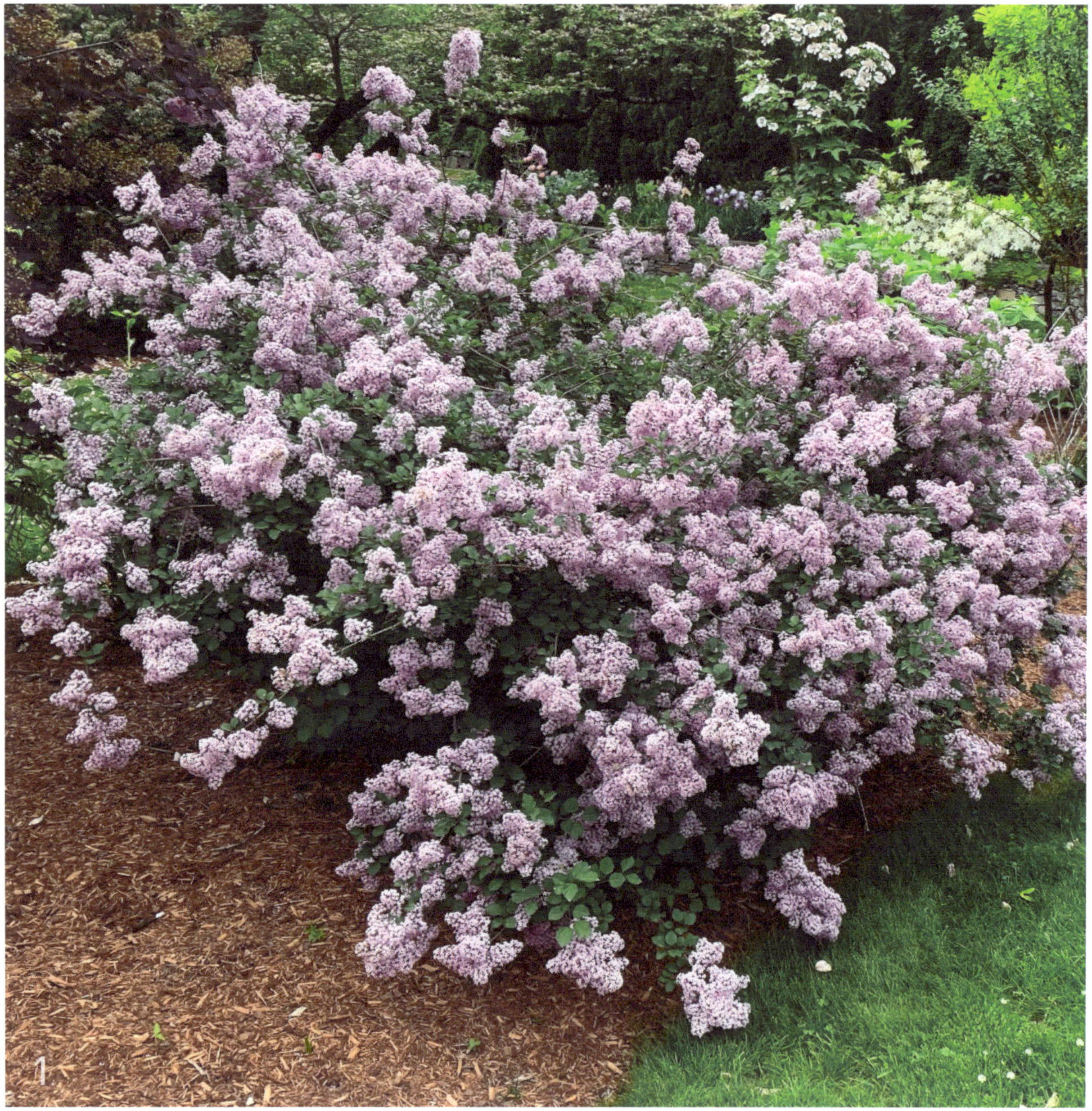

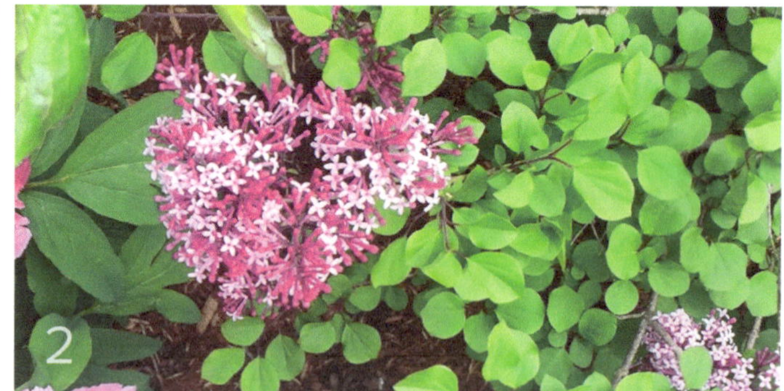

1. Different from the common lilac, *Syringa vulgaris*, this shrub has small leaves and blossoms. It was given to me by a student. It resembles 'Miss Kim', a Korean lilac shrub that has larger leaves. The buds are dark purple. As they open, the lighter lavender of the blossom is revealed.
2. Detail shows the dark buds and the open, lighter tiny blossoms.
3. I tilted this basket on its side to create a backdrop and to make use of the grid to stabilize the tall iris. The other iris is combined with the lilac to create a mass that contrasts with the interesting spaces in the woven pattern of the basket.
4. The curved lines of the vase are extended with lilac branches. A dense group of flowers in the middle holds the arrangement together.
5. A lilac and dogwood tsubo arrangement.
6. The alliums thrust out of the lilac mass in this arched container.

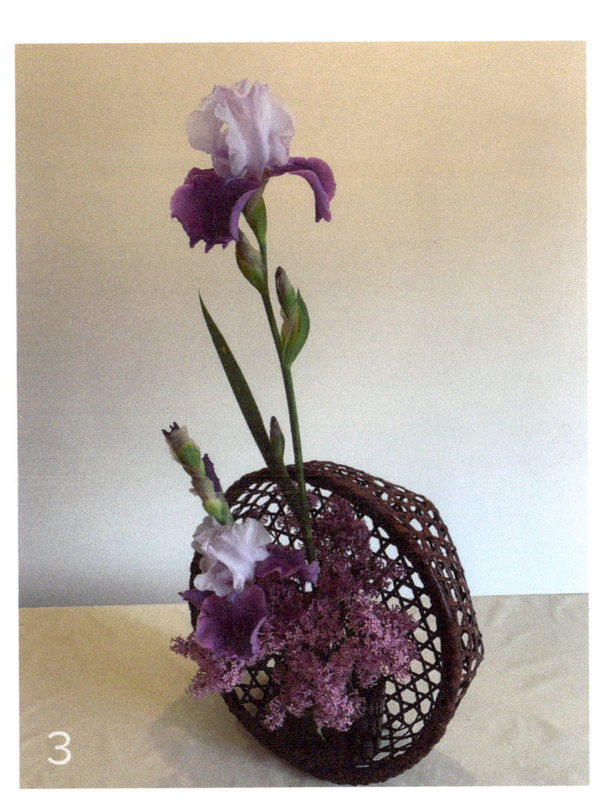

3

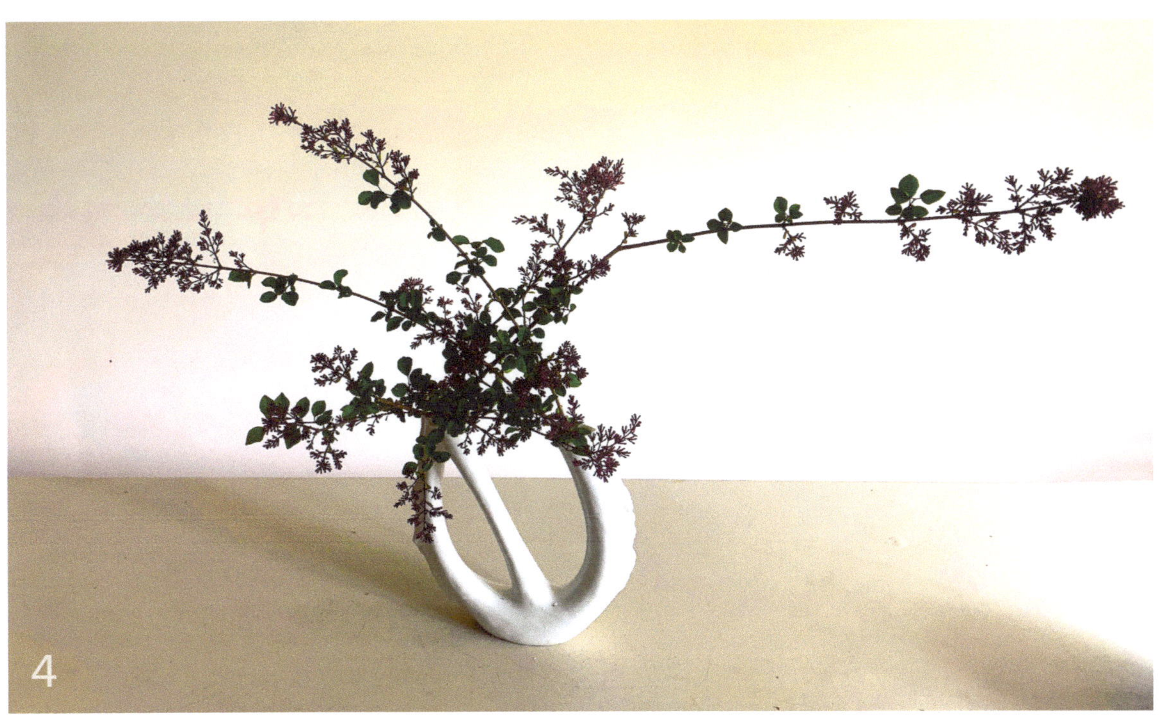

4

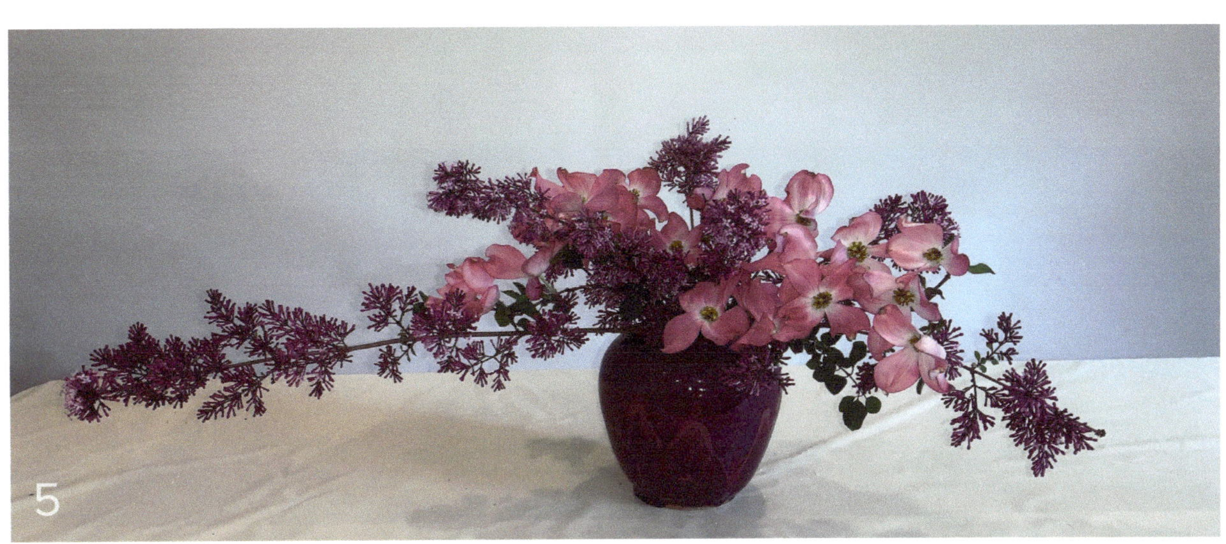

5

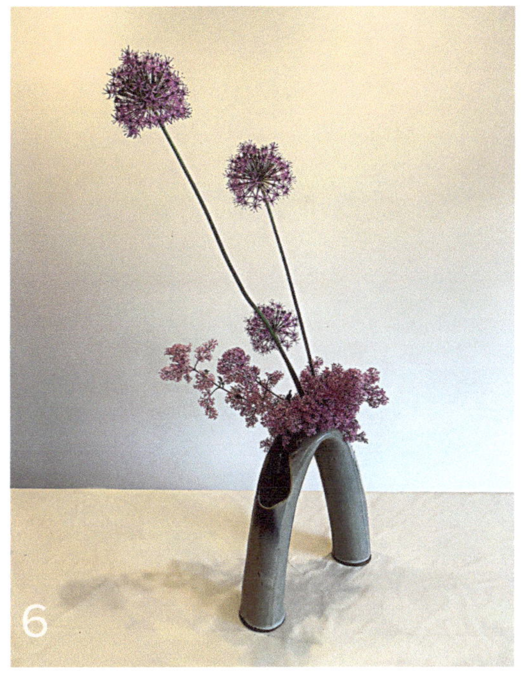

6

Magnolia, Star *Magnolia stellata*

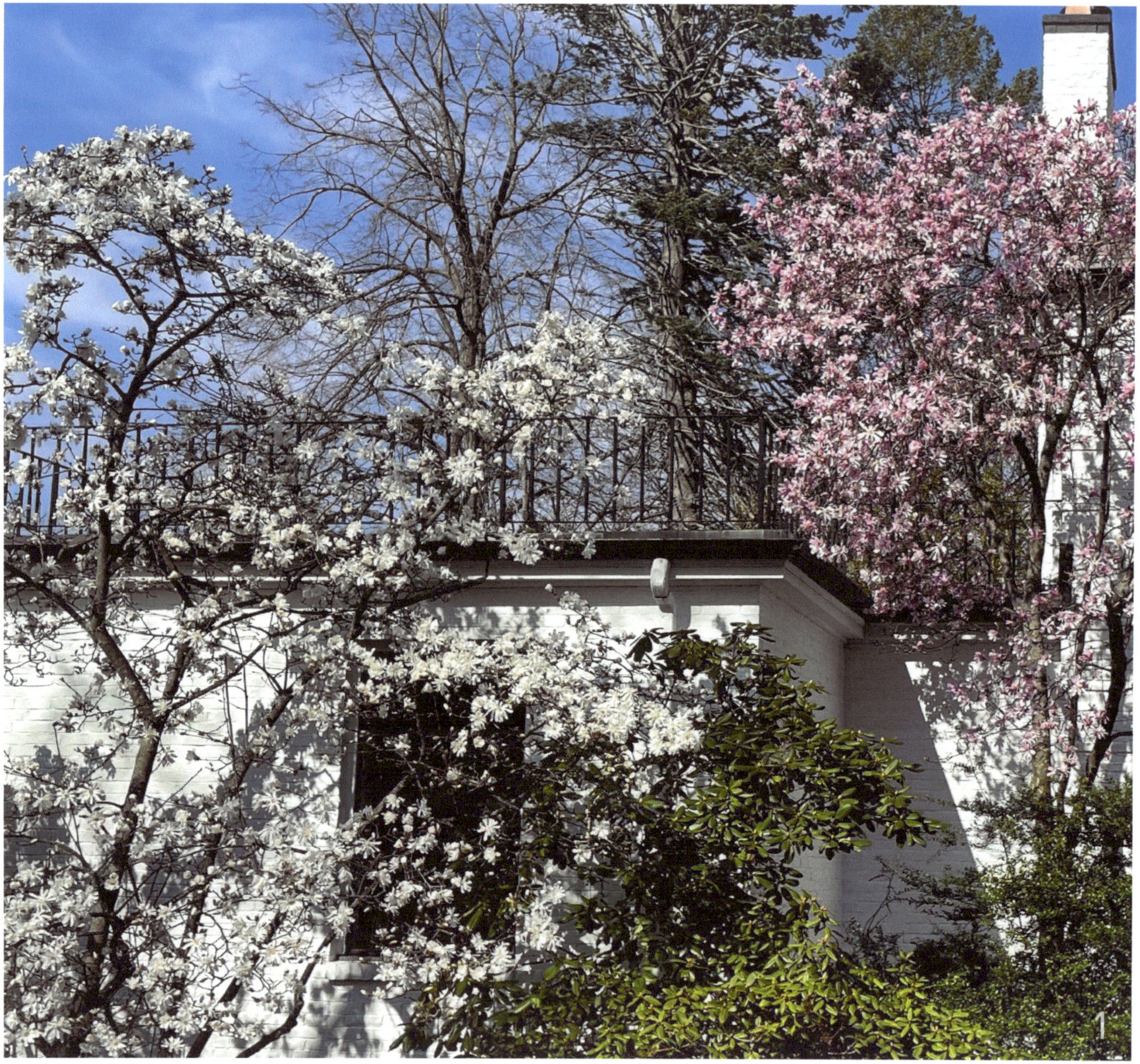

1. The star magnolia has lovely blossoms. Here you see the pink tree on the right and the white on the left. Sadly, I find it hard to condition the flowers of my star magnolia. So, most frequently, I use the branches with their velvety buds in the wintertime.
2. Close-up of the opened blossom.
3. Magnolia branches with buds outline the space where azaleas pose.
4. A new vase my husband made with curved ridges inspired me to use this curved branch with buds just beginning to open.
5. The winter buds form a soft frame for the roses and baby's breath.
6. A riot of petals swarm around this container of the matching colors.

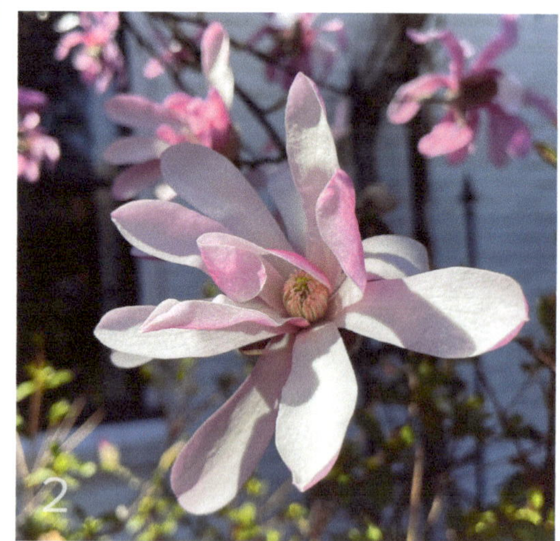

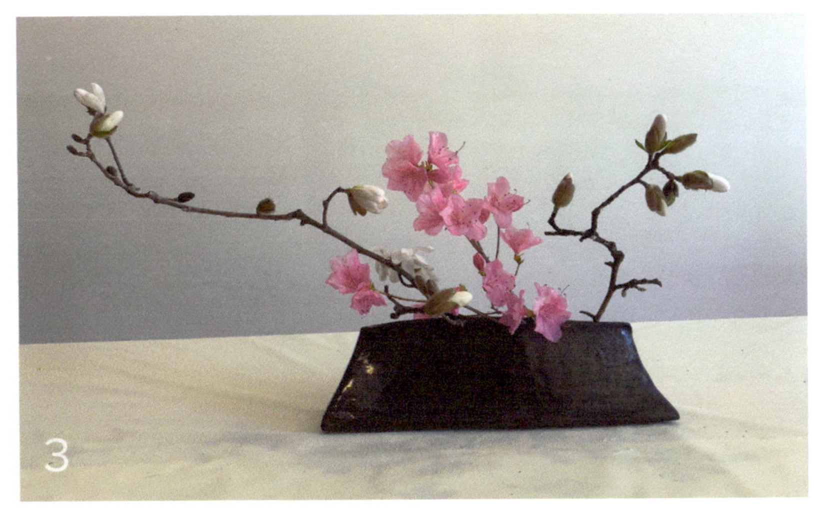

3

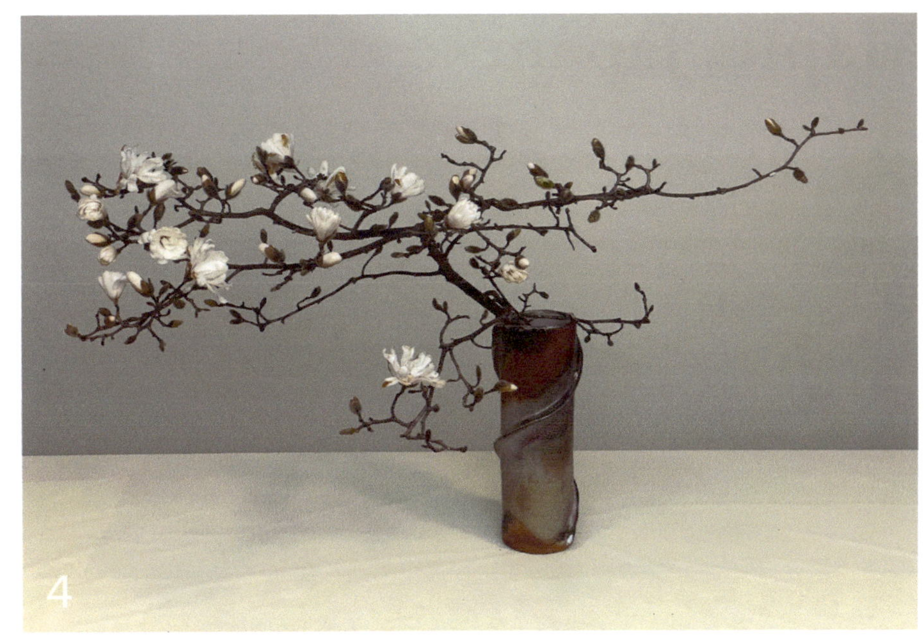

4

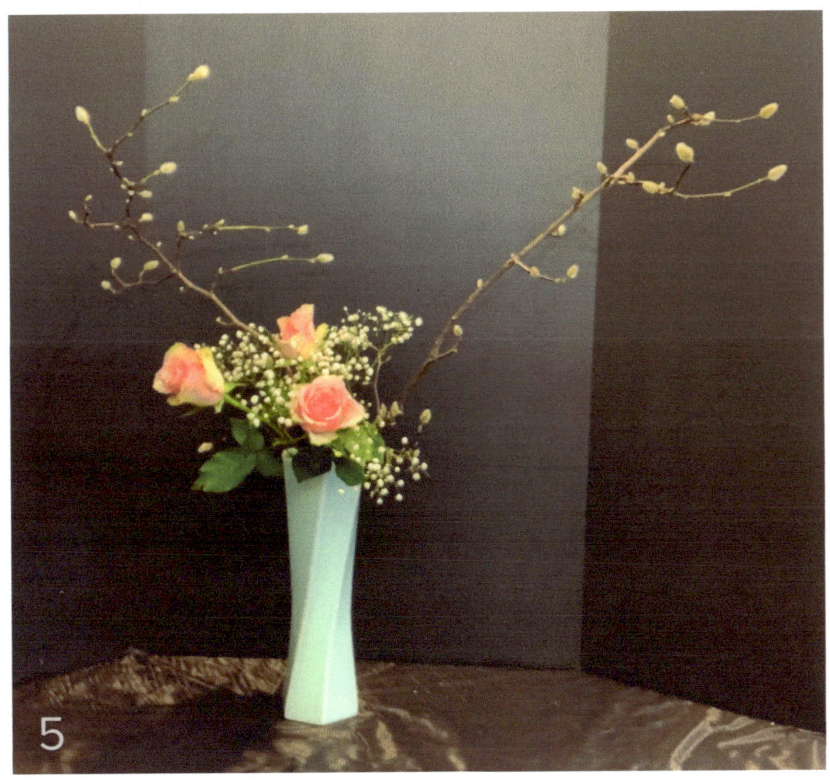

5

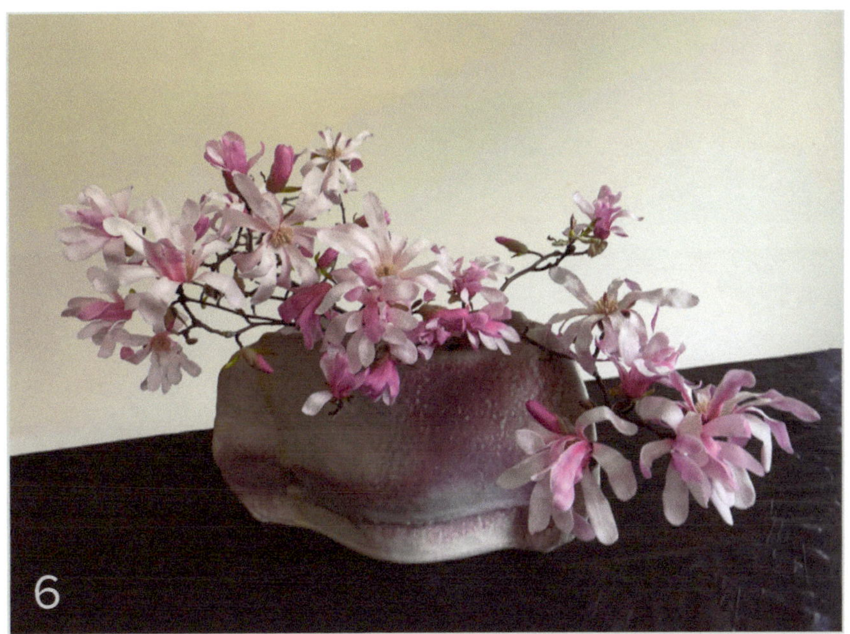

6

Maple, Japanese
Acer palmatum var. *dissectum*

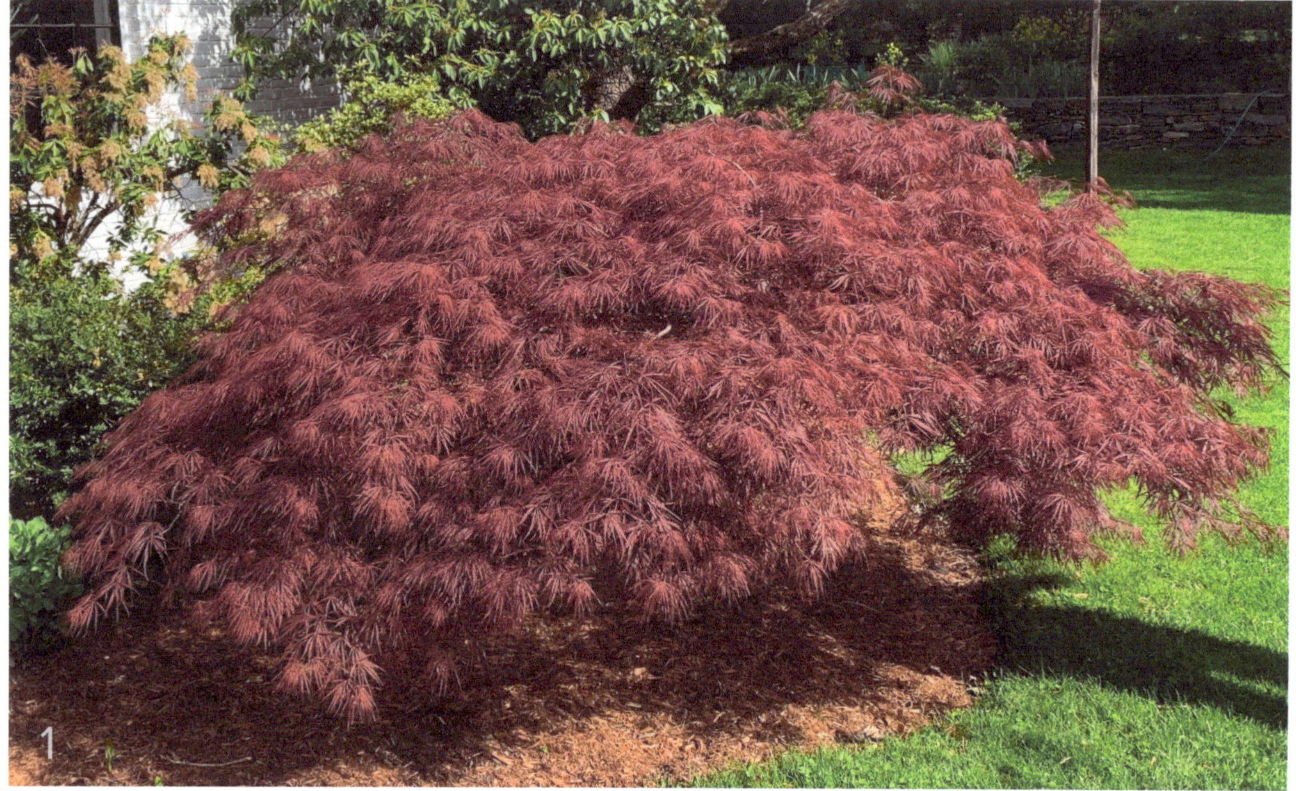

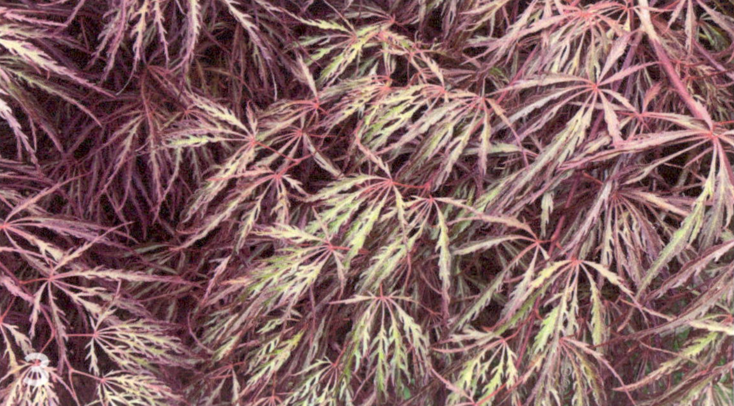

1. This tree is shrub-sized. It is a wonderful red in the spring and summer. I don't know the specific variety of this cut-leaf maple, because it was already growing on the property when we purchased it. For arranging, it is best used horizontally.
2. Detail of cut leaves.
3. In late summer, its leaves develop a green hue.
4. This Japanese maple is juxtaposed with the maple wings of a Norway maple whose leaves have been removed.
5. Caladium leaves and mini carnations strengthen the horizontal line of this arrangement.
6. A creative miniature design showing the maple leaves and some leucothoe blossoms.
7. Here, the boat-like container floats peonies and maple branches.

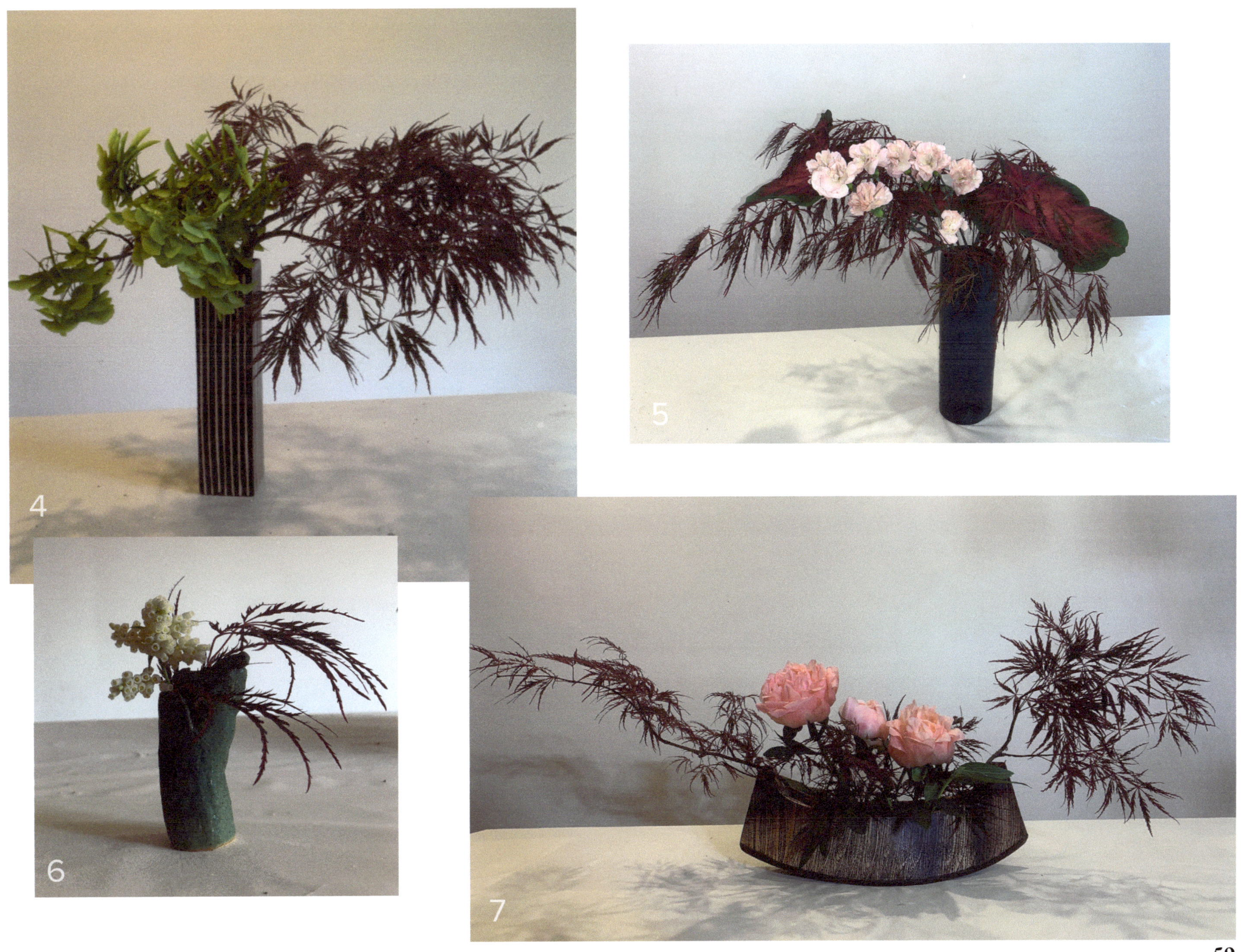

Maple, Norway *Acer platanoides*

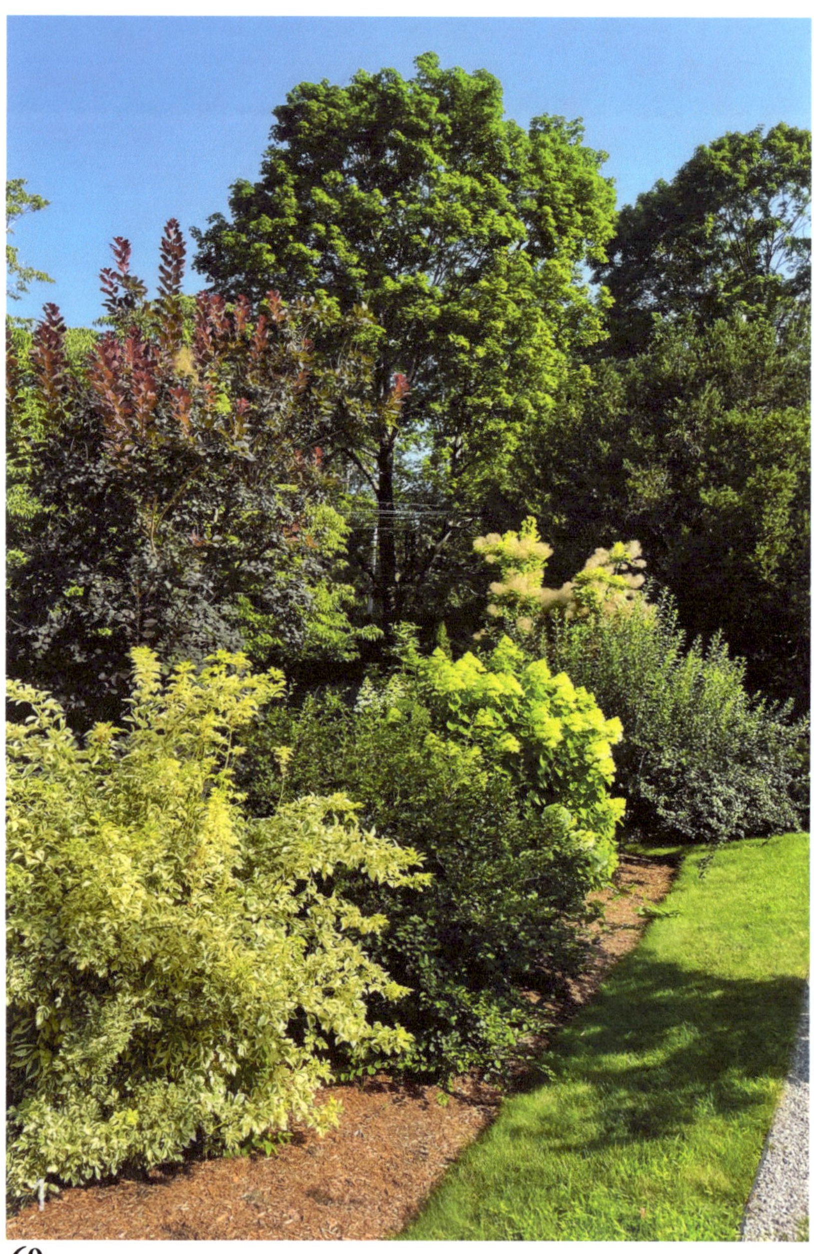

1 In Newton, Massachusetts, Norway maples were planted along many of the residential streets. In the photo to the left, it is the tallest tree in the center. Norway maple is now recognized as an invasive species, but our town only removes them when they die or become a hazard. In the time we have lived in this house, the town has had to remove two of them on our property. Maple branches are easy to cut and put in a kenzan or split for nageire mechanics.

2 The tiny blossoms form a pom-pom.

3 The leaves and maple wings cluster on the branch. I remember as a child picking these maple wings, splitting them and putting them on my nose!

4 The spring branches are decorated with tiny balls of blossoms. Lily and andromeda complete the design.

5 This summer, some of my Norway maple was trimmed at the top by an arborist. The full branches were too massive to use, so I cut off all the leaves, leaving the maple wings. I found these fun to use, as in this nageire with iris from our garden and branch with maple wings.

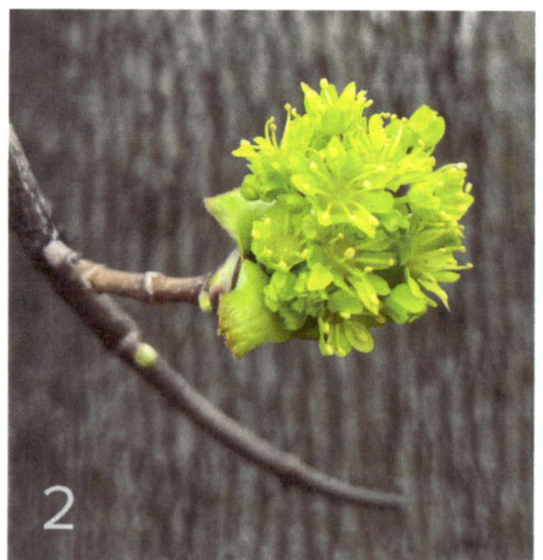

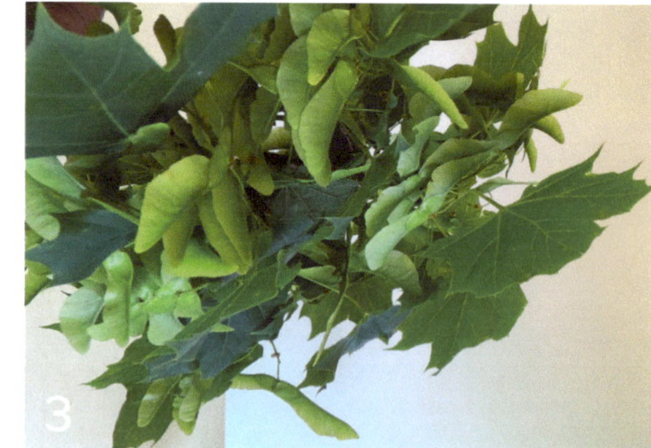

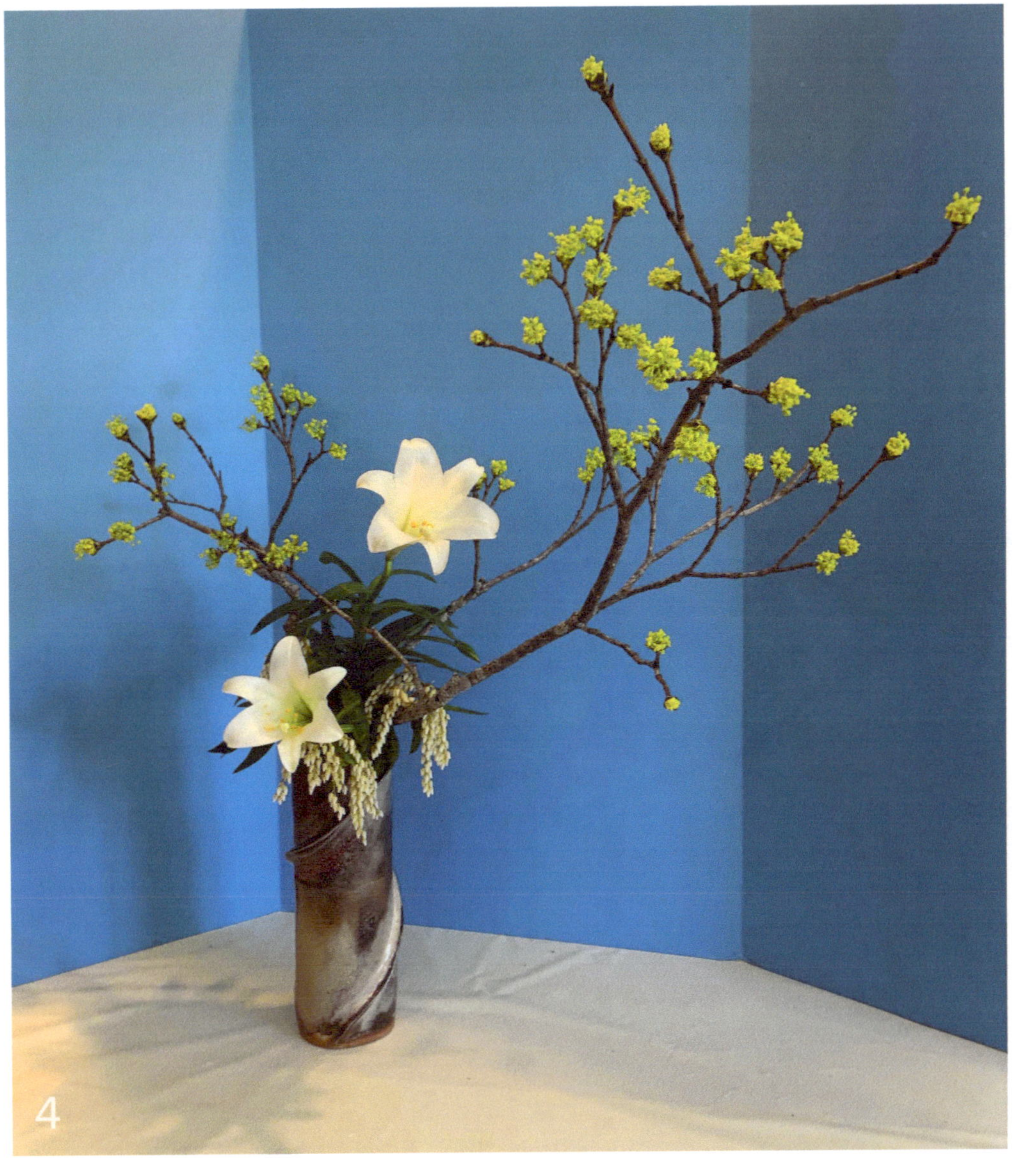

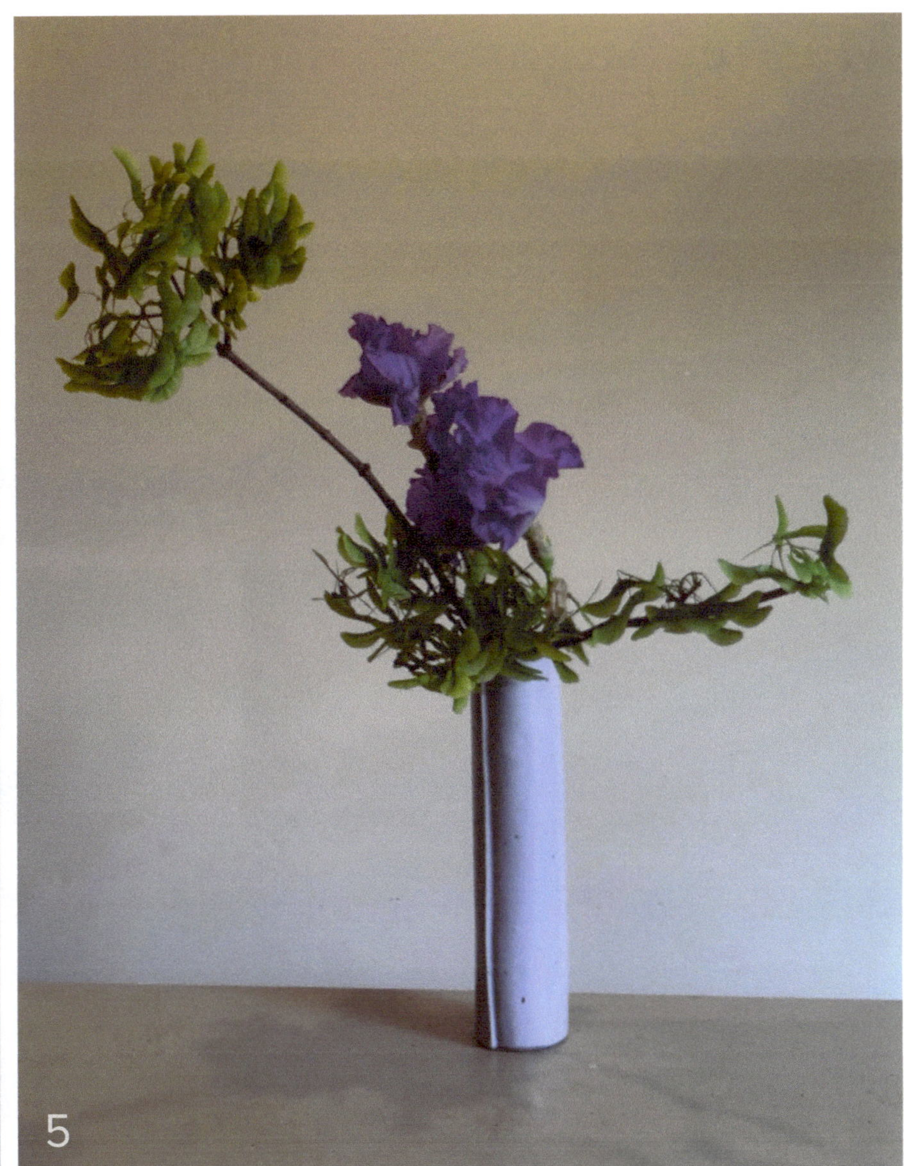

Maple, Sugar *Acer saccharum*

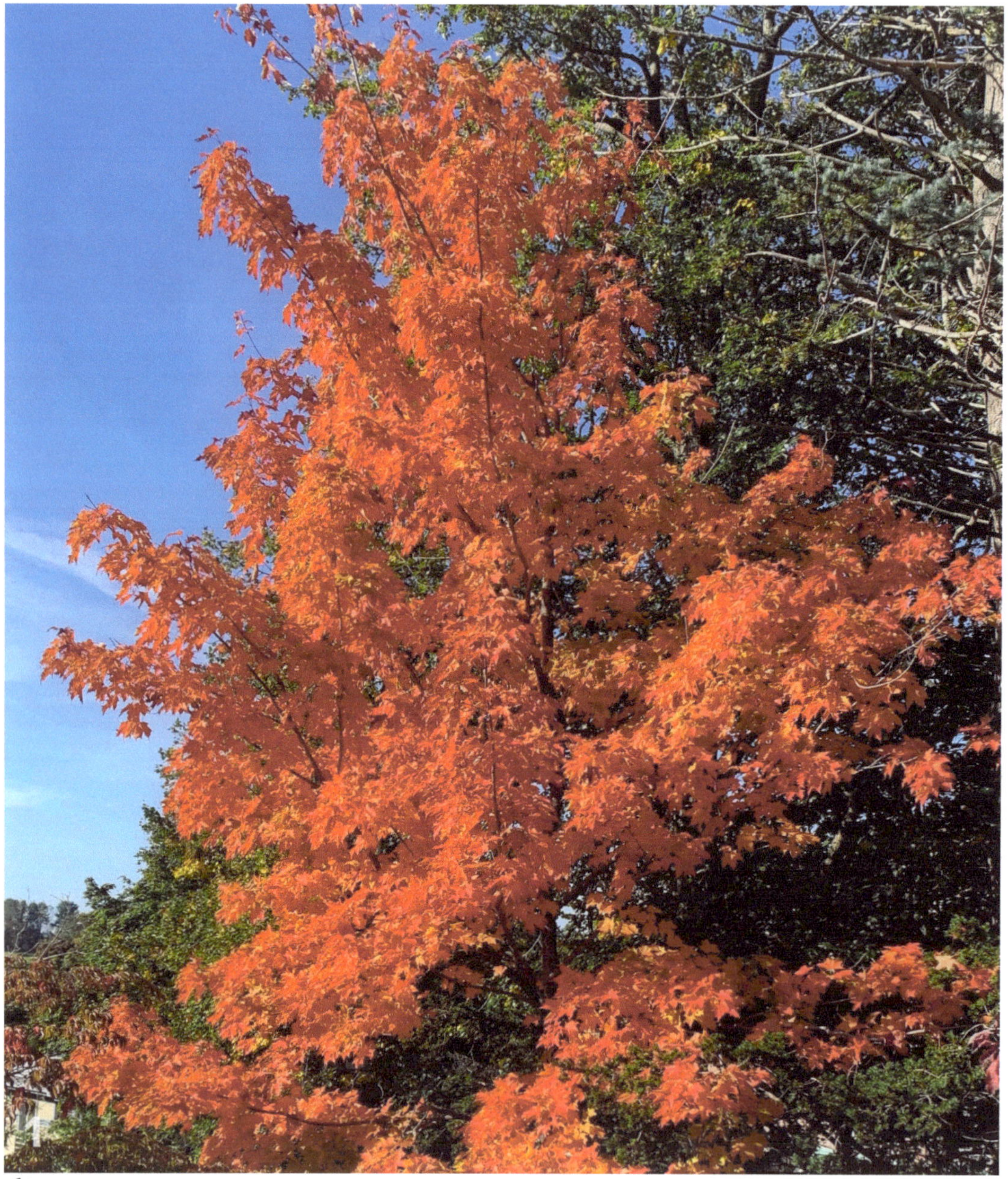

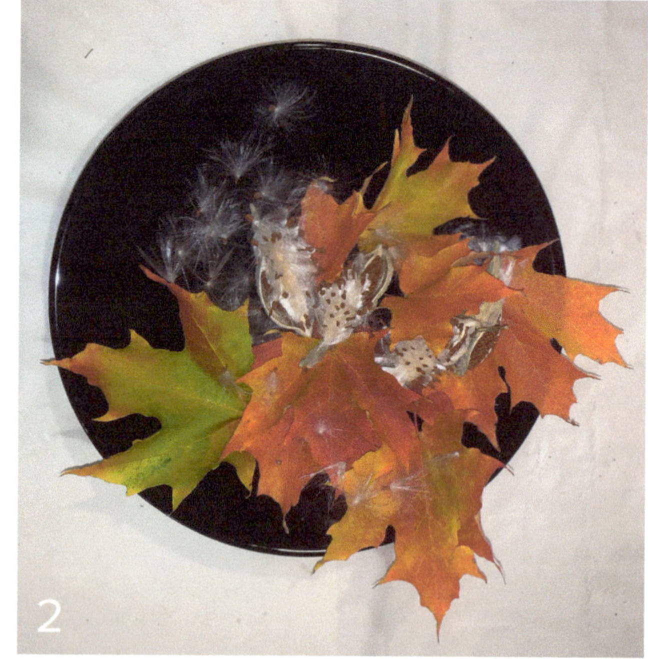

1 This is another kind of maple that turns a beautiful red in the fall. Although the leaves are fairly large for using in arrangements, we prize the beautiful autumn hues they bring.
2 The leaves and milkweed pods are arranged in this shallow dish (viewed from above) showcasing the beauty of the leaves.
3 This Halloween arrangement of chrysanthemums, persimmon fruits, spider orchids, beautyberry, snowberry, and manzanita branches is brightened with sugar maple leaves.

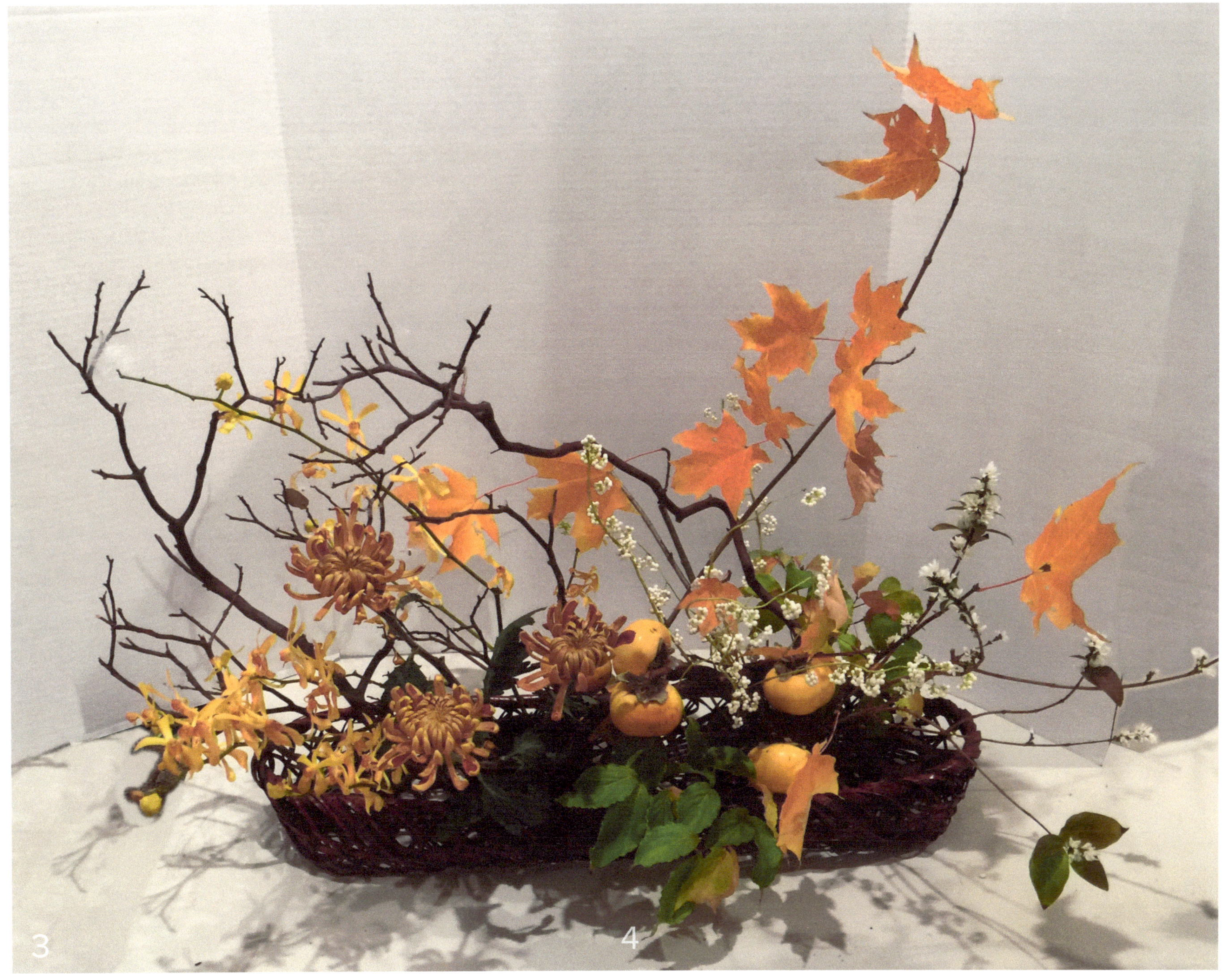

3
4

Mountain Laurel *Kalmia latifolia*

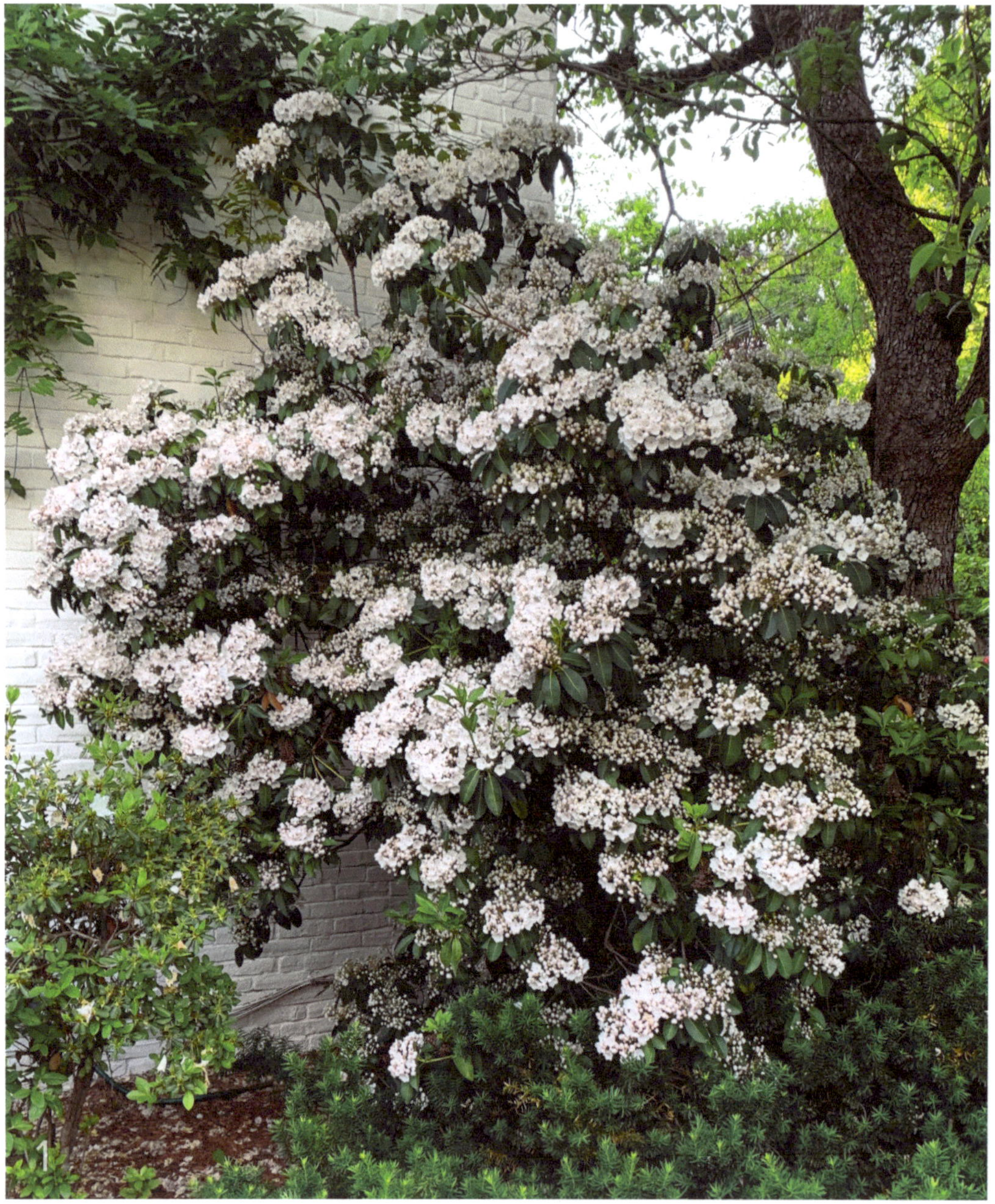

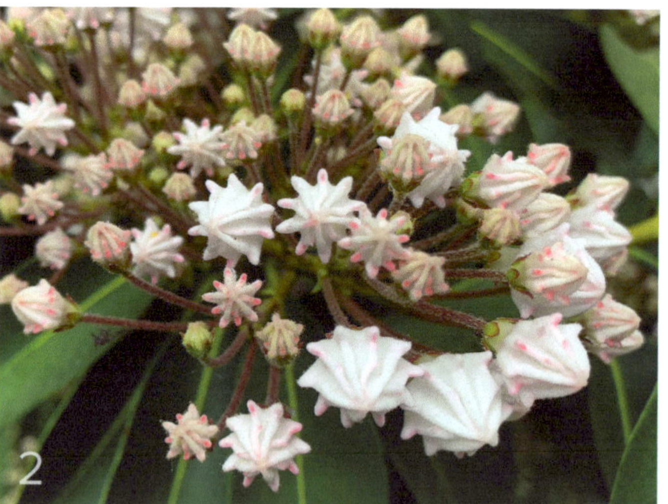

1   We were blessed with a large planting of these evergreens next to the house. Snow falling off the roof doesn't seem to harm them. They bloom a bit later than the rhododendron. In our garden, the groups of flowers, called trusses, are white with pink buds. I have seen a wide variety of beautifully-colored ones in neighbors' gardens. The seed heads are even interesting after the blooms have faded. The leaves are medium-sized and pointed.
2   Fascinating detail of the surface of the buds.
3   Mountain laurel in bloom with royal purple smoketree, with the inflorescence that gives the smoketree its name.
4   Seed heads with nasturtium in a miniature design.
5   A pink glass container holds this diagonal line design of pink blossoms and green smoketree.

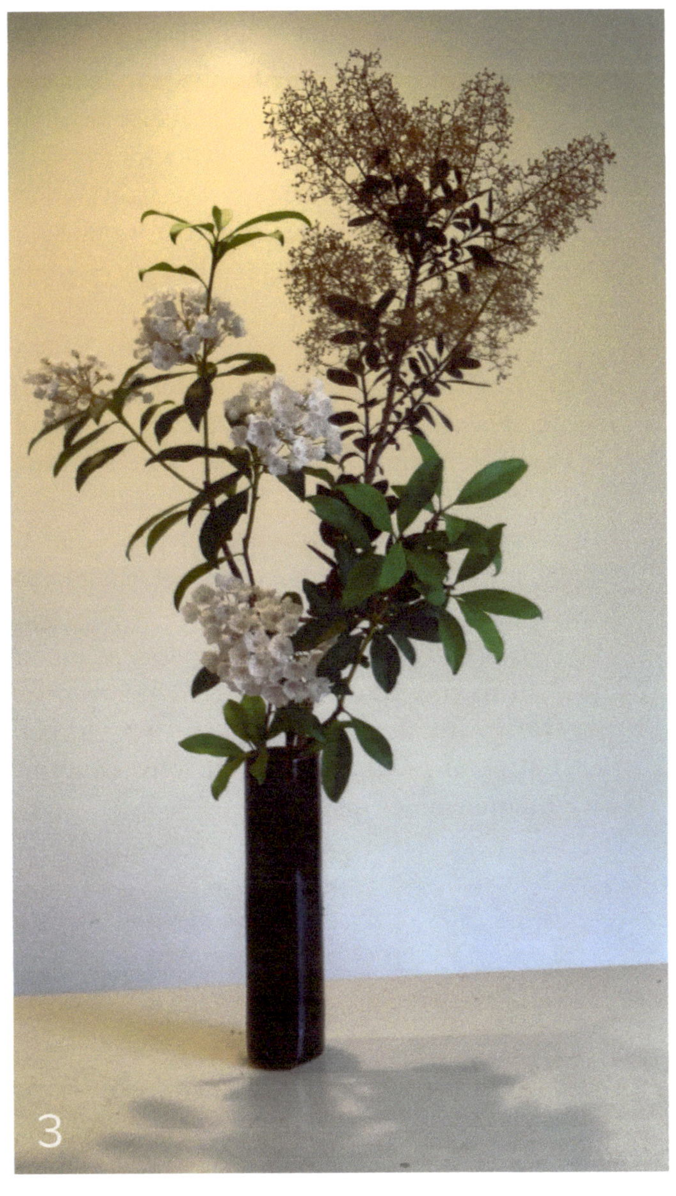

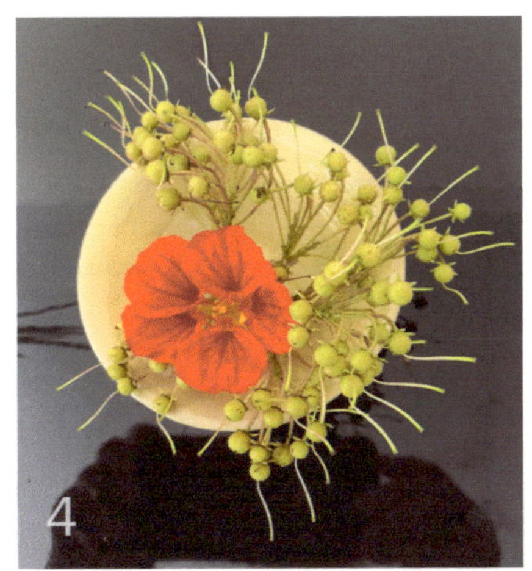

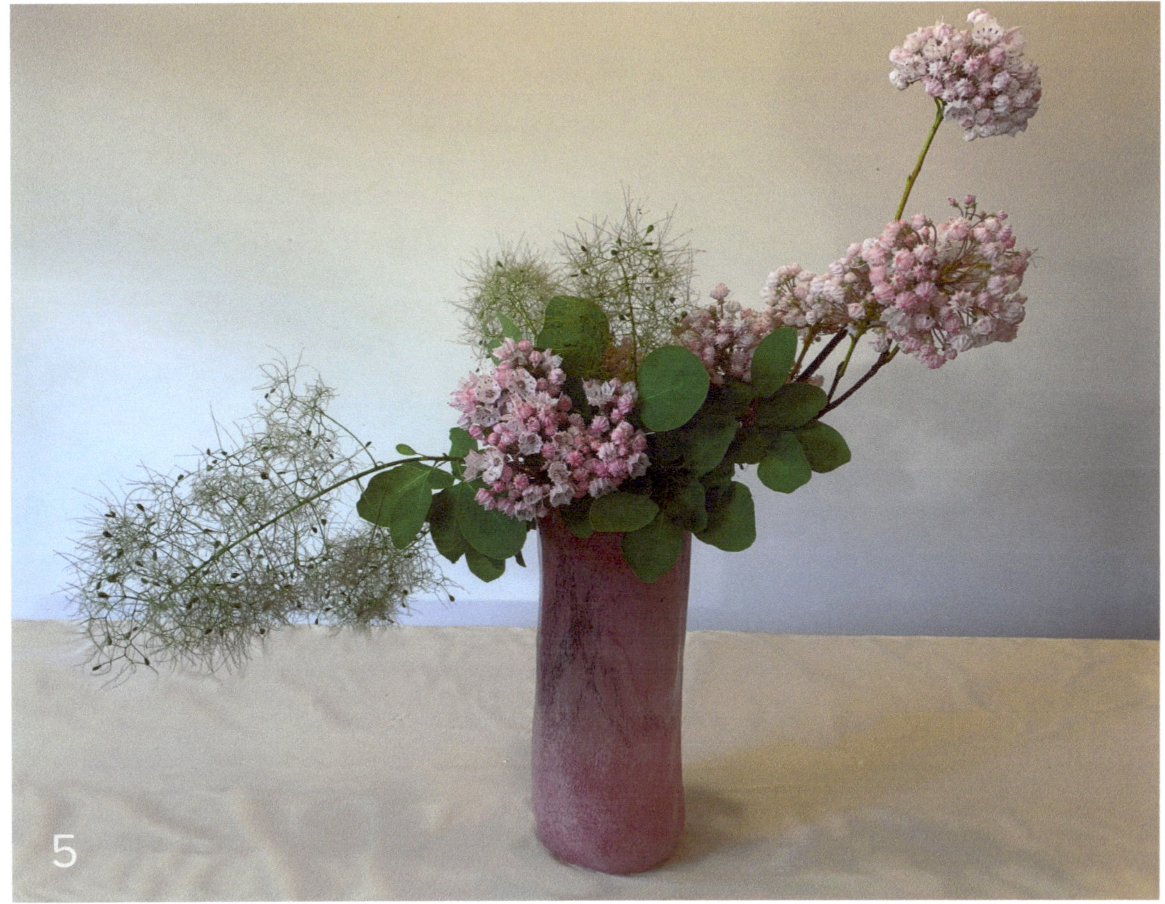

Pieris japonica

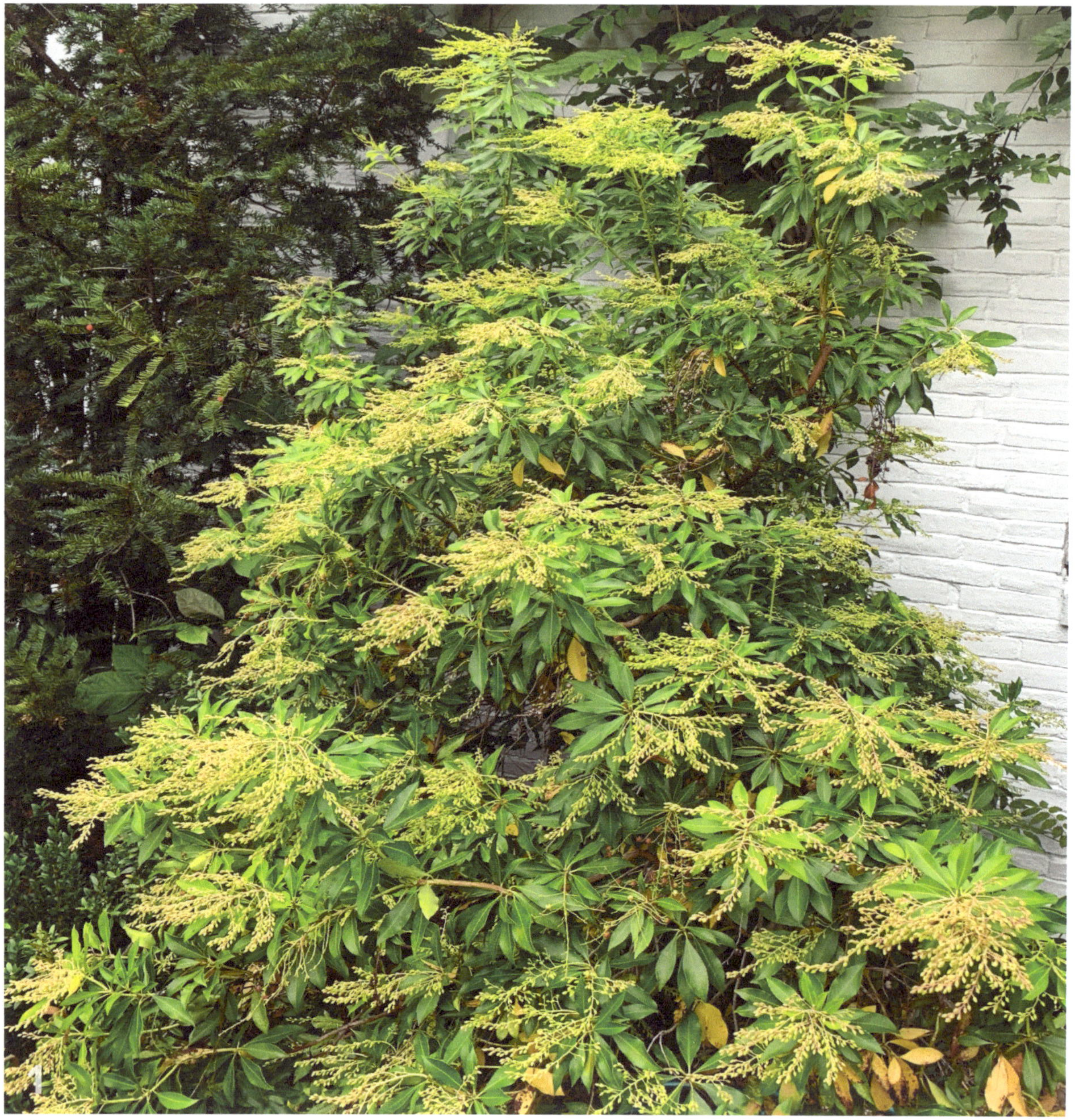

1 Commonly called andromeda, this shrub is evergreen. The blossoms are beautiful white bells that become little green berries. The structure that holds the blossoms, and subsequently the fruits, adds a delicate texture to the plant. The stems can become quite thick and strong as they age.

2 Detail of blossoms.

3 These ikebana freestyle designs (photos 3 and 6) are made with just one kind of material. They are arranged to show stems, leaves, and seed heads. This arrangement is fixed in a kenzan in a moribana container.

4 Andromeda, PJM, and chrysanthemums are fixed by wedging in this container that is too narrow for a kenzan.

5 The *pieris* blossoms play with the fuji mum and the PJM in this traditional urn. The leucothoe gracefully extends the design.

6 *Pieris japonica* balances on a nageire container with no mechanics inside.

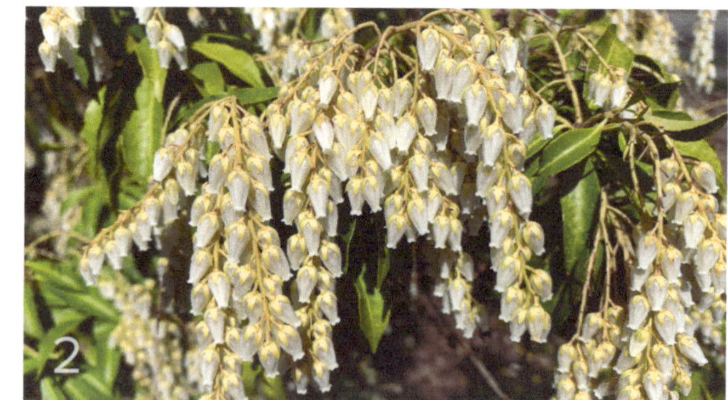

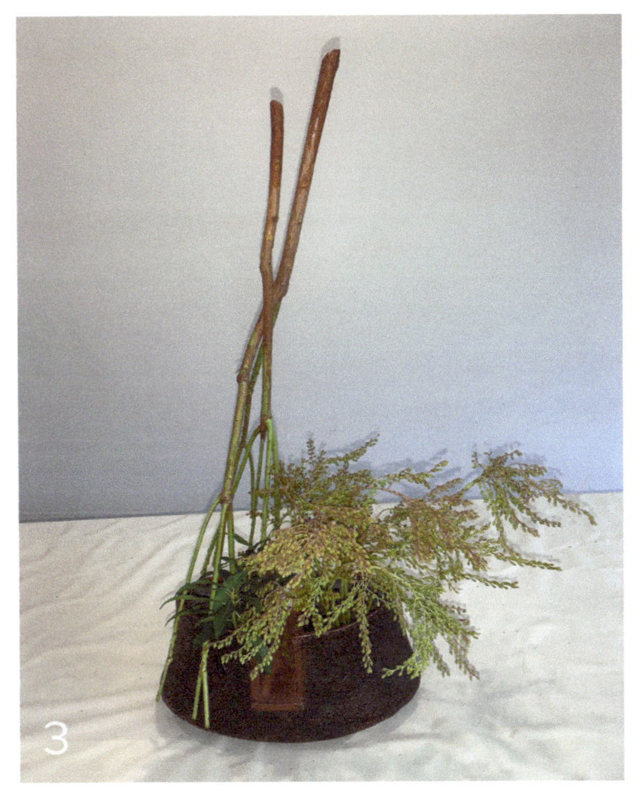

3

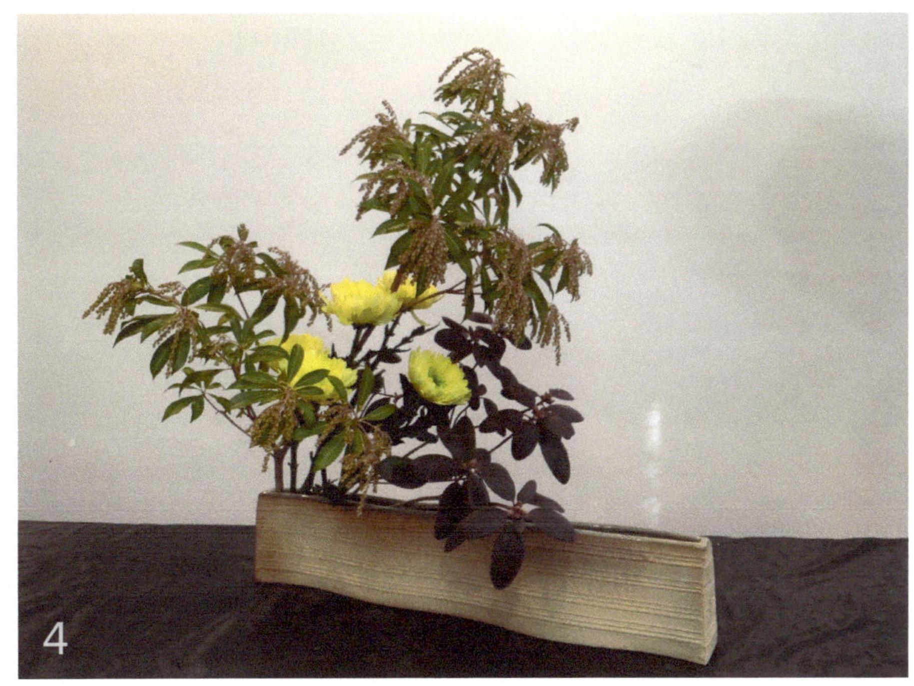

4

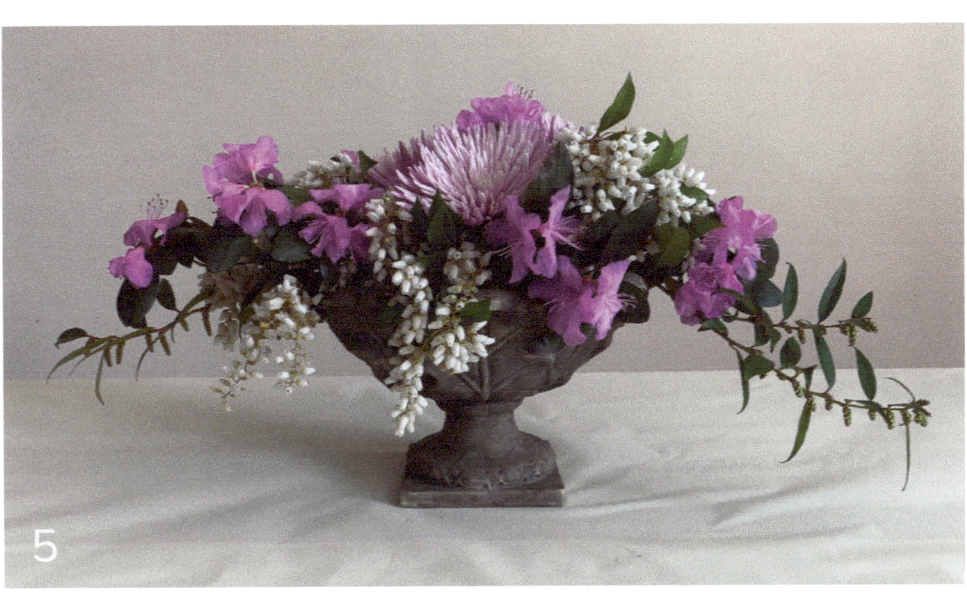

5

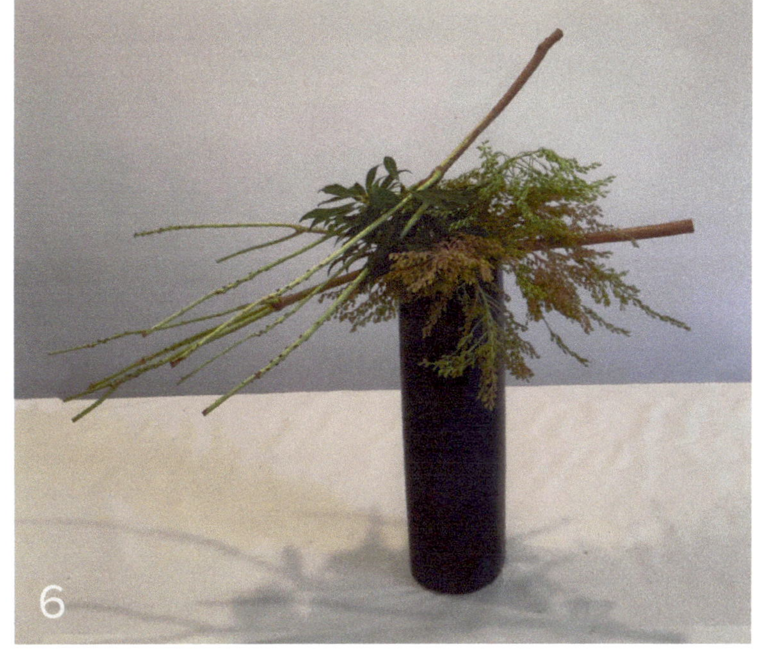

6

Pine, White *Pinus strobus*

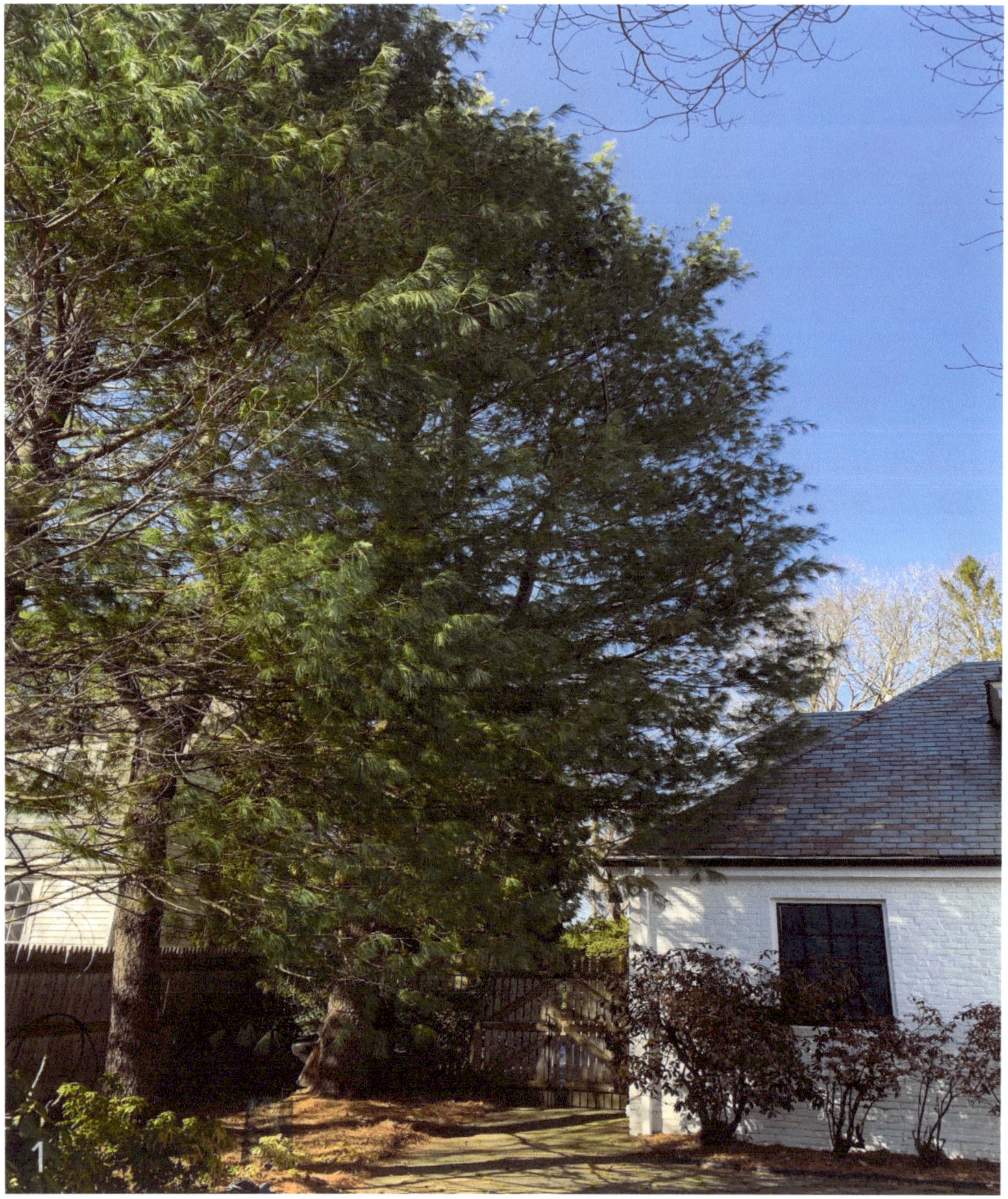

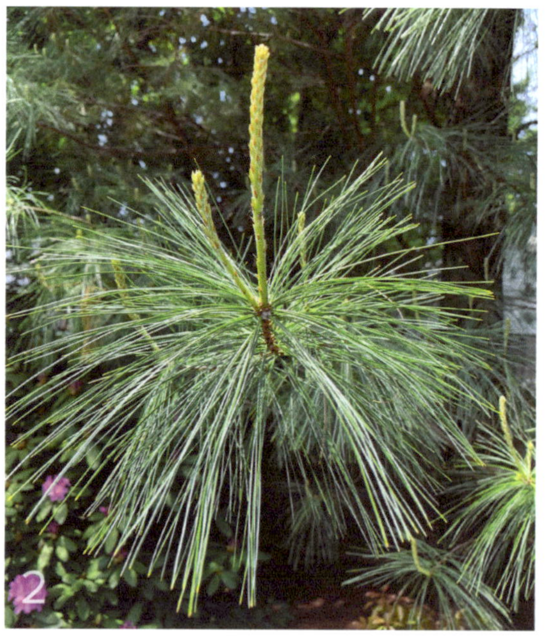

1. This lovely evergreen tree shields our house from the neighbors, even in the wintertime as in this picture. The needled branches are graceful. For a few weeks in June, their yellow pollen coats our porch.
2. Here are the new candles and the needles. In Japan, the method of managing the shape and size of the pine tree is to remove all or part of the candle that grows into the new branch.
3. A holiday design decorates our hearth. Pine, red carnations, arborvitae, variegated bamboo leaves and holly are arranged for a festive look.
4. Pine branch and needles represent a stark winter scene.
5. A winter arrangement of narcissus flowers from a forced bulb and white pine. This container expresses winter with slanted snow falling.

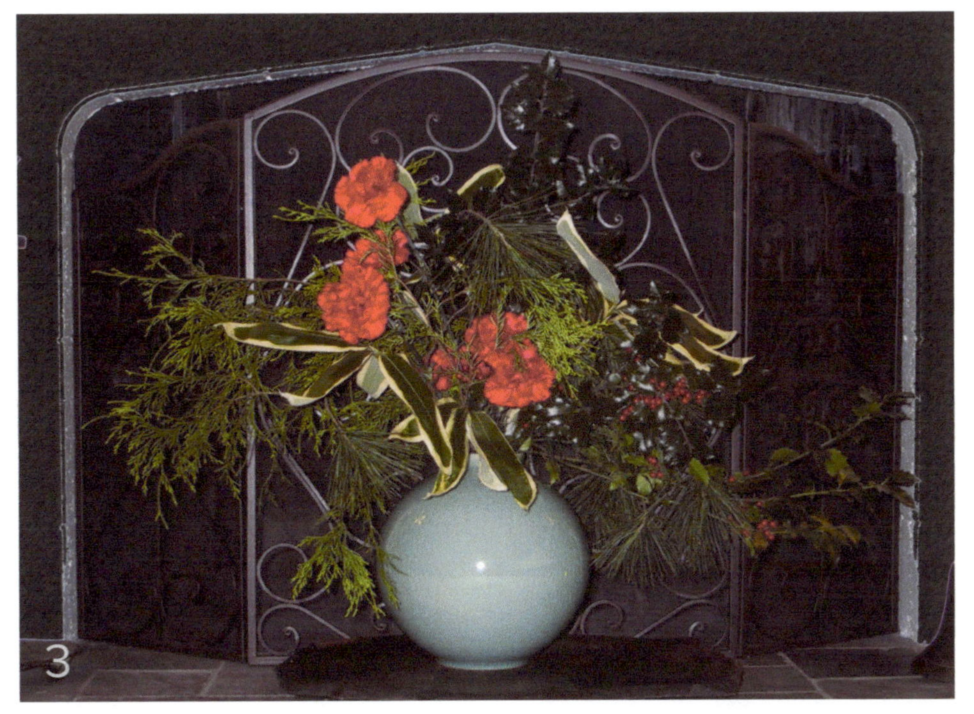

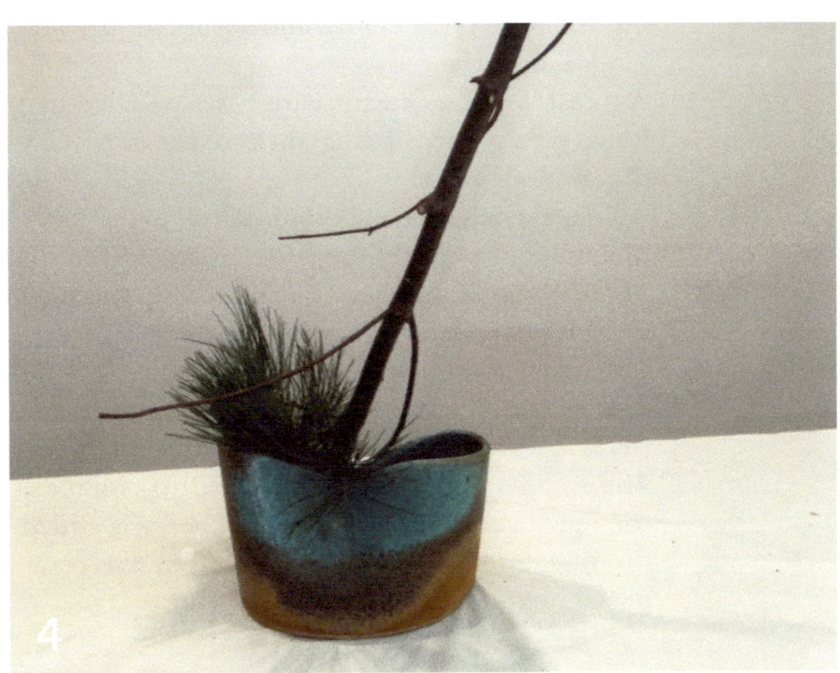

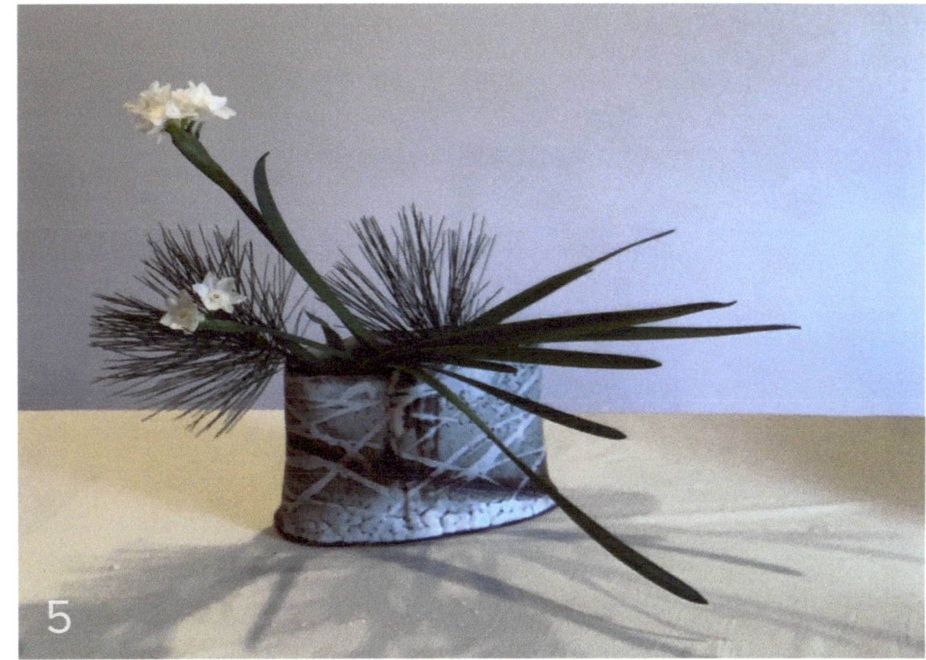

Rhododendron

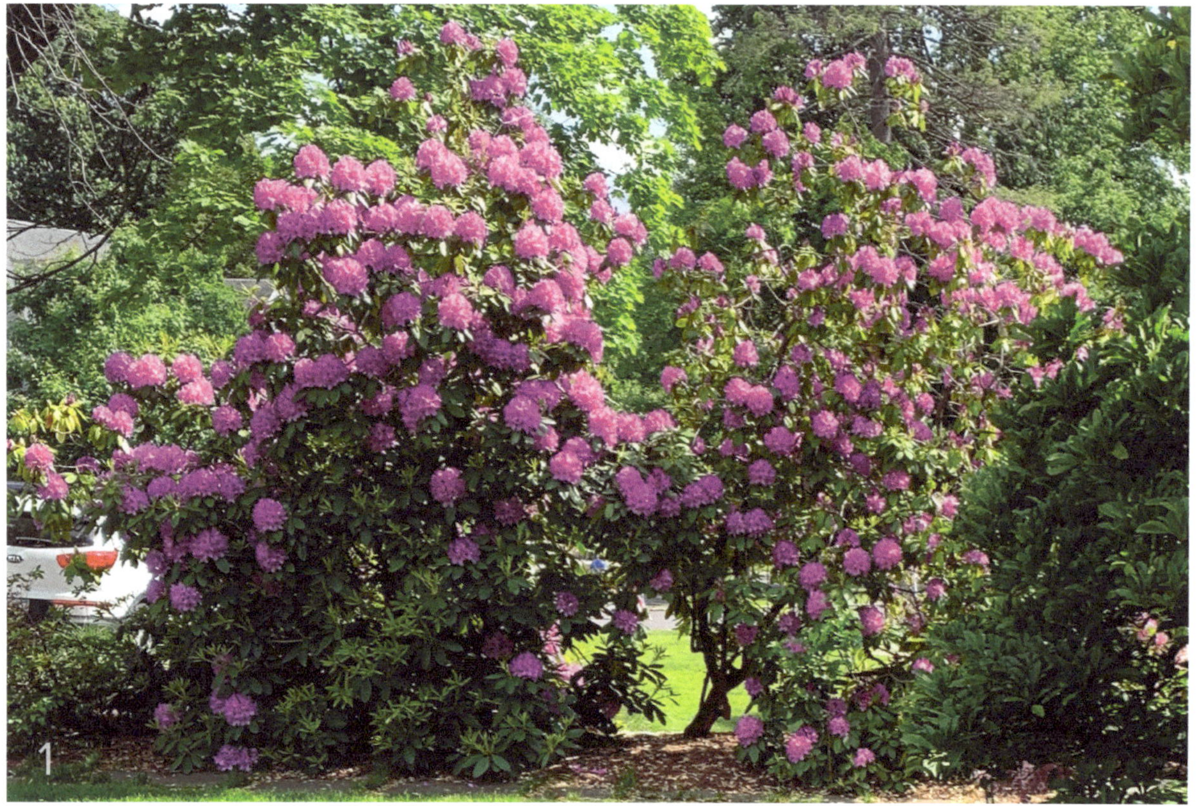

1 These evergreen shrubs can grow quite large. Their flowers are groups of many blossoms organized in a truss. Colors can be white, pink, purple, or red. Rhododendron are wonderful to use in large arrangements. Sometimes the older shrubs have interestingly-shaped branches. The branches are quite brittle, but they are larger in diameter than azalea branches. They grow and bloom well in the shade. In the sun, they may bloom better, but their leaves may burn, particularly in the winter.

2 A close-up of leaves showing buds.

3 Close-up of a truss.

4 This u-shaped container supports flowers, leaves and branches of only the rhododendron, showing the variety of colors and forms in just one kind of material.

5 A freestyle arrangement with roses perched like hungry baby birds being sheltered in a nest by the rhododendron.

6 An interesting branch holds buds up high.

7 The mass of pink rhodie with the iris in the slit of this large container contrasts with the lone branch on the left in its own space.

8 This iron container was made in the Sogetsu Atelier and shipped to me. It is quite large so the richly-colored blossoms fit in the three top holes. The smaller PJM leaves are added to complete the mass. A branch of Kwanzan cherry is added for line. Sogetsu arrangements often are composed of line, mass, and color.

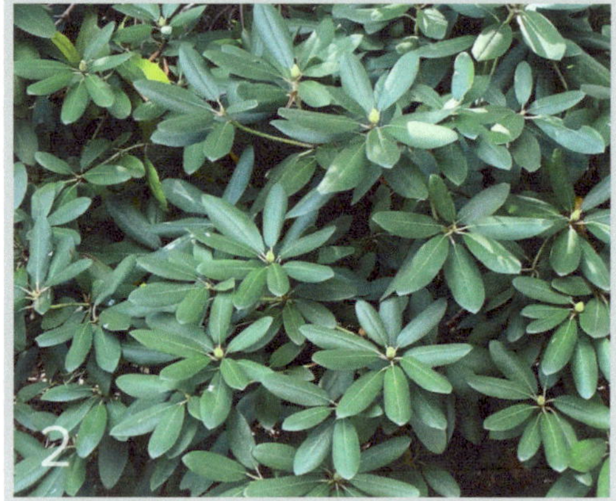

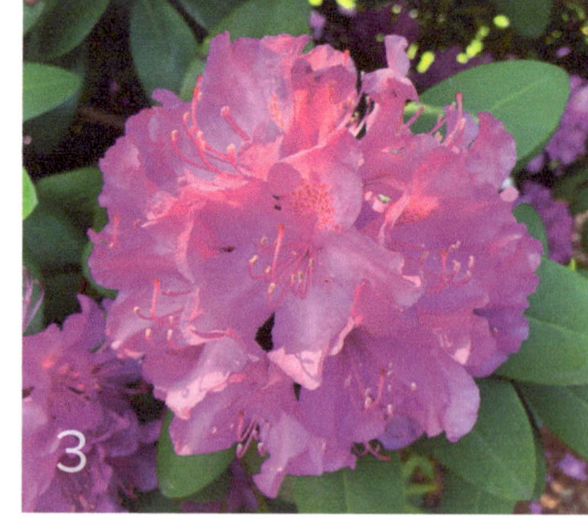

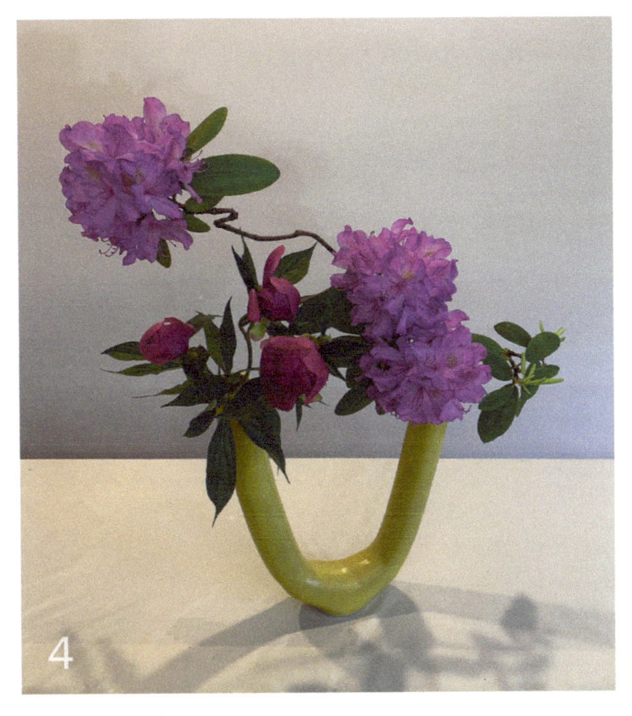

4

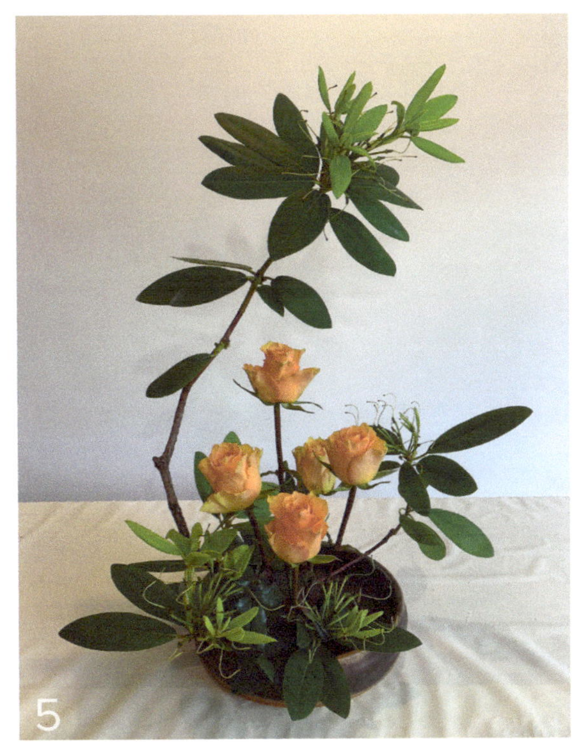

5

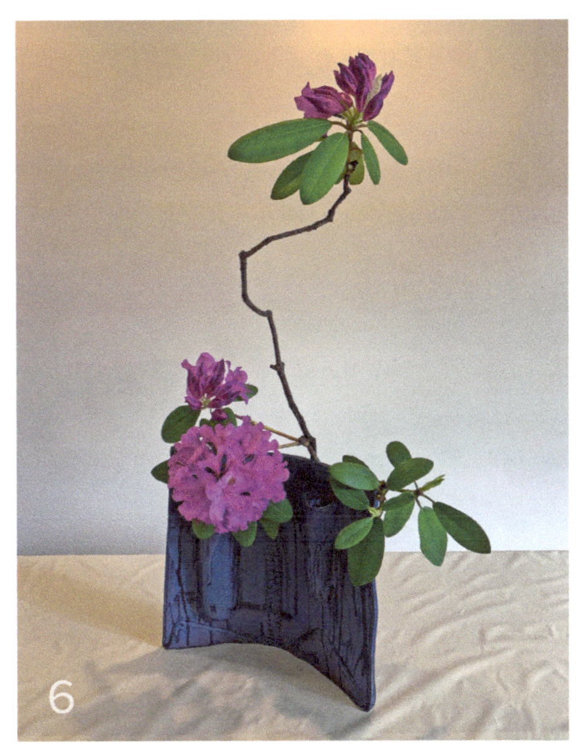

6

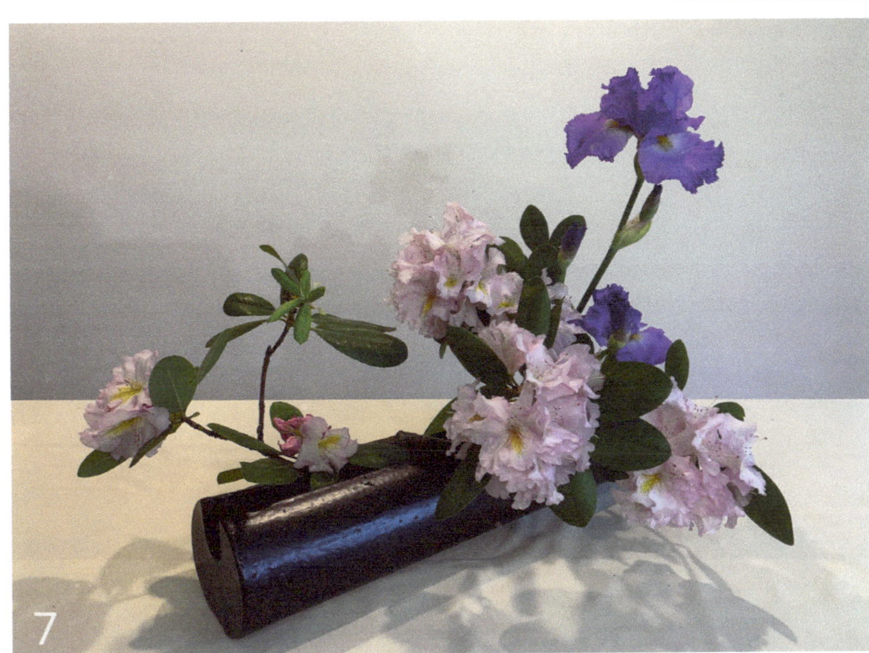

7

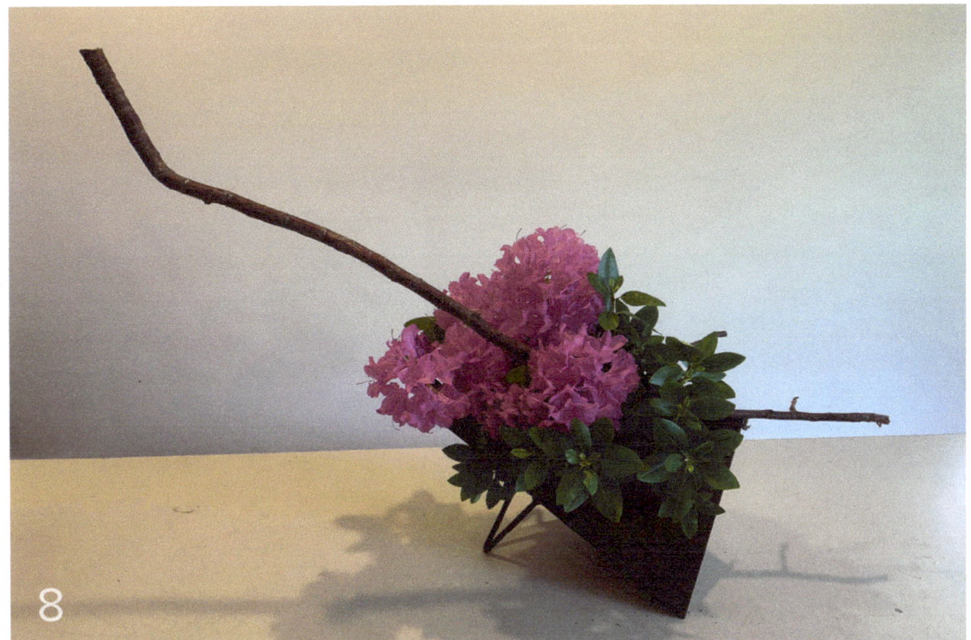

8

Rhododendron, PJM

1   These evergreen plants look like a cross between rhododendron and azalea. Both the leaves and flowers are smaller than other rhododendrons', but with the same brittle stems. PJMs are very satisfactory plants around the foundation of a house. These hybrids were developed here in Boston by the Mezitt family of Weston Nurseries. PJM stands for Peter J. Mezitt. They are the most-planted rhododendron in the Northeast today.

2   Spring flower buds and their leaves.

3   Here are the fall colors of PJM between branches of evergreen leucothoe.

4   This arrangement features a weeping mulberry branch painted silver and PJM blossoms.

5   PJM flowers surround the container and kiwi vine outlines space and plays around the blossoms.

6   Early spring maple tree flowers complement PJM in a mass-line arrangement.

7   Curly willow and sunflowers are combined with PJM fall-colored leaves in this freestyle nageire.

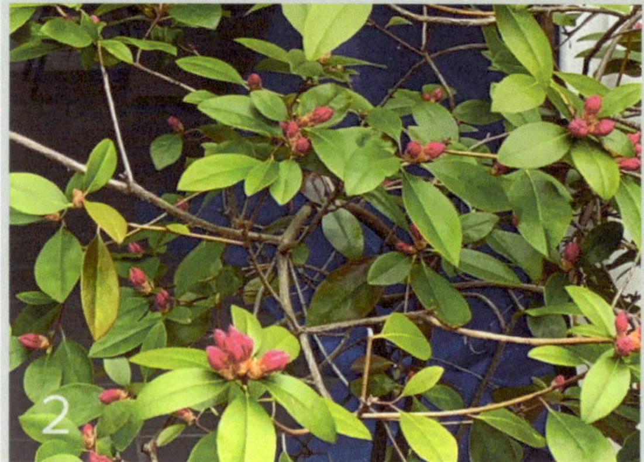

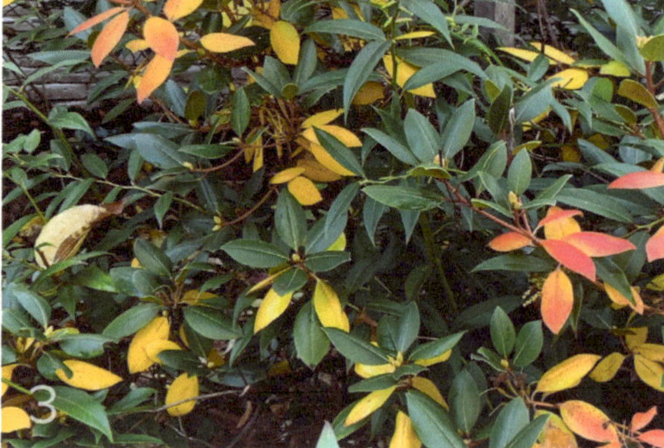

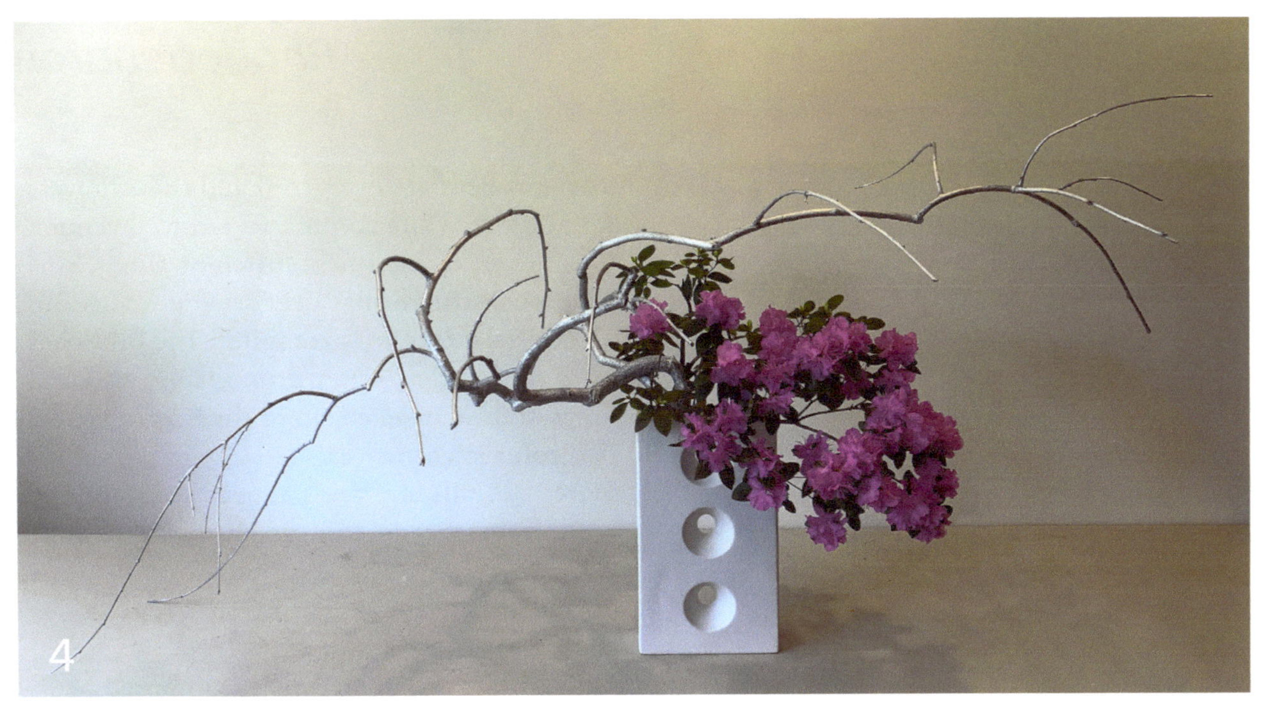

4

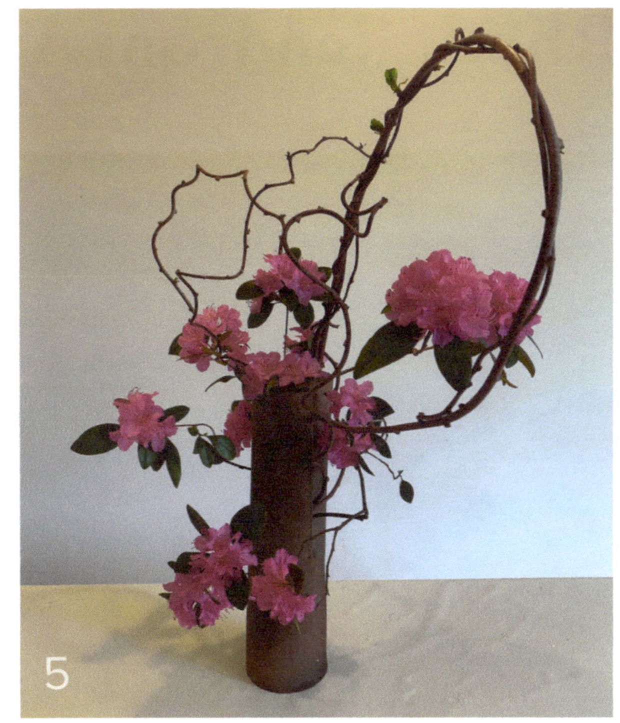

5

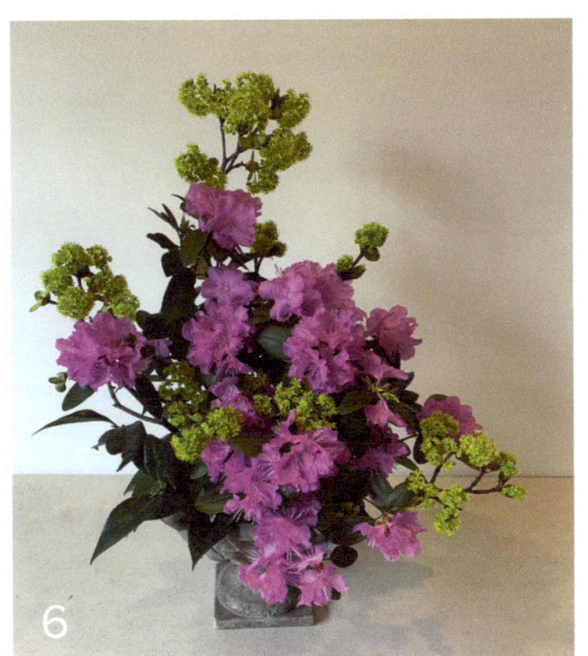

6

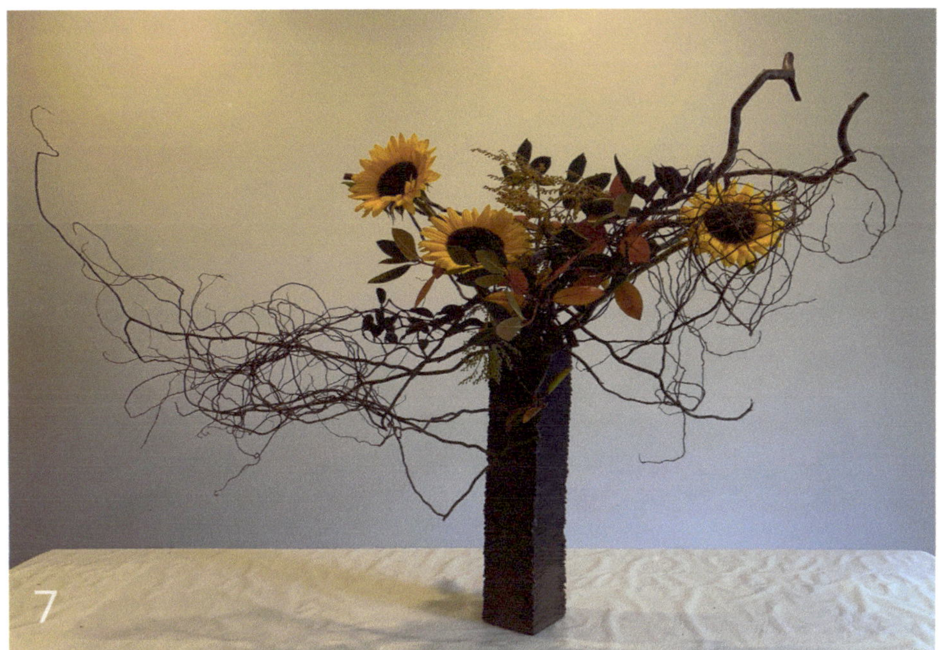

7

Rhododendron, Azalea *Rhododendron*

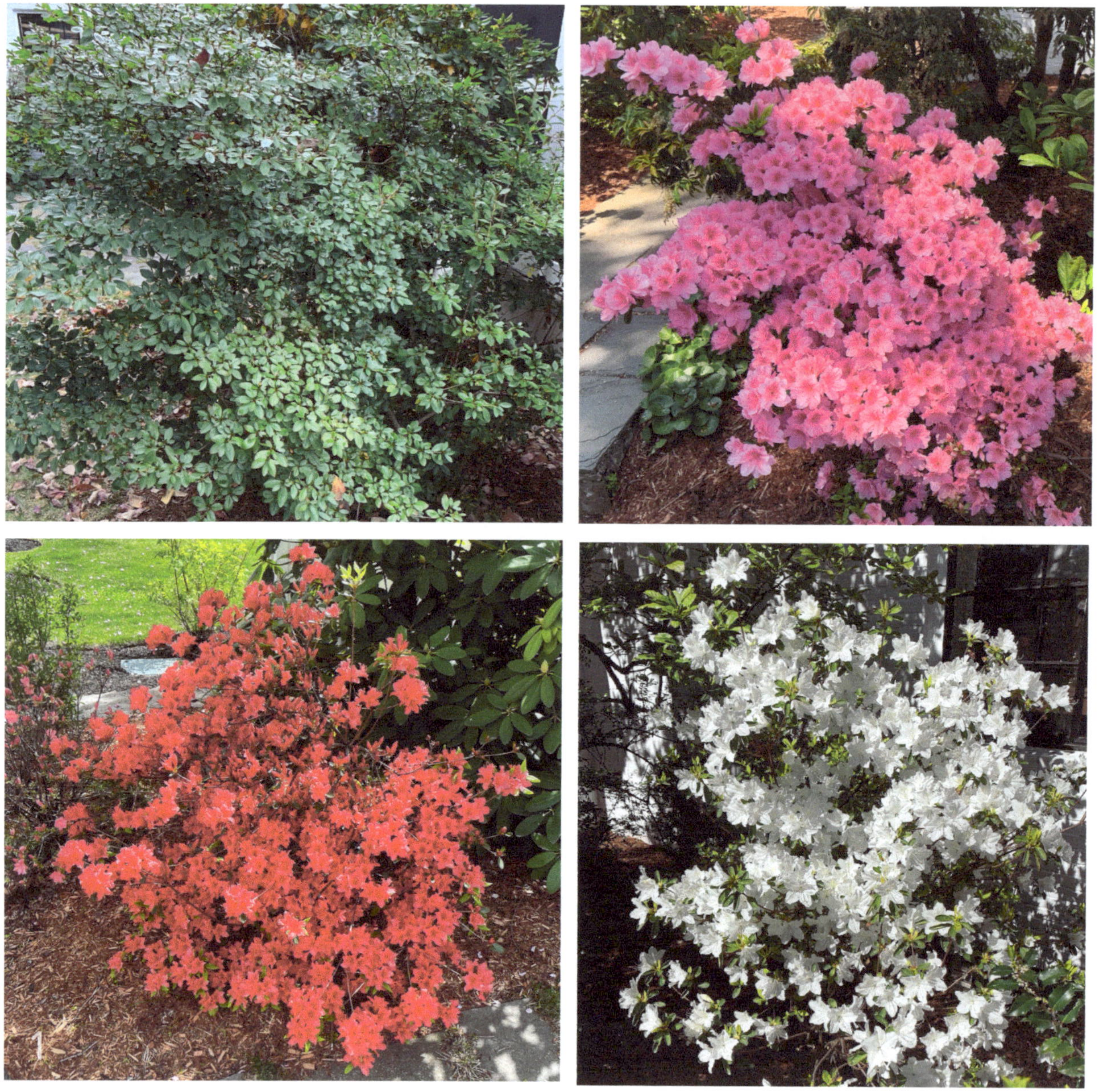

1. These azaleas are evergreen and their flowers range from white to pink to red to lavender. They seem to bloom at different times, so I have a colorful display over several weeks and a good selection for arranging. The branches are a bit brittle so they do not split well and are best used in a kenzan or directly in water.
2. Fall color in the leaves.
3. Here, the allium stems repeat some of the pattern in the container. The white azalea brings the color of the container up into the arrangement. The Miss Kim lilac repeats the purple of the alliums.
4. Unconventional material is combined with fresh azaleas in this arrangement. The "unconventional material" is packing material that came with tropical flowers.
5. Miniature design using cotoneaster branch and a single azalea blossom.
6. This azalea arrangement, with darker rhododendron blossoms and hosta, won first place in a flower show.

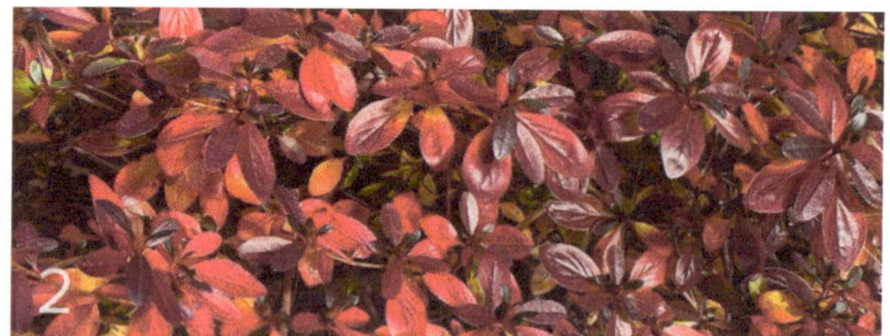

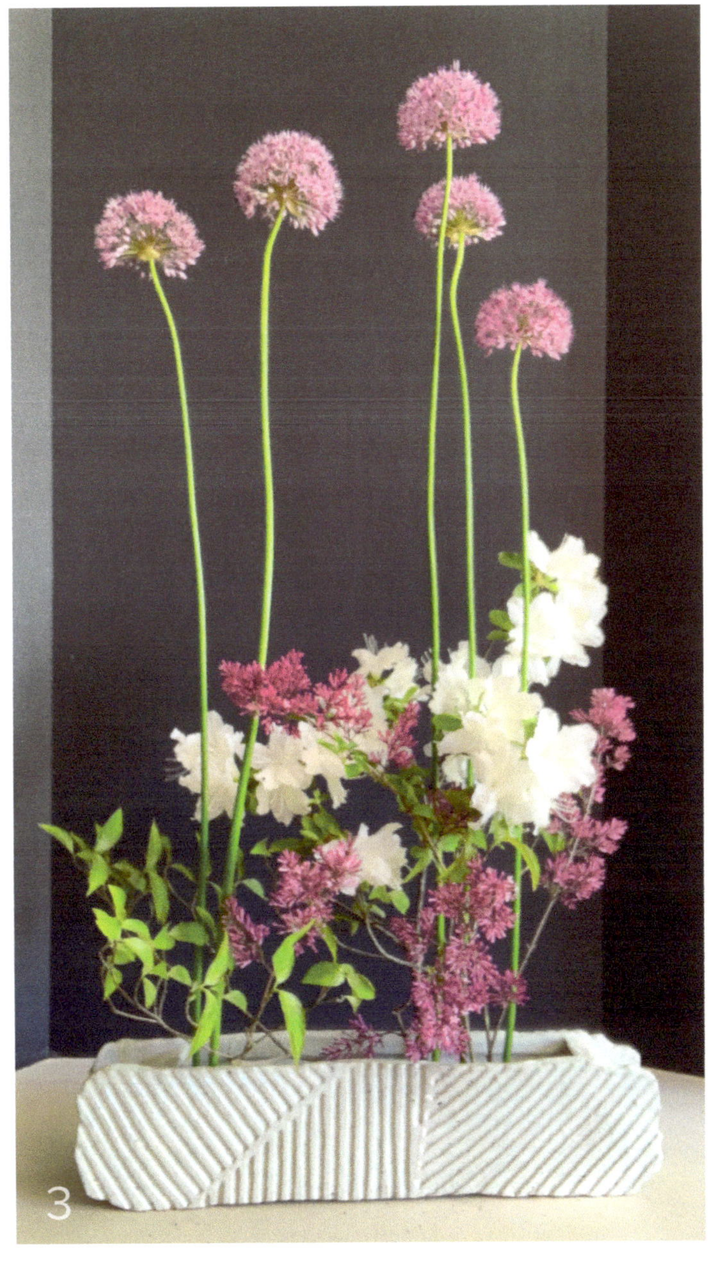

3

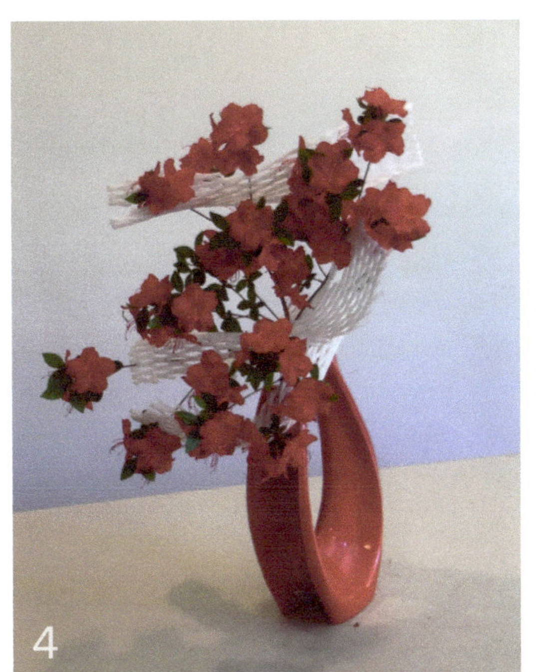

4

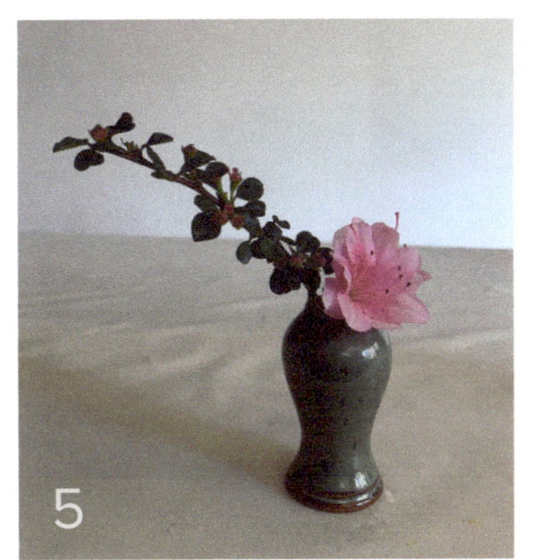

5

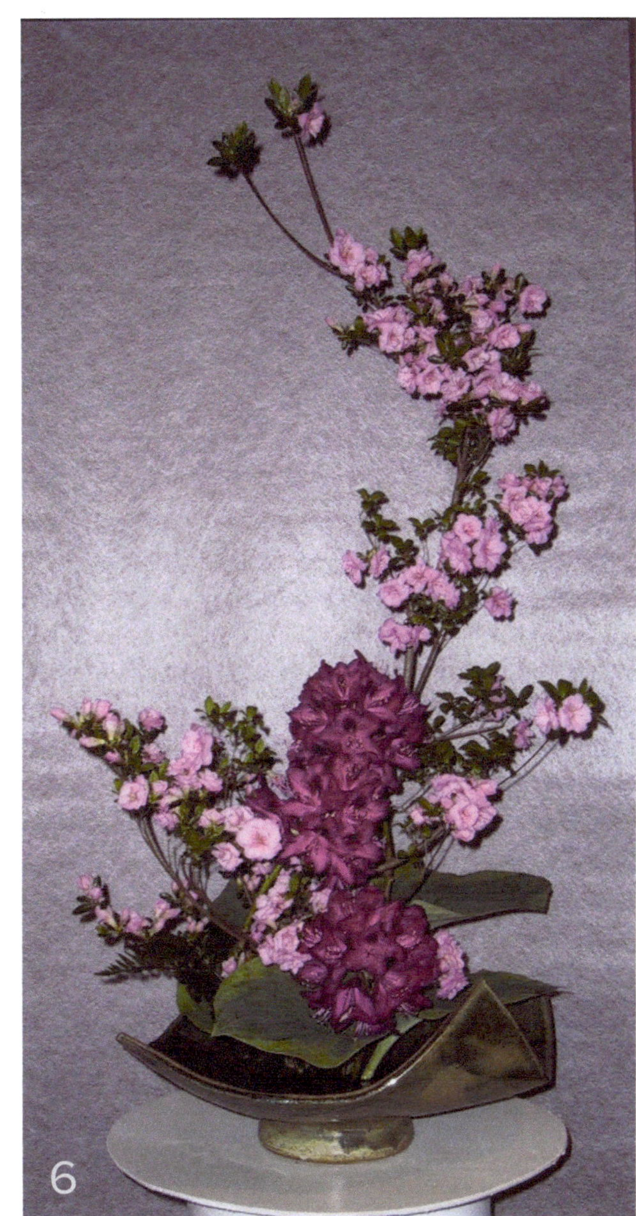

6

Rhododendron, Azalea (Deciduous) *Rhododendron*

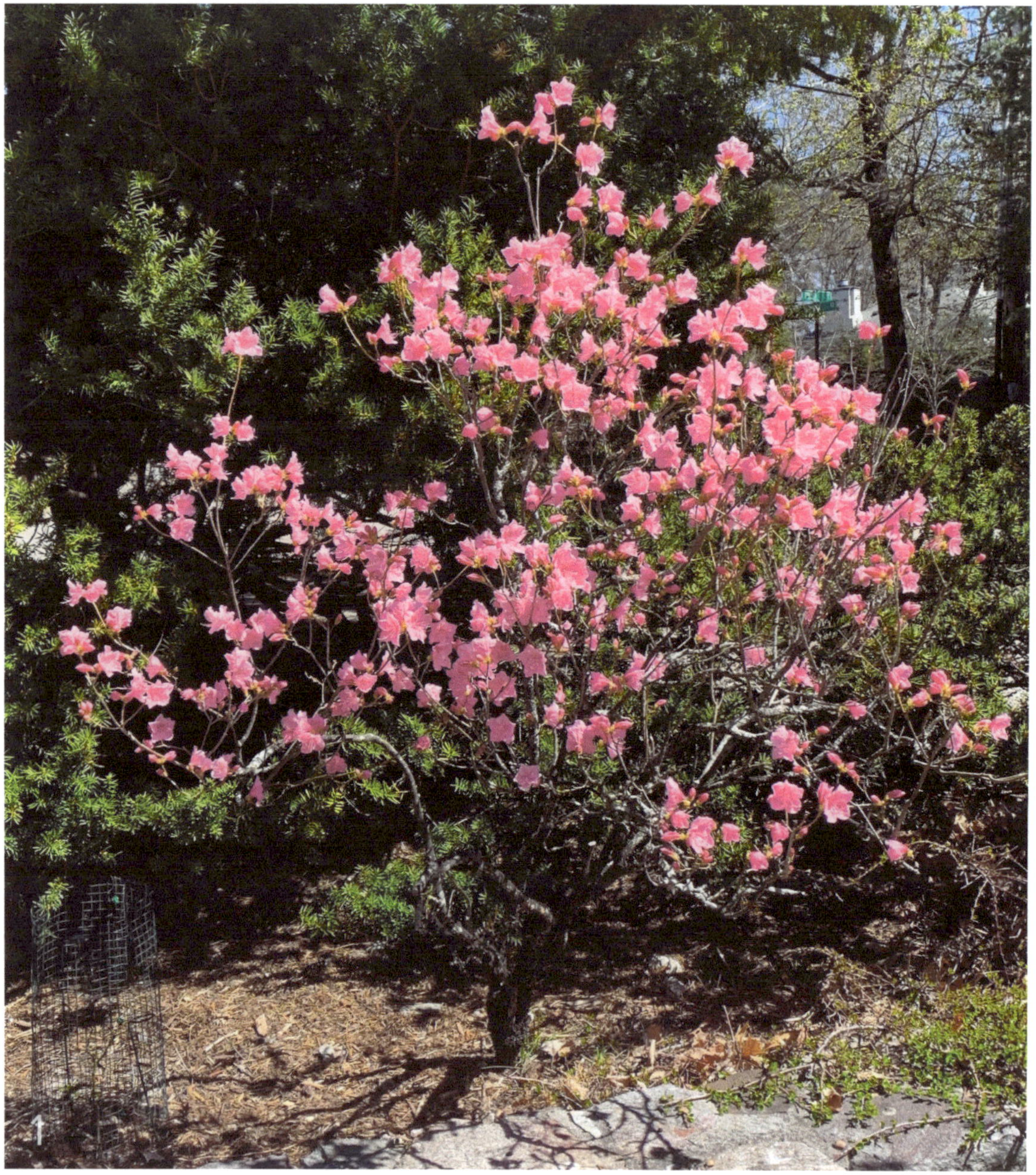

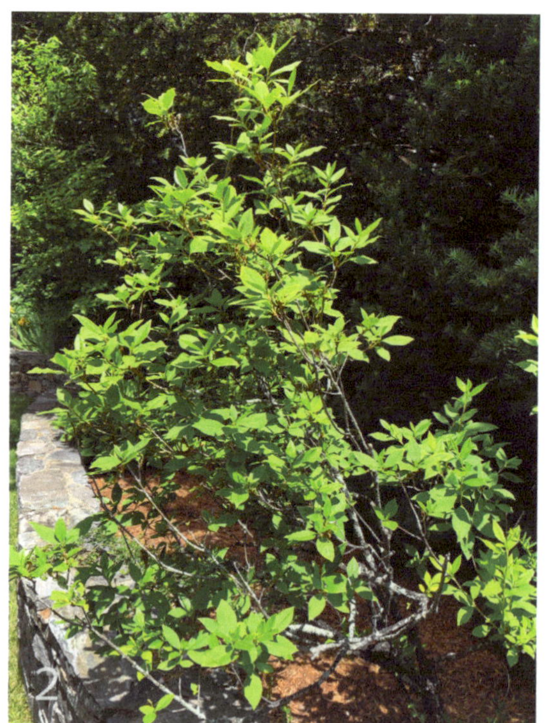

1. This shrub is one of the first to blossom in my garden. As a deciduous plant, it loses all its leaves in the winter. In the spring, the flowers blossom before the leaves open.
2. The azalea later in the spring.
3. A delicate spring arrangement in a Japanese basket. The white spirea dances with the star magnolia and the azalea threads a line through the arrangement.
4. Two self-made porcelain containers, inspired by Greek ruins, hold these charming branches.

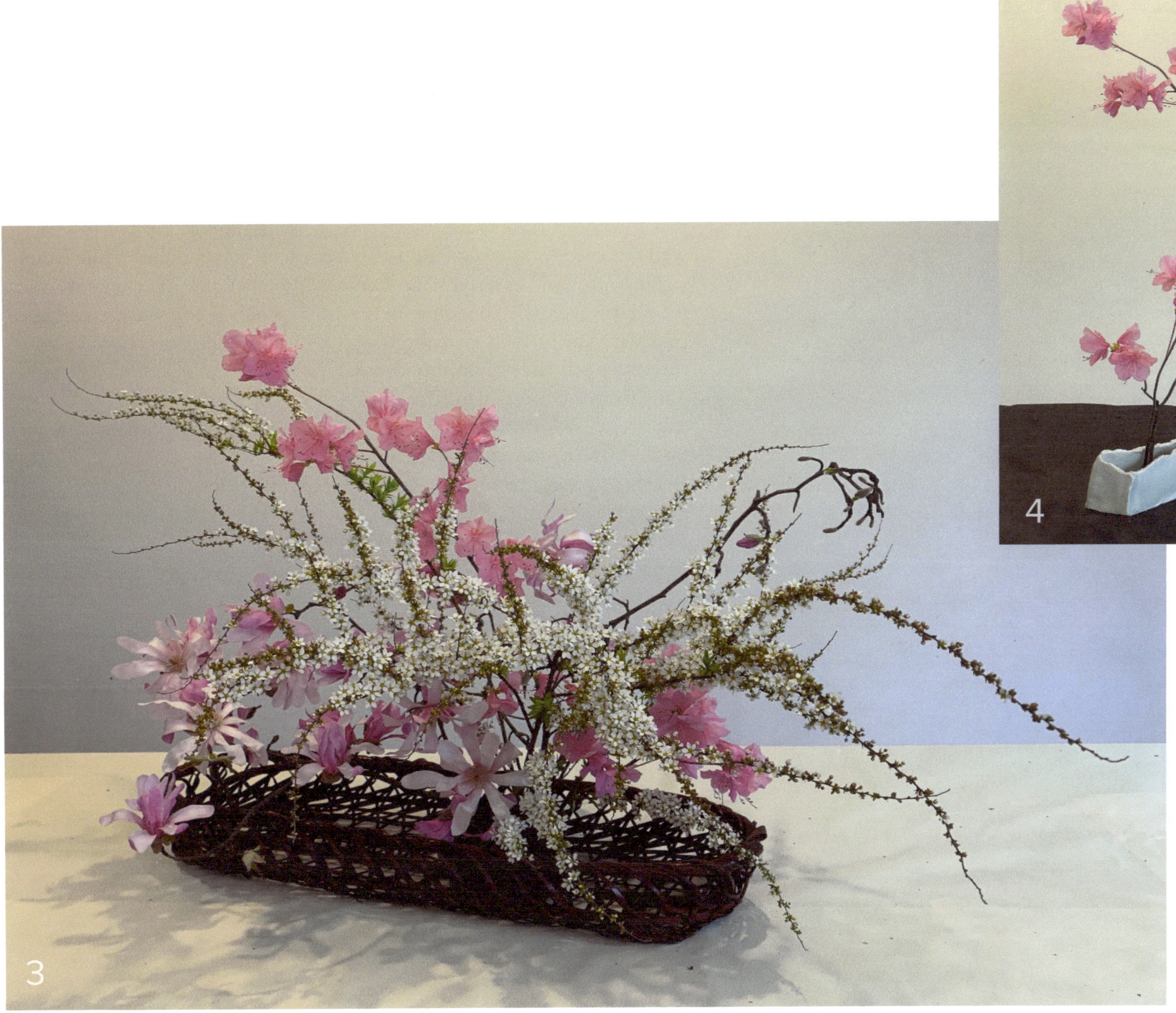

Smoketree, 'Royal Purple'   *Cotinus coggygria 'Royal Purple'*

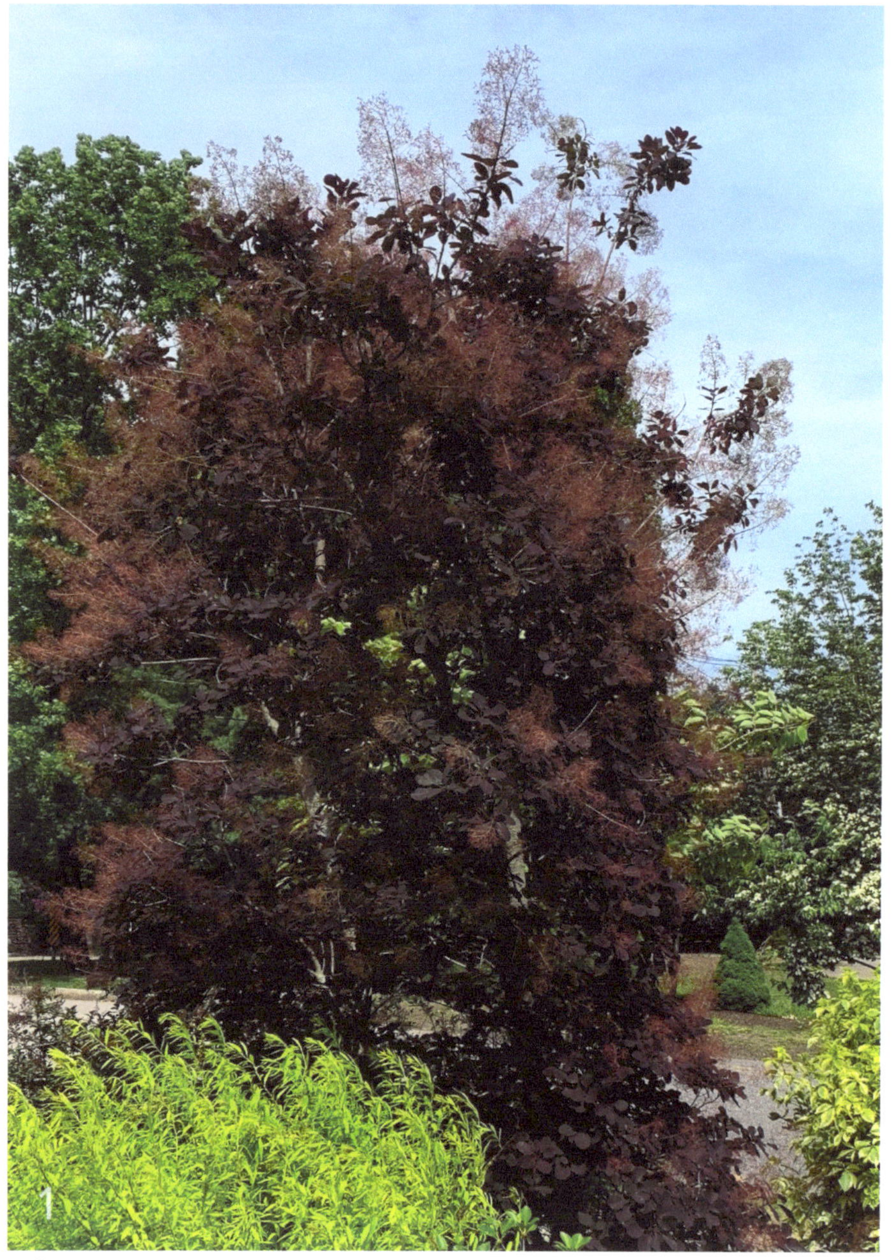

1   I love seeing the smoketree when it is in bloom and afterwards when the smoke holds on for weeks. The smoke plumes consist of tiny hairs attached to the flower stalks. In my last home, we planted it and waited many years. It finally bloomed the year before we moved. Unfortunately, my Royal Purple smoketree in Boston loses its smoke very soon after it is formed. I have tried to learn why this happens. We try to keep it well watered. Some have said it is beacause it is a male, while others say it is just this variety. Who knows? The dark purple leaves are very nice. However, they become increasingly green as the season progresses. First year growth is straight and strong. Older branches are more interesting as they form side shoots.

2   Tiny flower clusters whose stems become the smoke.

3   This creative mass design contains yellow peonies, smoketree leaves and inflorescence, and a monstera leaf.

4   In this nageire, the smoketree embraces pink iris.

5   Smoketree line material creates space in this variation one slanted moribana, with roses to attract attention.

6   Here the smoketree leaves contrast with the grouped flower stalks. Pink iris flowers complete the design.

7   This floor arrangement is cradled in an iron sculpture: birch, smoketree, fuji mums, red rover, viburnum, and a dried branch which continues the angular lines of the container.

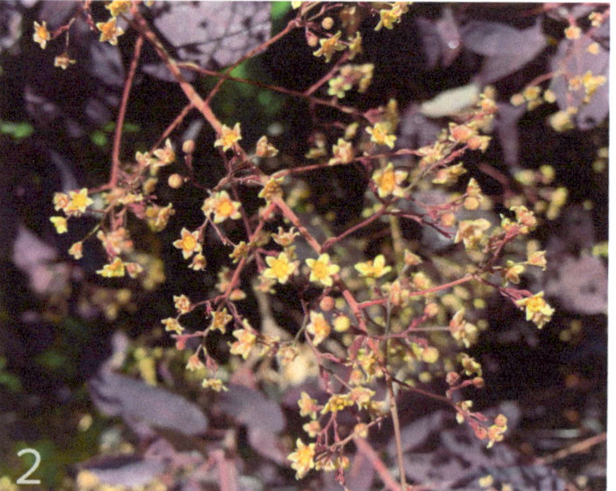

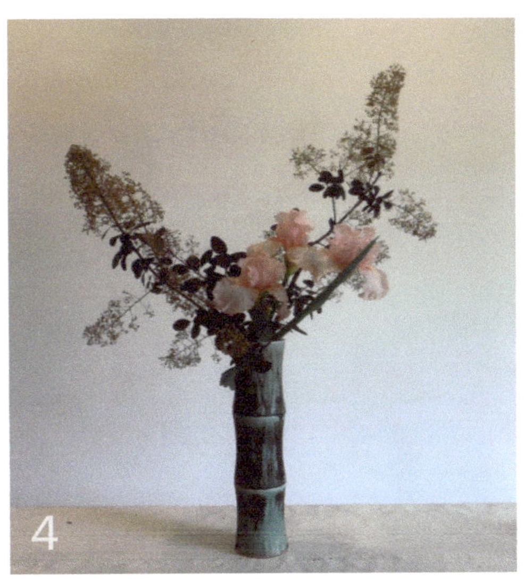

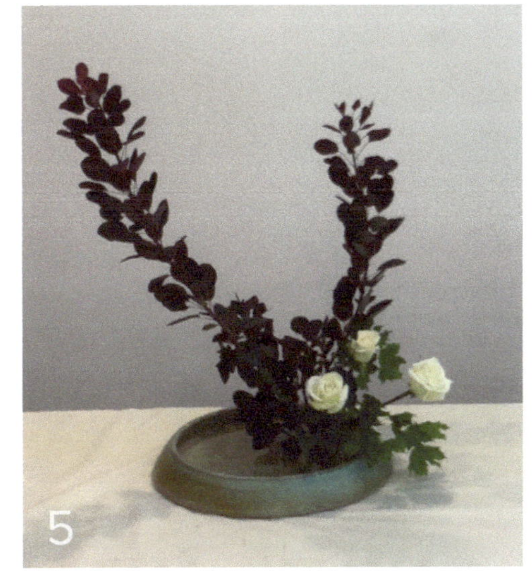

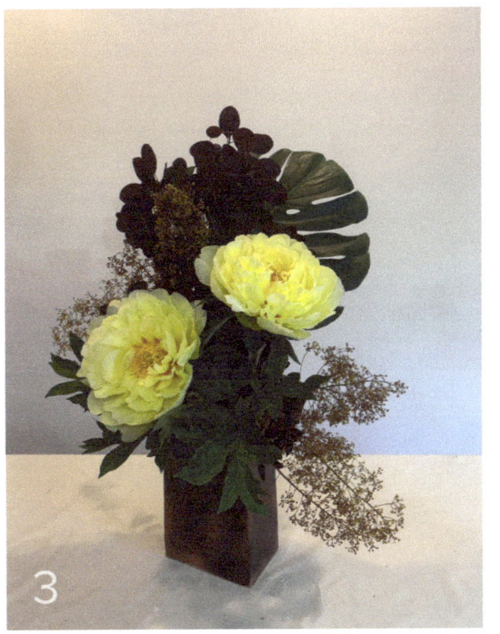

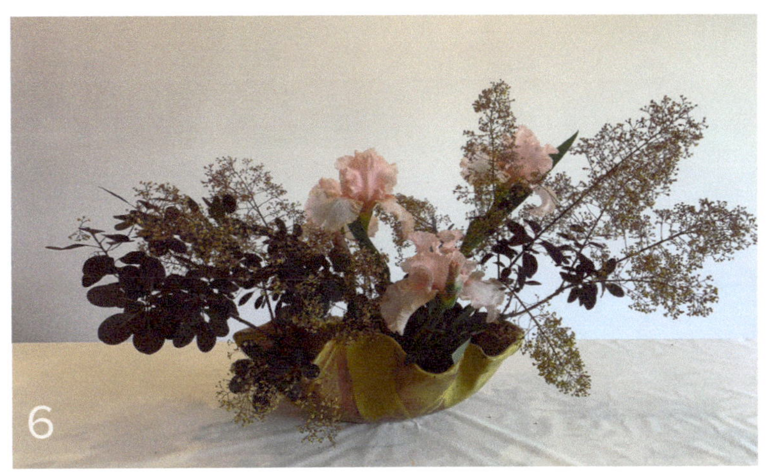

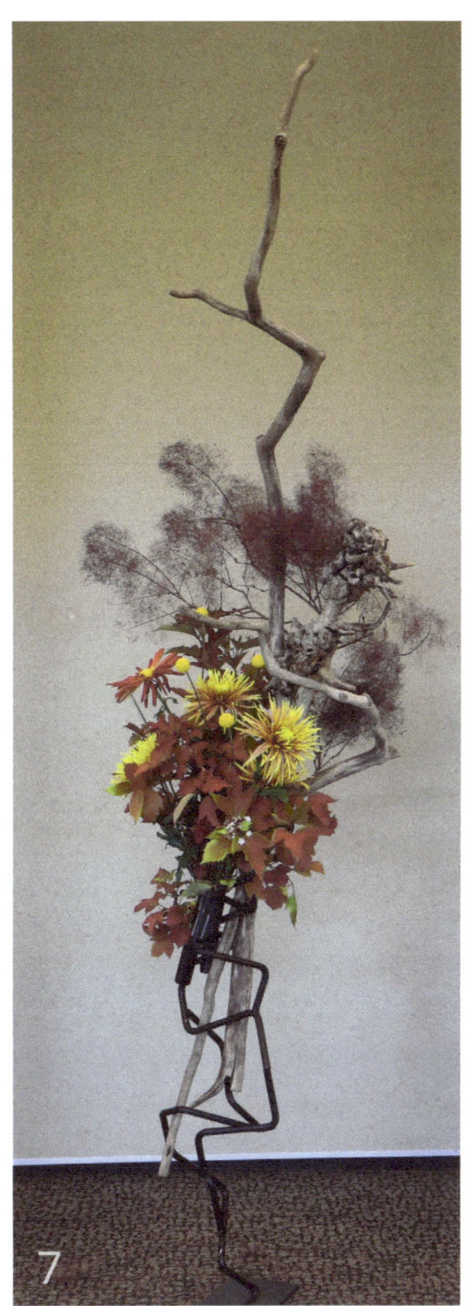

Smoketree, Golden Spirit

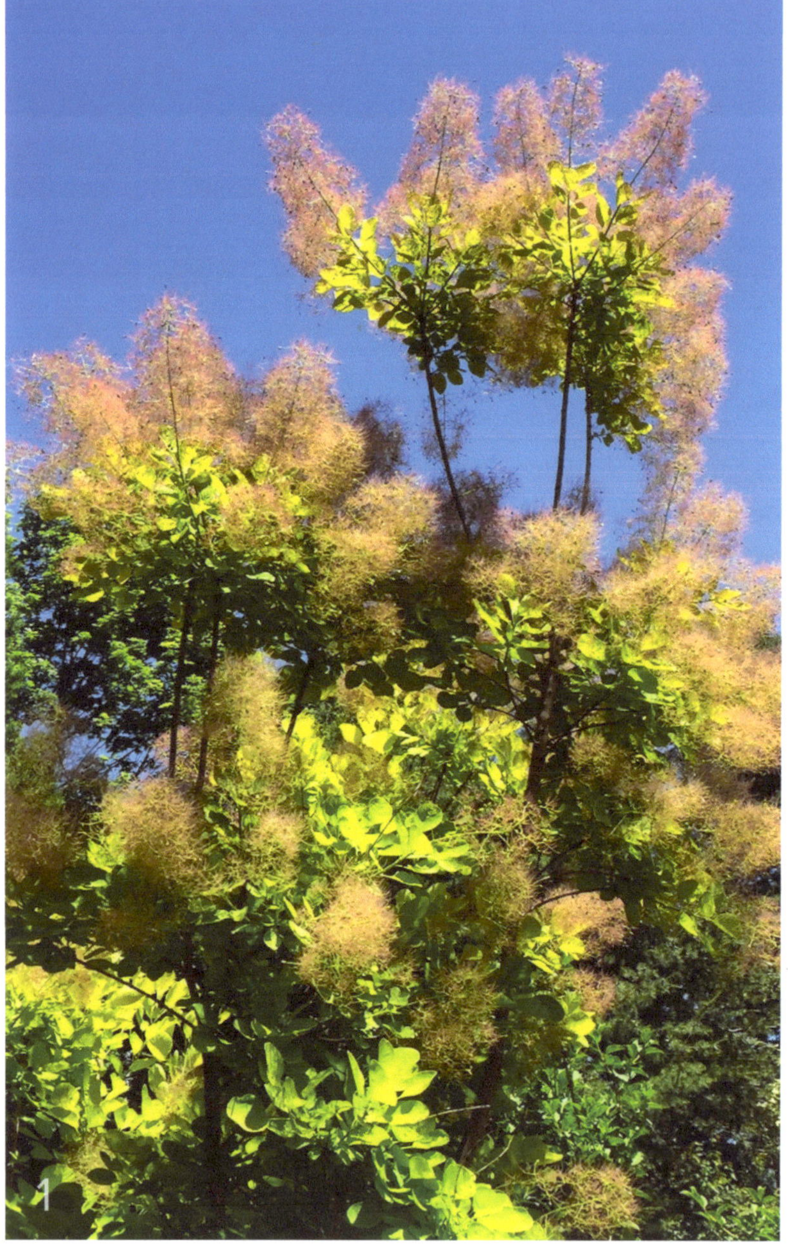

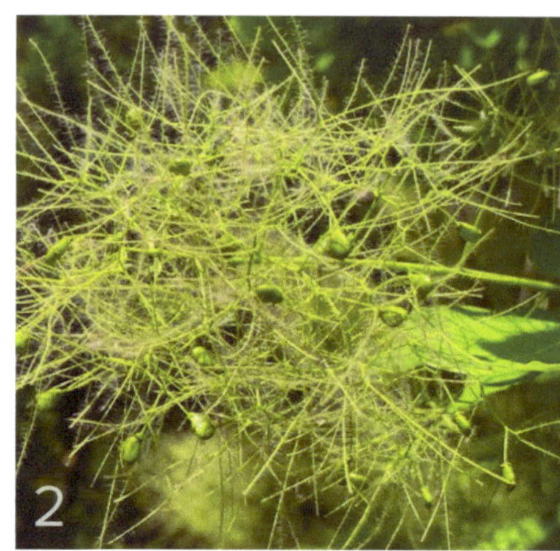

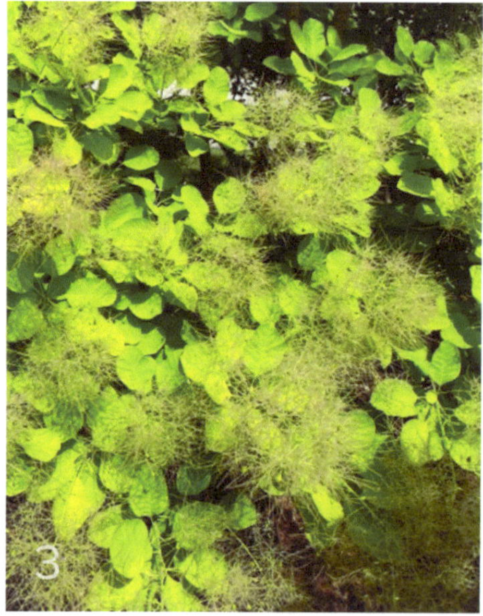

1. This smoketree has beautifully-colored spring green leaves and golden smoke which lasts on the tree until fall. The smoke matures quickly and takes on a rosy hue.
2. After the flowers bloom, the stems hold tiny green seeds.
3. Smoke covers the whole tree.
4. This smoketree arrangement is accented with yellow foxtail lily, *eremurus*, and purple allium.
5. I placed the smoke to activate spaces defined by wisteria vine in this nageire arrangement.
6. This is an all-around arrangement with green leaves of aging smoke flower and bearded iris from our garden. Both tree and flower are beautiful viewed from any angle.
7. An arrangement of two colors of smoketree spilling out of this pink container with mountain laurel in the focal area.
8. Early buds of the smoketree are coupled with delicate iris blossoms in this basic slanting nageire.

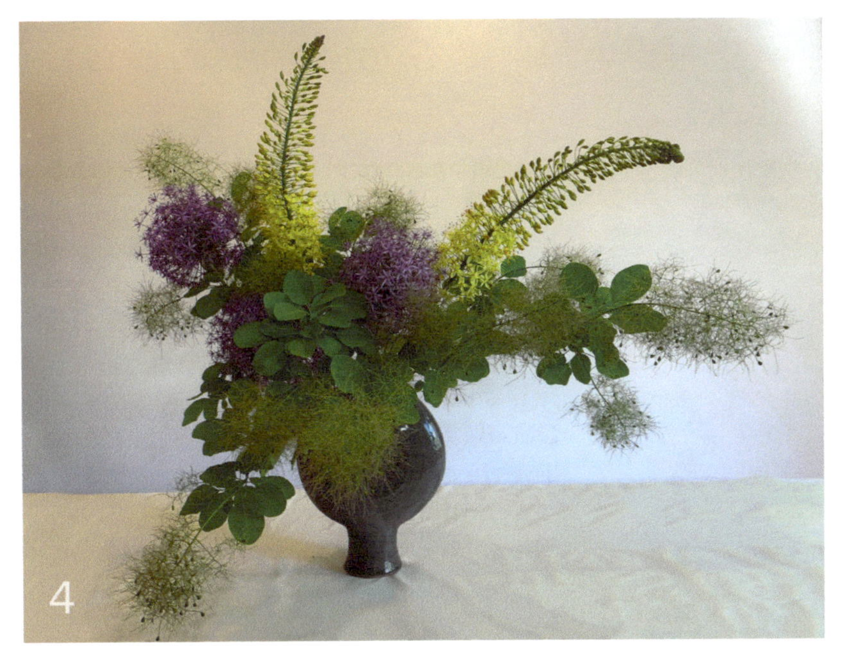

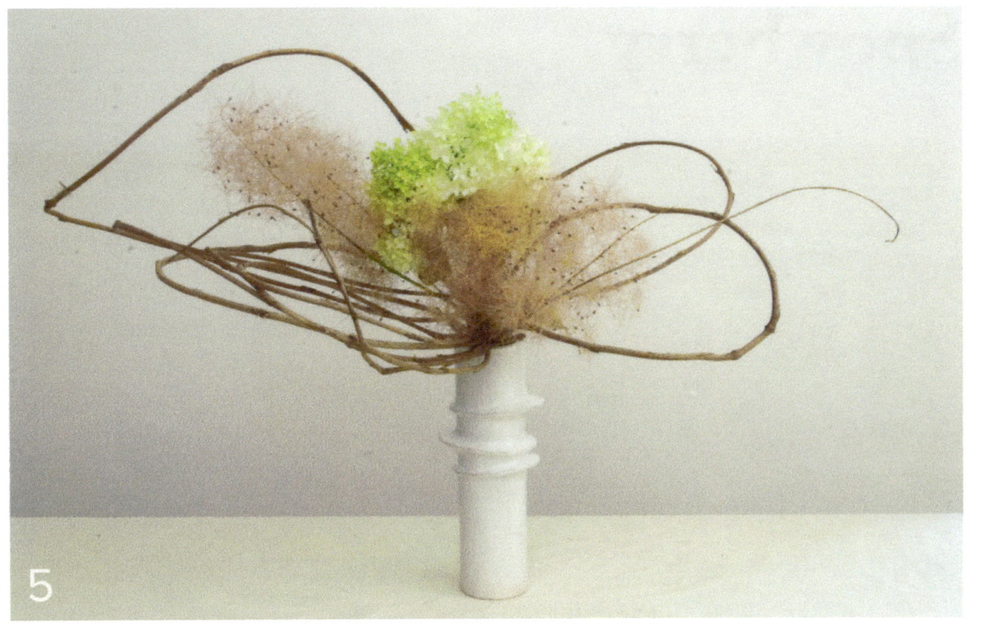

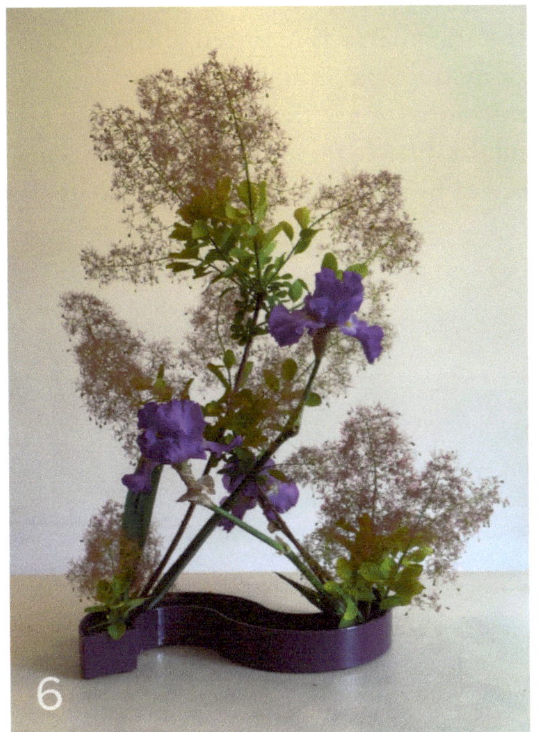

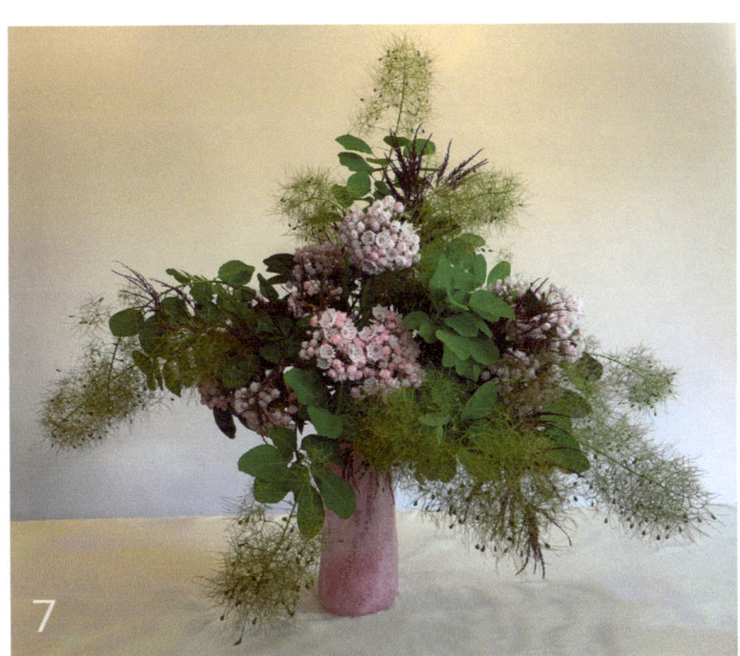

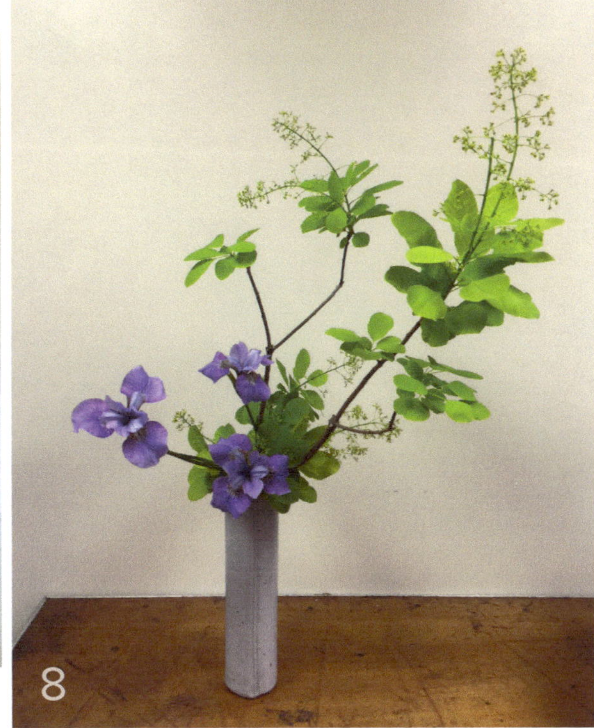

Snowberry   *Symphoricarpos albus*

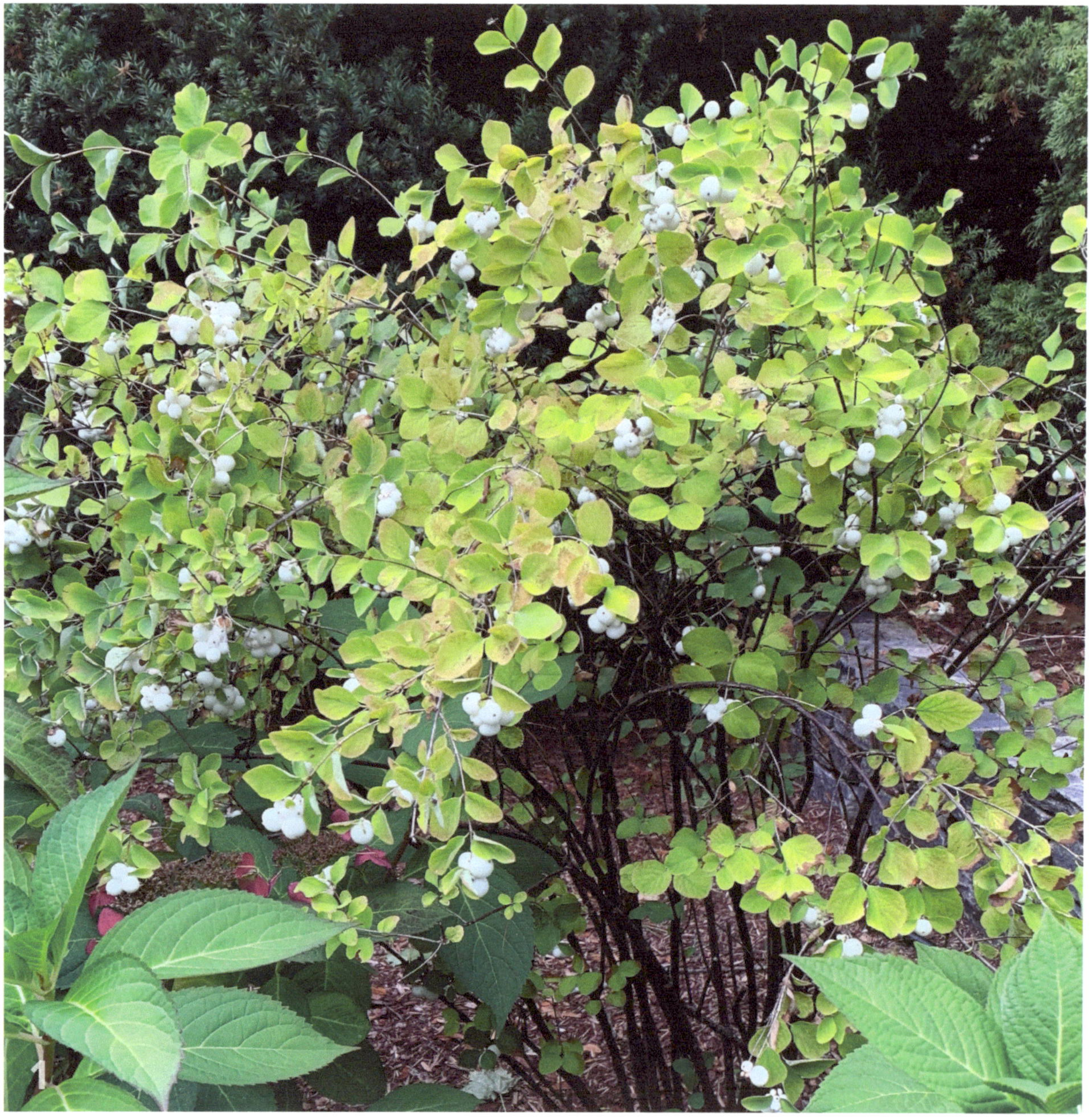

1. This is another plant that delights flower arrangers. I am charmed by the white berries hanging in bunches on thin stems. If the stems are moved, the berries bounce enchantingly. I usually take the leaves off when arranging with the branches. I have grown it successfully in sun or shade.
2. Detail of the fleshy white berries
3. The tiny flowers which produce the berries at the ends of the branches.
4. The color of the hanging amaranthus matches the red container for a unifying effect. Their form creates a miniature fairy forest from which the snowberries emerge.
5. Here, the snowberry is featured with fall-colored euonymus and a single zinnia.
6. This traditional mass design is decorating a functional table. It includes eucalyptus, carnations, sea holly, andromeda, and snowberries.

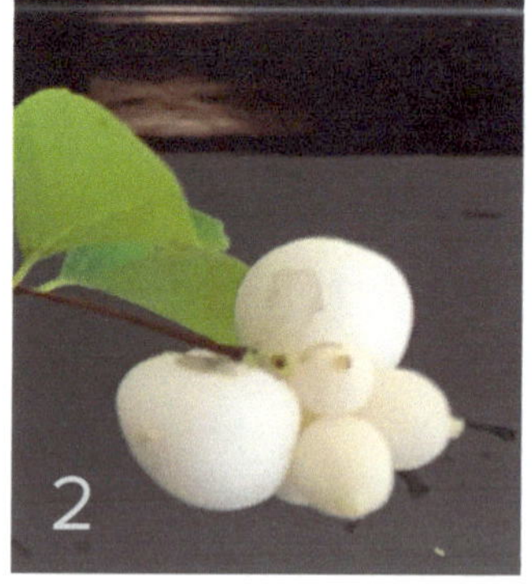

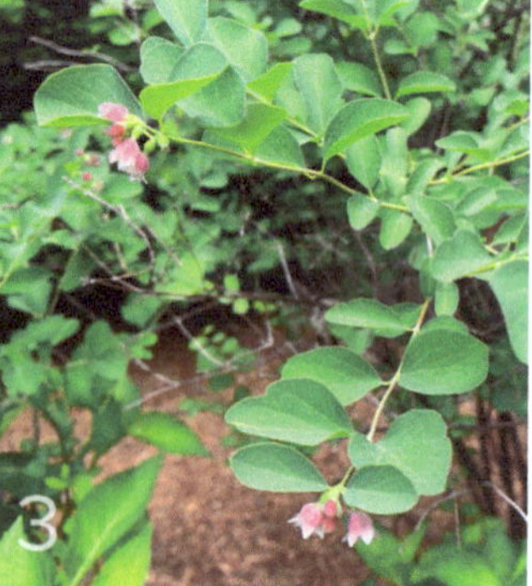

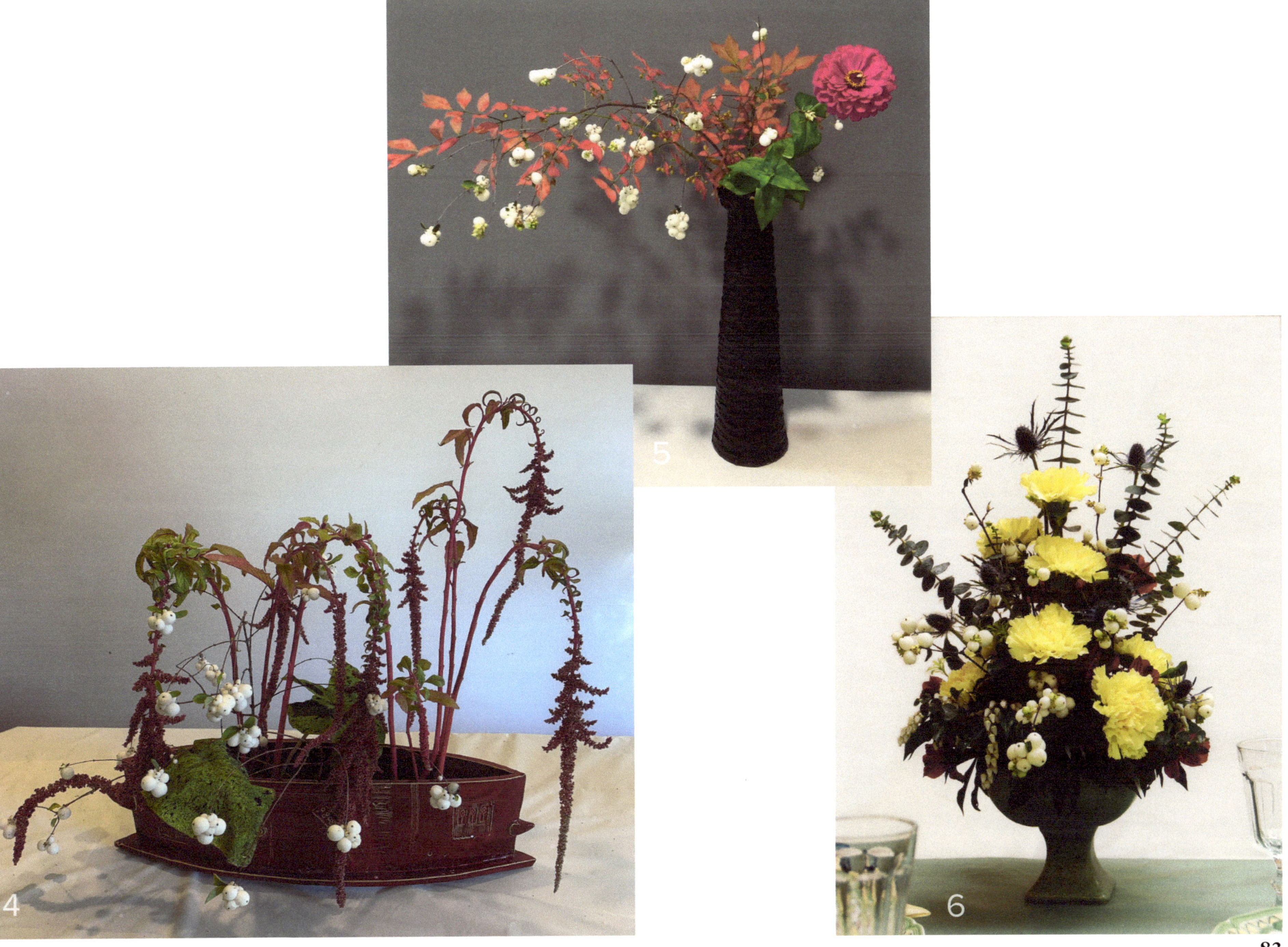

83

Spirea 'Ogon'

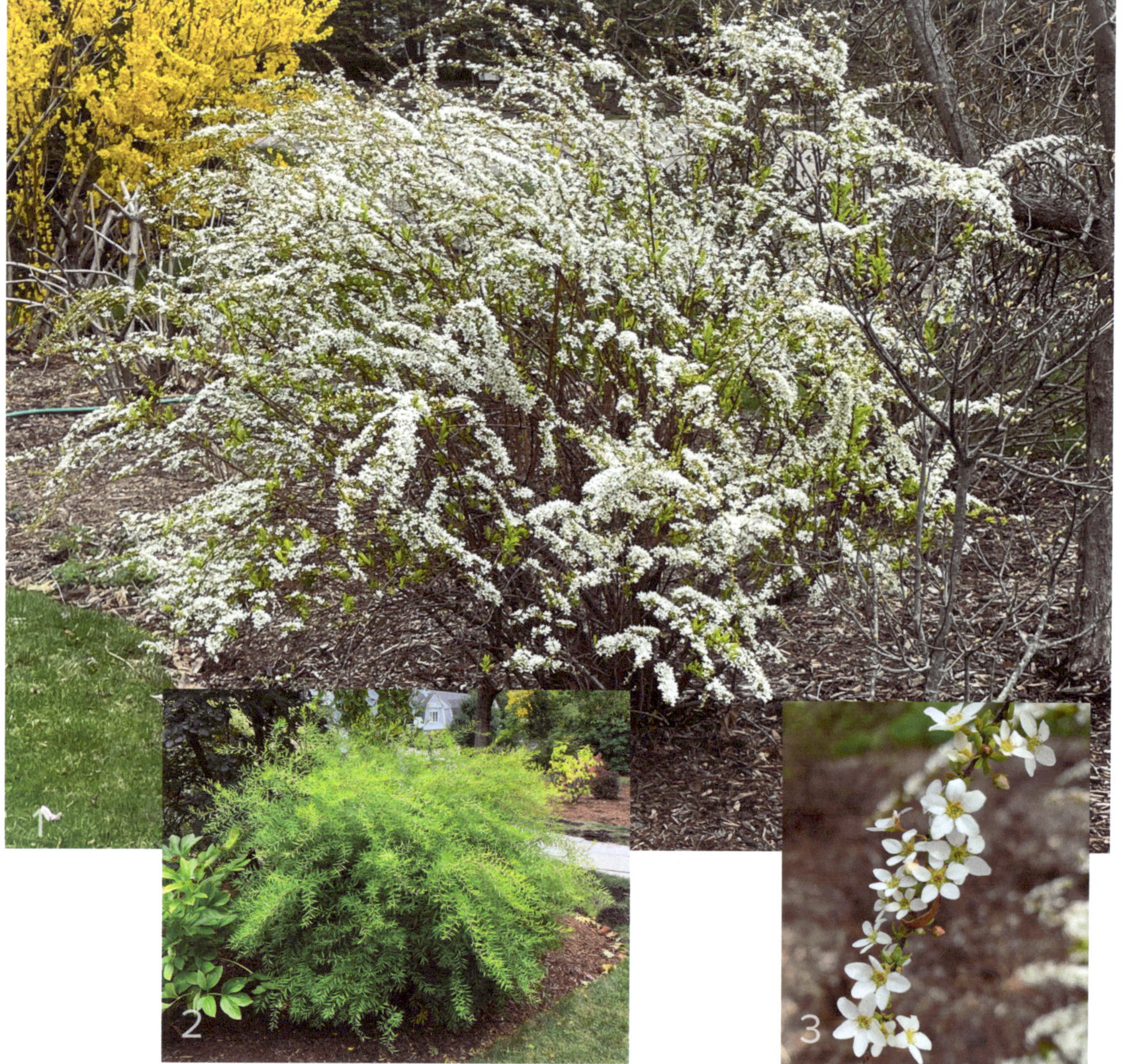

1 This lovely early-blooming spirea is one of my favorites. The branches have graceful lines. The delicate white flowers appear in rows on the branches. The light spring green of the leaves is delightful. The branches are quite thin and brittle. I can cut branches often and never notice anything missing.

2 The leaves open to this beautiful green after the blossoms fade.

3 Detail of blooms.

4 White spirea and yellow chrysanthemum mass contrasts with the empty space in the container. The purple of the sweet peas brings richness to contrast with the strong color of the container.

5 This is the spirea in fall colors with chrysanthemums and fasciated willow.

6 Here, I have contrasted the spirea with a branch of Norway maple to show similar curves but very different leaves and branching.

7 Bamboo anchors this wave of spring flowers, including forsythia, azalea, and spirea.

8 White container with spirea sheltering purple sweet peas.

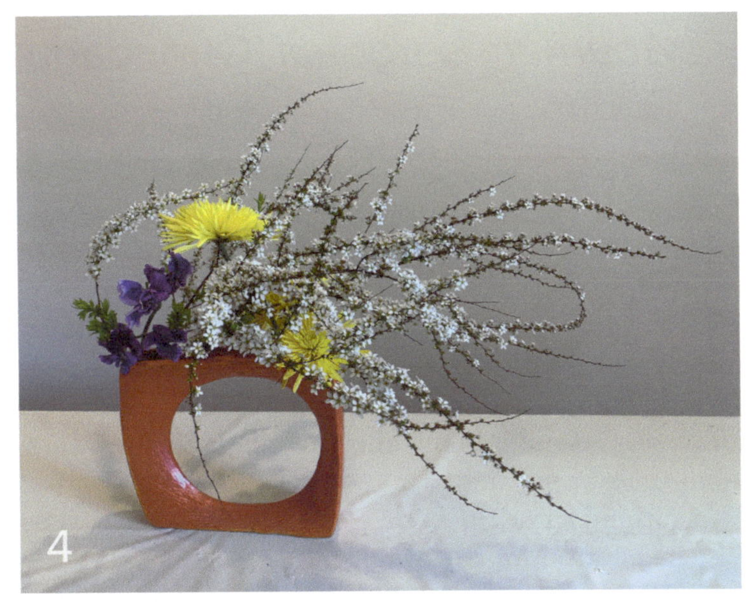

4

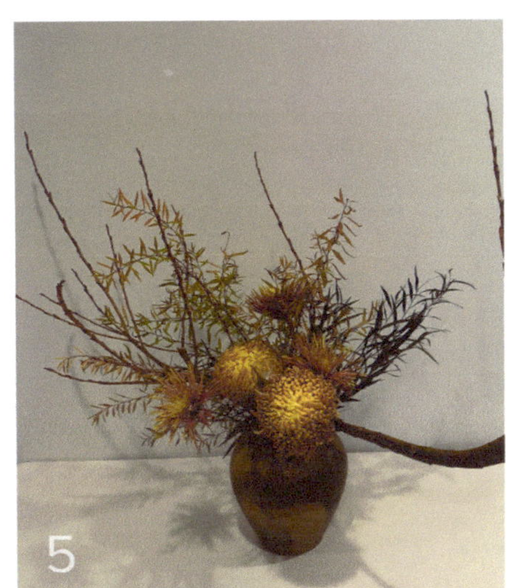

5

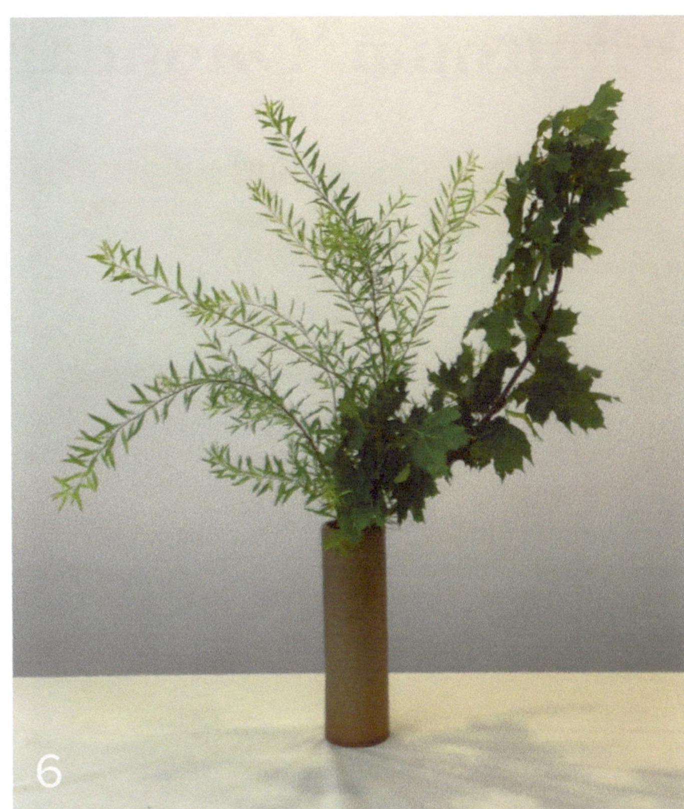

6

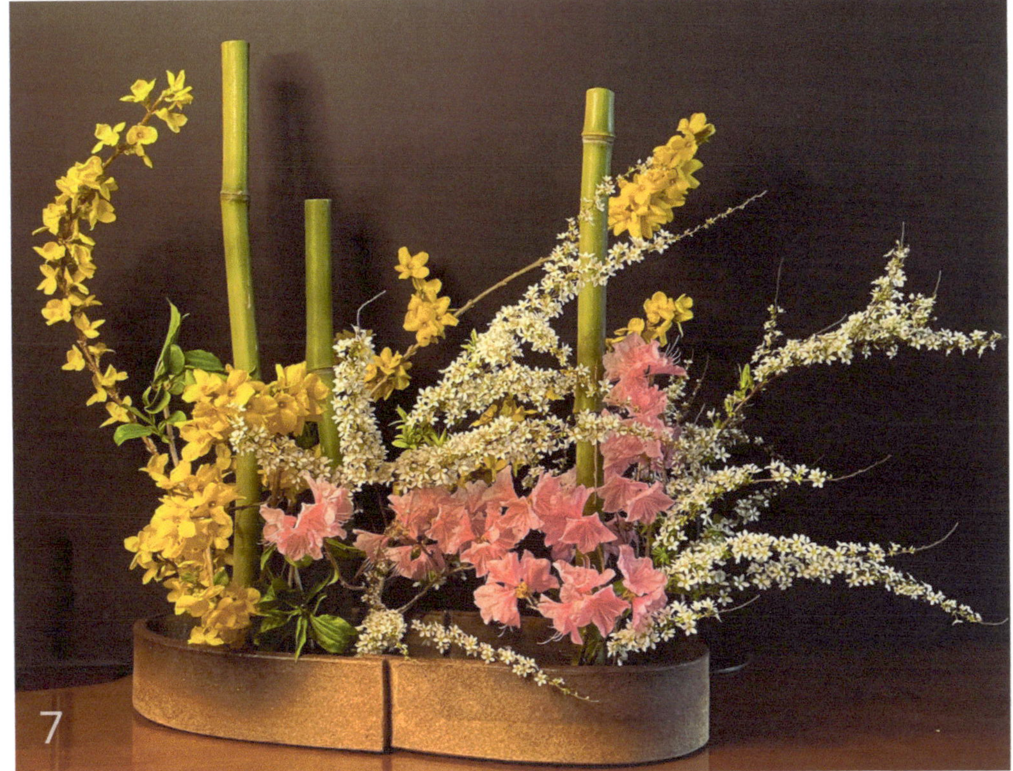

7

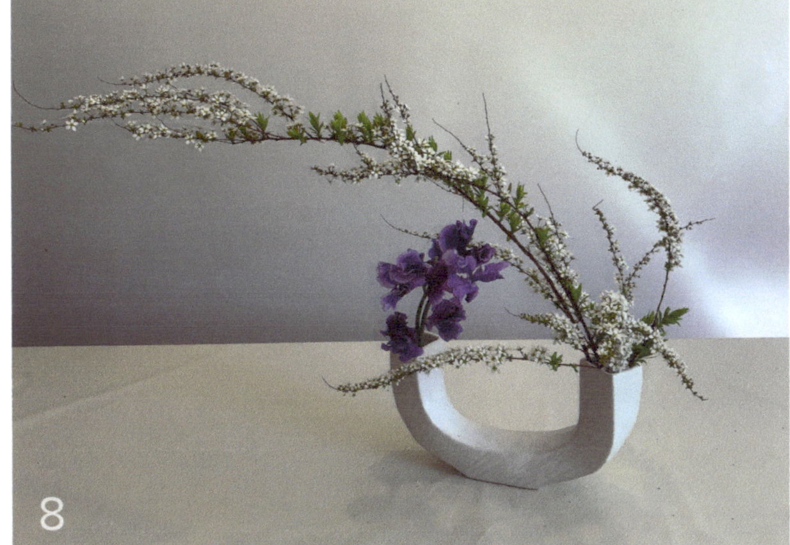

8

Viburnum 'Onondaga'

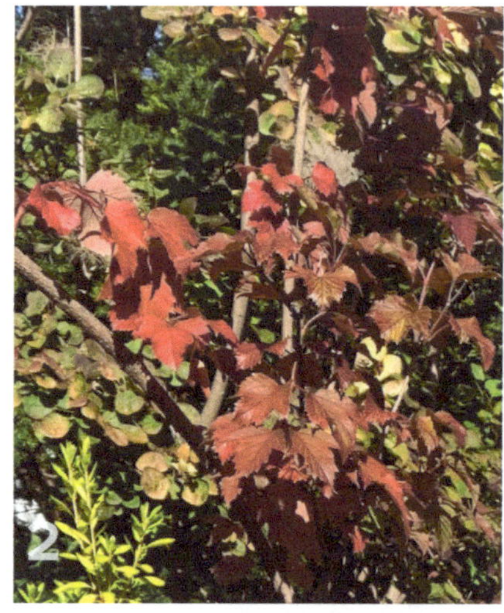

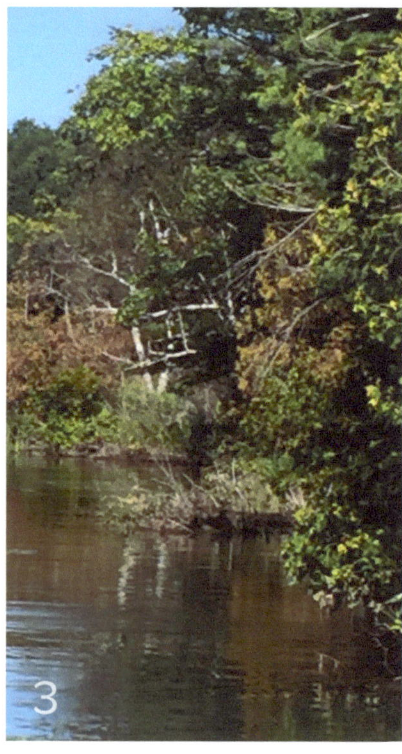

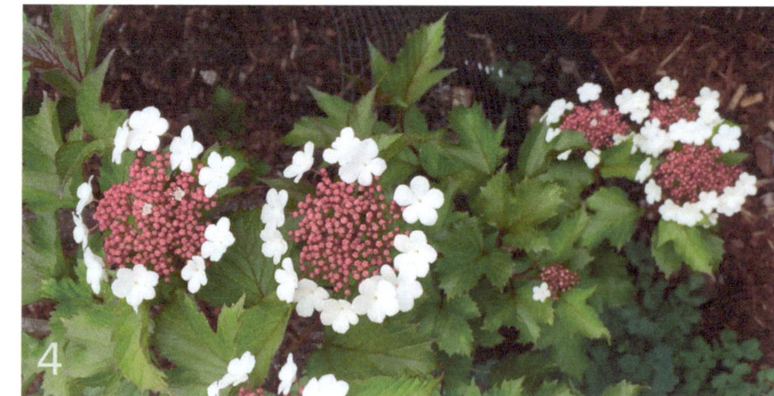

1   White flowers appear in the spring on branches with leaves. In the summer, red berries form. In the fall, the color is magnificent, changing from red to mahogany over time. A friend recommended this 'Onondaga' variety and it has proved a great addition to the garden. It seems to not have insect problems. However, some rodents like the stems and I lost all but one stem a few winters ago. Now, new shoots are appearing and we hope they are safe in the hardware cloth fence we put around it.
2   Red autumn leaves.
3   The inspiration for the arrangement opposite was the pattern of the white birch branches among the leaves.
4   Detail of the flowers.
5   The red leaves at the top show the beautiful color of this shrub in the fall. Sunflowers and chrysanthemum surround the birch branches, spirea, and dark smoke leaves. White beautyberry and gomphocarpus dance in the spaces. This is a 4-foot-high floor arrangement that welcomed guests to a flower show at Tower Hill Botanic Garden in Massachusetts.

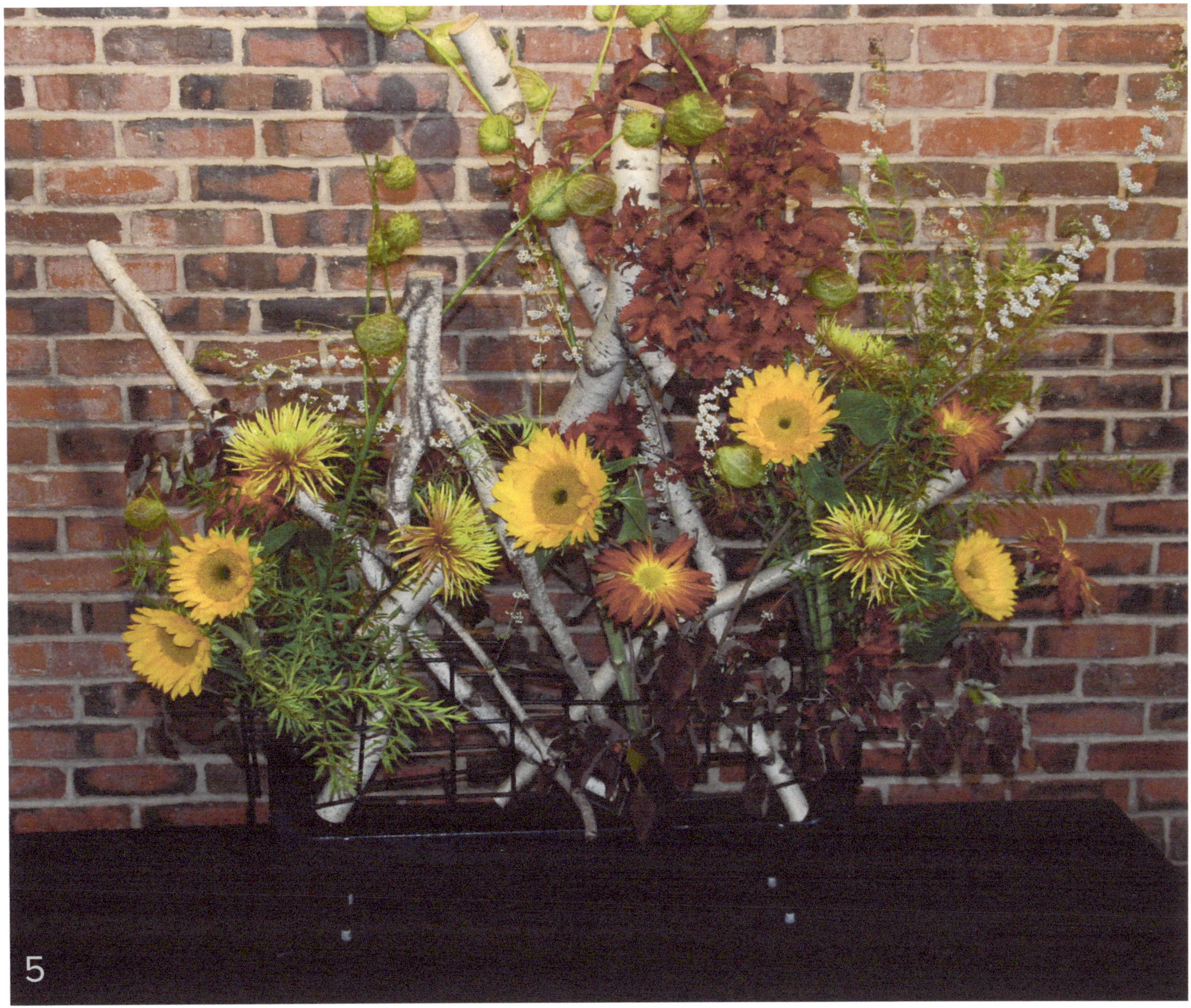
5

Wisteria, Chinese

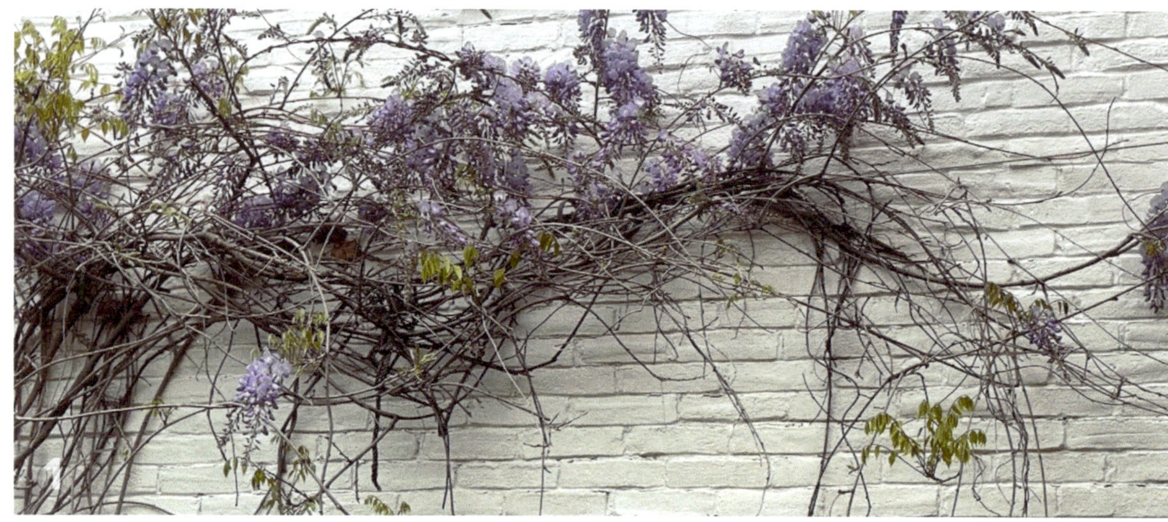

1 This early-blooming wisteria grows to the right of our front door. After visiting Italy and seeing how they managed these vigorous-growing vines, my husband strung wires over the window to encourage the wisteria to grow the way we wanted.
2 The leaves arrive after the flowers fade.
3 Detail of a single raceme.
4 Here you see pods hanging from a single branch. The amaranthus color matches the top of the container.
5 A nageire basket with a single blooming branch of wisteria.
6 The vine is placed to echo the shape of the container. The flowers are grouped to create a strong focal area and to let the spaces show.

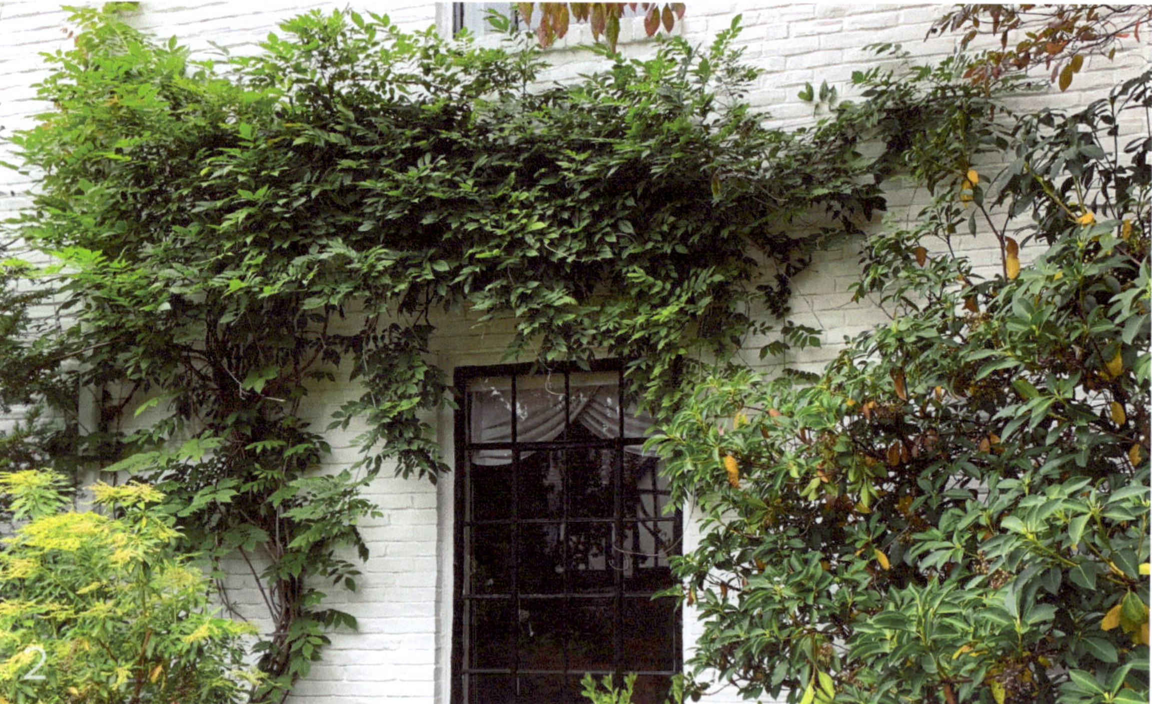

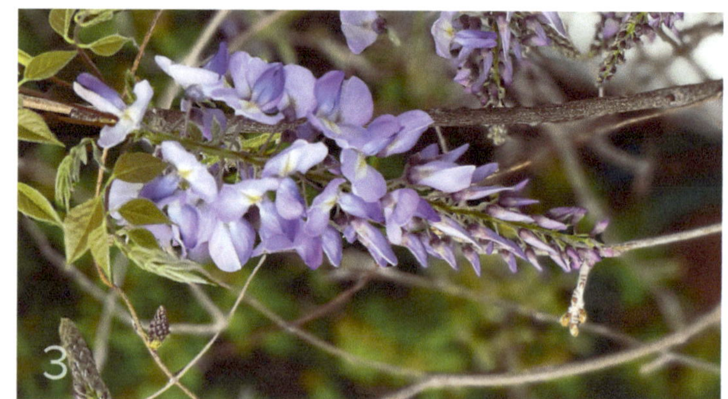

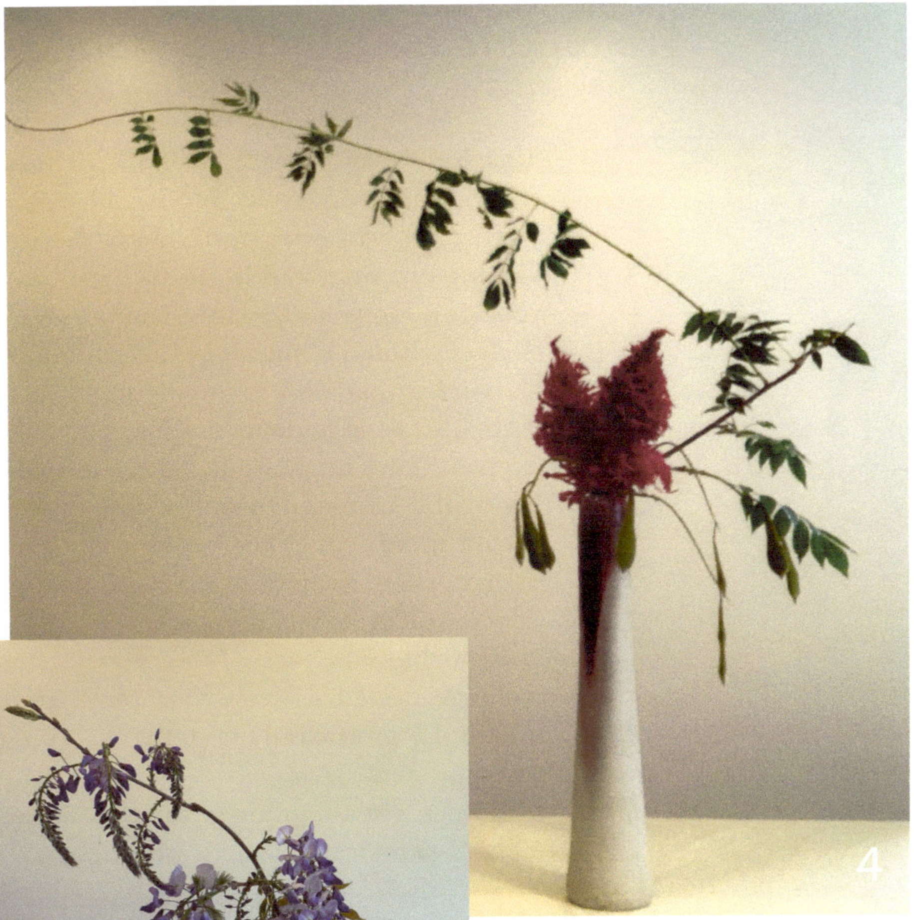

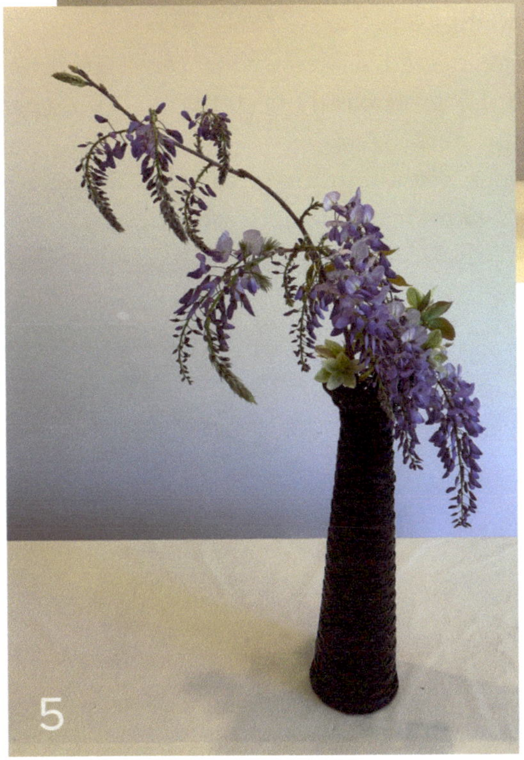

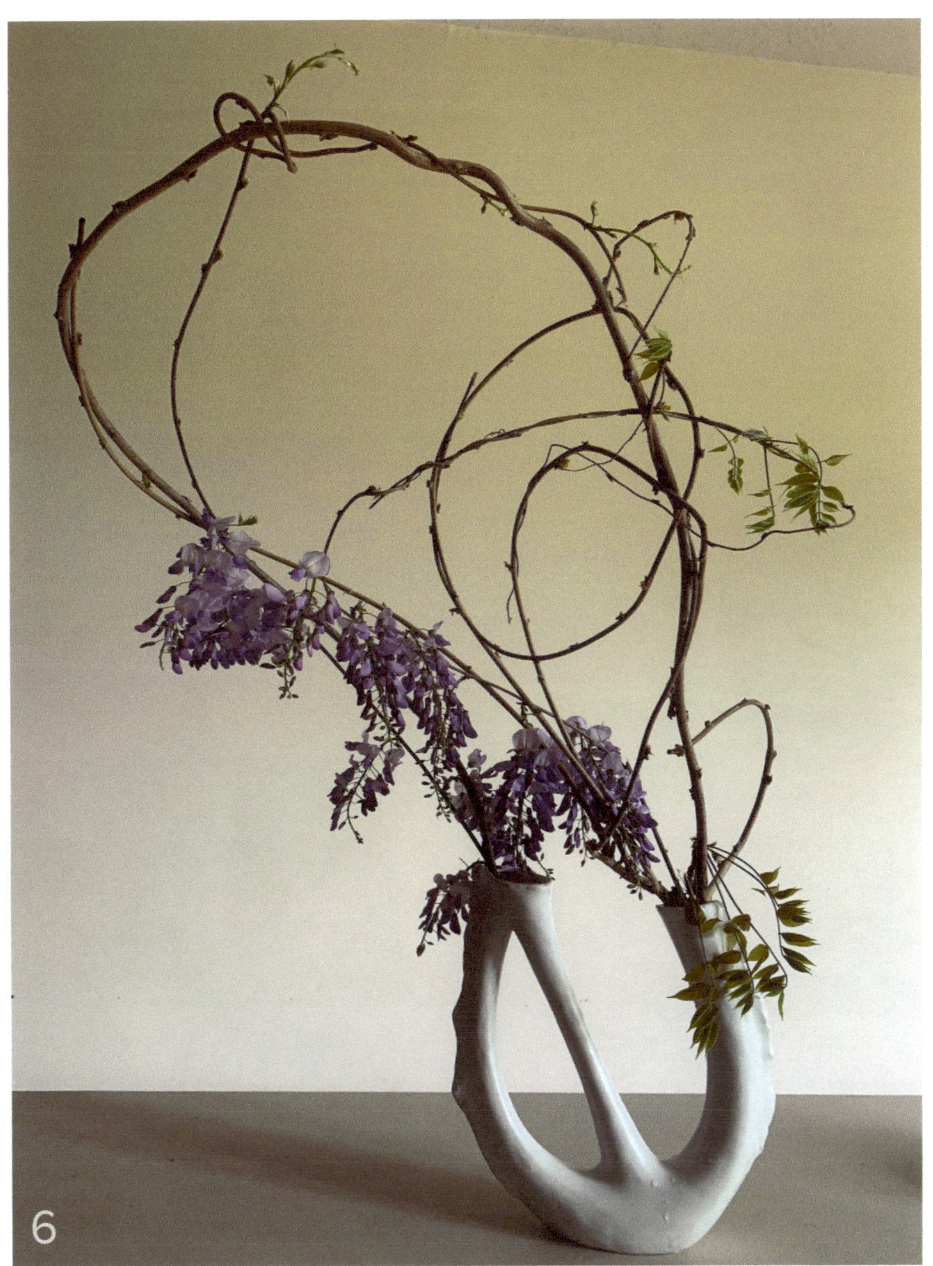

Wisteria, Kentucky 'Aunt Dee' *Wisteria macrostachya* 'Aunt Dee'

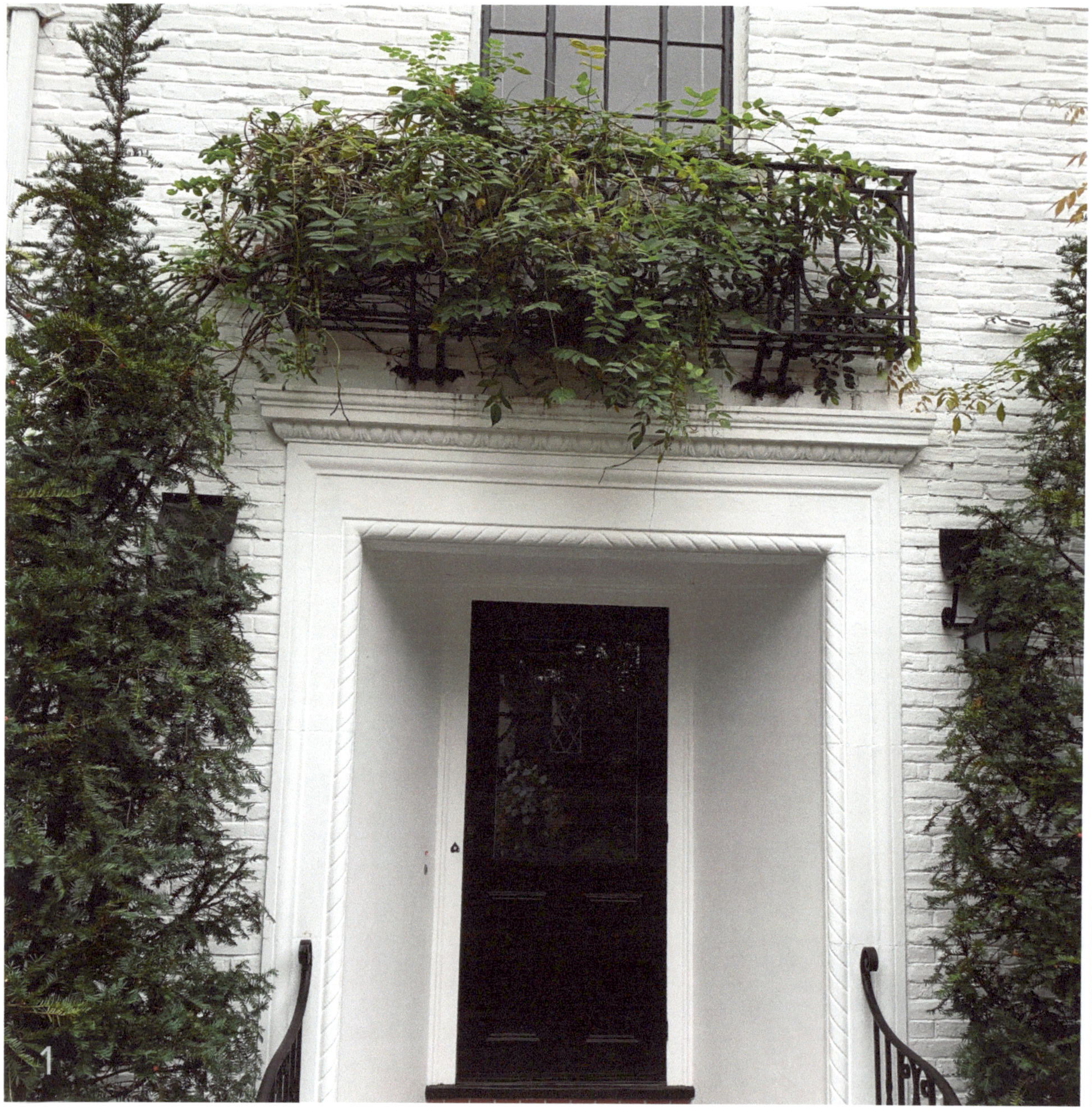

1. This Kentucky wisteria grows on the iron railing above my front door. It blooms later than my other wisteria, with the leaves coming out first, and it grows vigorously. If you look from above, this vine twines anti-clockwise. The vines need trimming once or twice a year, so I get many vines to play with. The arrangements on this page may be from either of my wisteria vines—it is nearly impossible to distinguish the vine once it is peeled and dried. When my husband prunes the two vines, he does so at the same time so they are all mixed up together!

2. Delicate blooms.

3. A single peeled wisteria vine plays around the smoke and foxtail lily stems in this nage-ire container.

4. I chose a glass container for this arrangement to support these delicate vines.

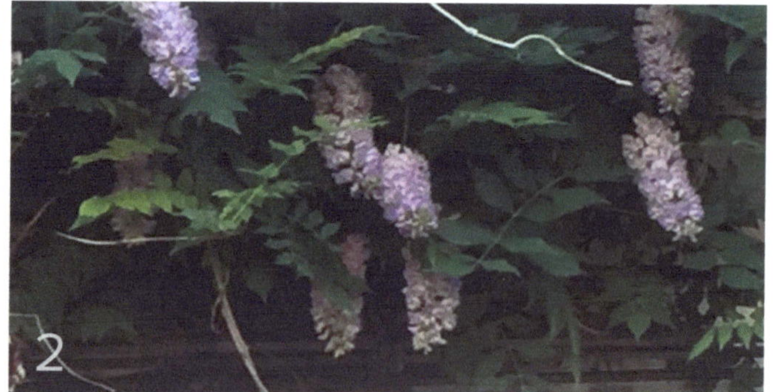

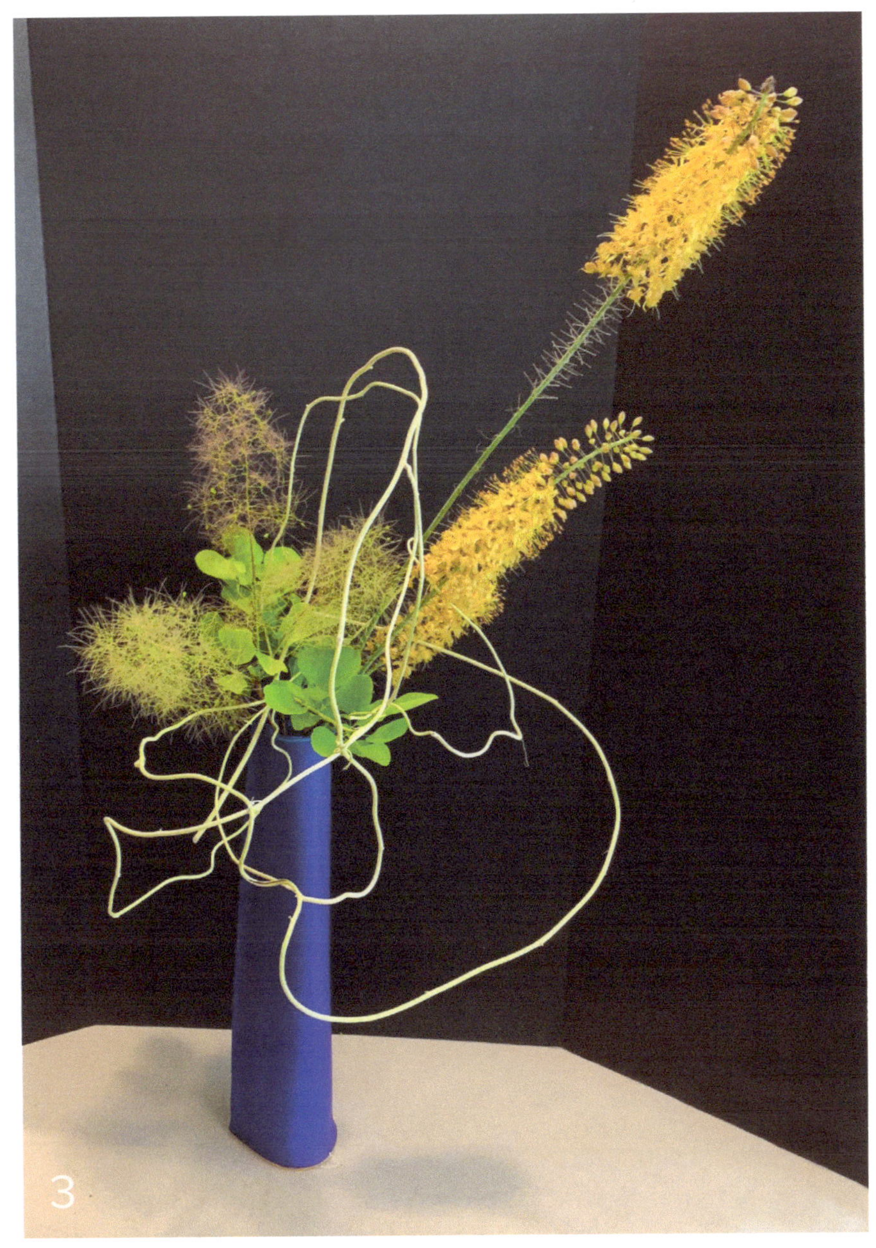

3

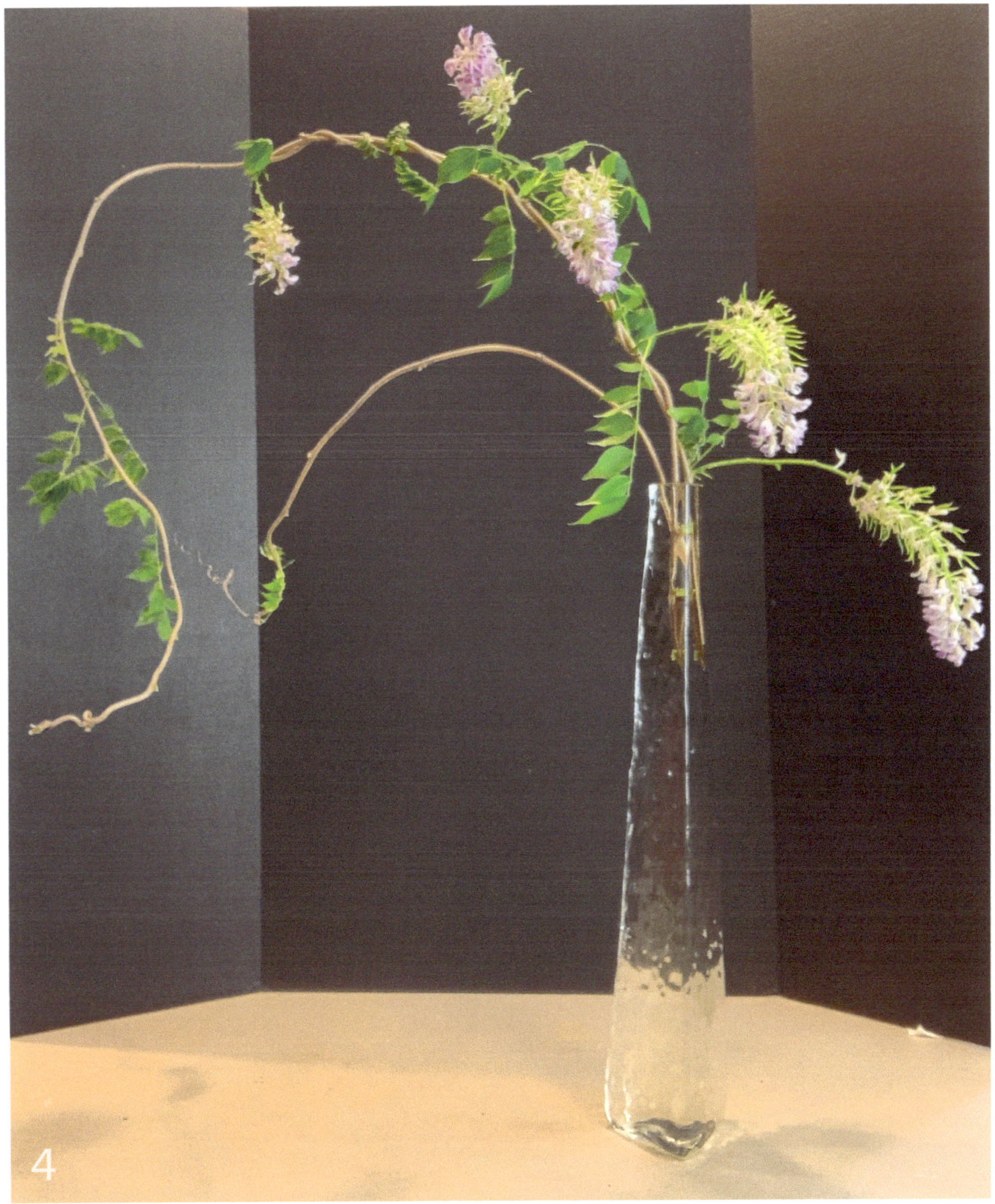

4

New Garden 2020

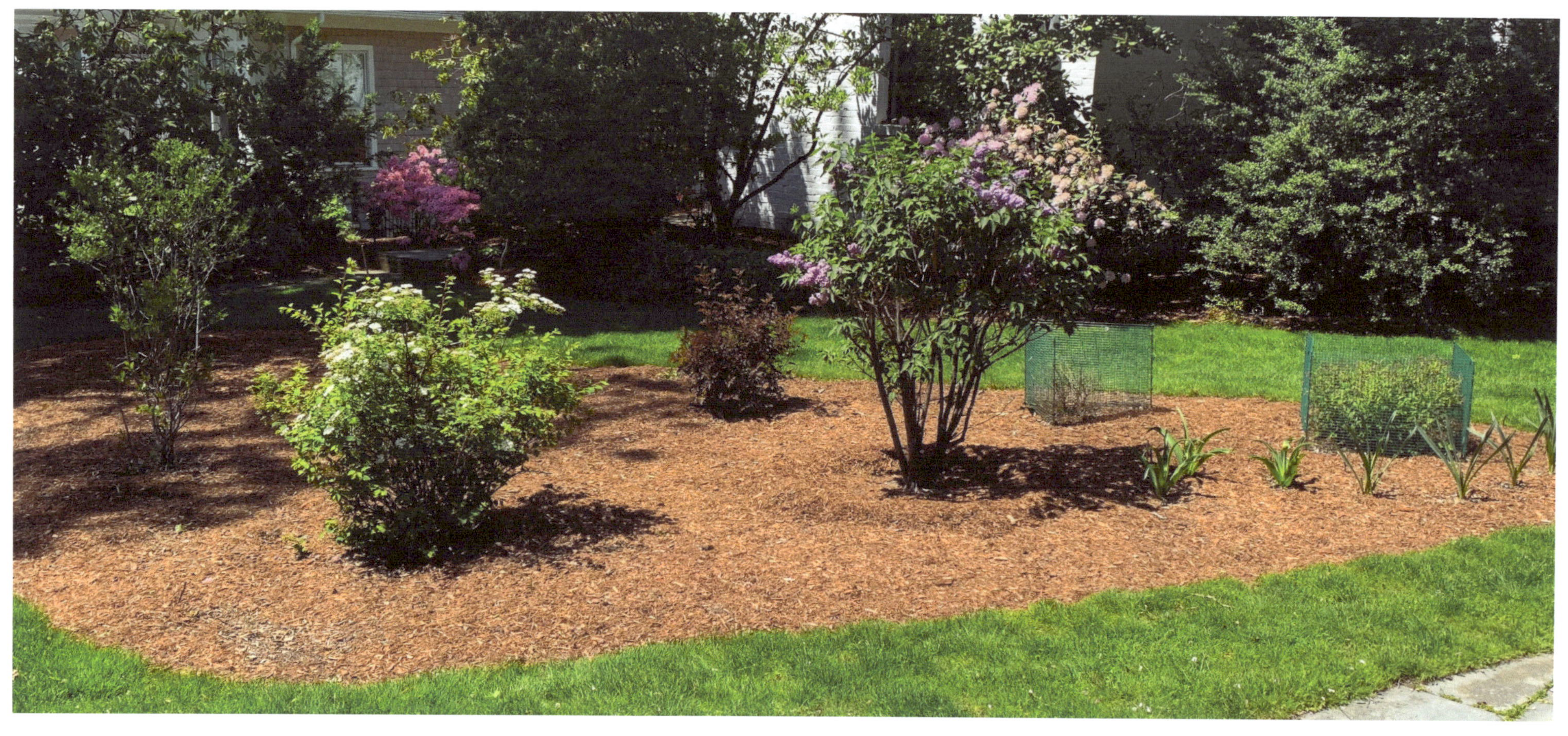

Red Winterberry   Spirea in bloom   Ninebark   Lilac   Broom (in cage)   Deutzia (in cage)

New Garden in the First Spring

All gardens are a work in progress. I knew some of my favorite plants were missing from my garden, so last year we tore up some more grass and added these plants:

Winterberry *Ilex verticillata* 'Winter Red' tall on left; *I. verticillata* 'Little Goblin' in front of Winter Red; *I. verticiallata* 'Jim Dandy' (male) planted nearby. Winterberry is a favorite source of berried branches. They range in color from cream to orange to red. They are separate male and female plants, so if there is no male nearby you will not see berries formed. They are deciduous, not evergreen. This is convenient, as the leaves fall off revealing the berries. The stems are strong and can be beautifully shaped.

Spirea, Bridal Wreath *Spiraea x vanhouttei* 'Renaissance'. I had large shrubs in our old yard which I cut often. It blooms later than our other spirea 'Ogon'. The arching branches are beautiful. Note the white blooms.

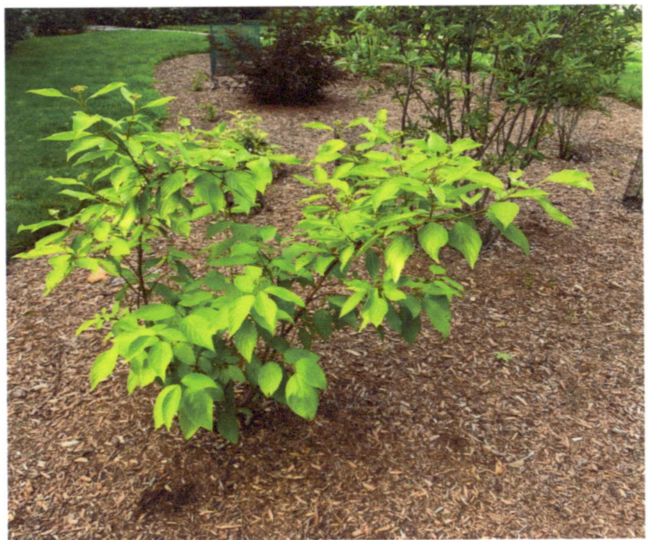

Lilac *Syringa vulgaris* 'Agincourt Beauty'. In bloom in the center, opposite. See the close-up of the bloom on this page, left.

Broom *Cytisis*. Protected from rabbit behind lilac.

Deutzia *Deutzia yuki* 'Cherry Blossom'. Protected from rabbits on right.

Dogwood, Red Twig or Red-Osier Dogwood *Cornus stolonifera*. Barely visible; hidden behind spirea

Ninebark *Physocarpus opulifolius* 'Coppertina'. Dark red between the lilac and the spirea.

Leucothoe *Leucothoe fontanesiana* 'Girards Rainbow'. Barely visible; moved behind the ninebark to avoid lawn sprinkler.

Hydrangea, Oak Leaf *Hydrangea quercifolia* 'Snow Queen'. We had to move this to the back yard to fence from rabbits—it's really big but not producing flowers this first year.

Red Twig Dogwood

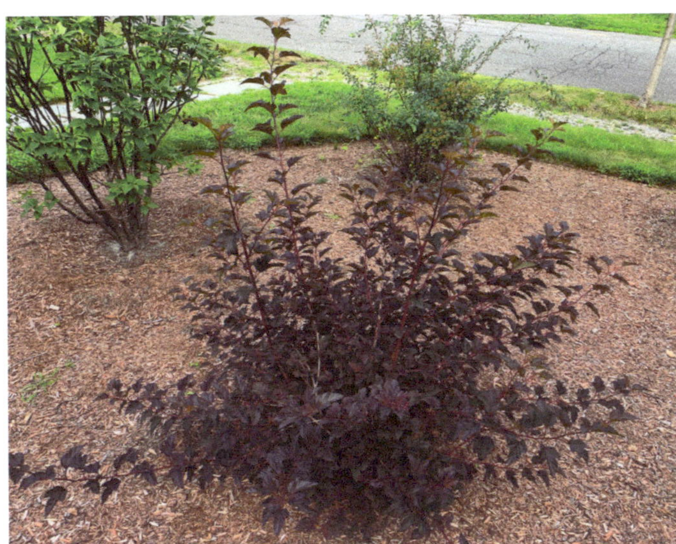

Ninebark

Leucothoe

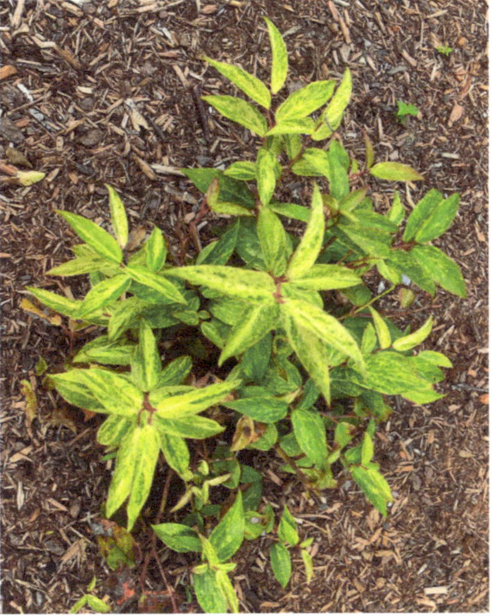

Containers

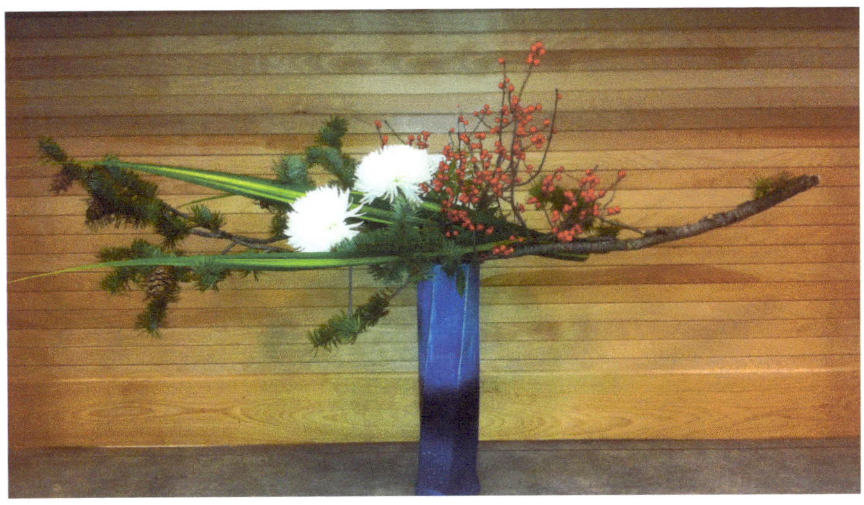

Acknowledgments

A rich environment created by my teachers and colleagues in ikebana organizations and garden club activities helped me grow in this creative field.

Forty years ago my first ikebana teacher, Joyce Overholtzer, became a model for me since she was both a Judge in the Garden Club and an ikebana teacher. Her teacher, Judith Hata, became my ikebana instructor and mentor. She is over ninety and still teaching and inspiring all of us.

From the Garden Clubs' Flower Show School, I learned the Principles of Design, which are invaluable in critiquing and improving my own designs and evaluating those of others.

I have continued to learn and grow by teaching ikebana. Thank you to all my students and fellow gardeners and Ikebanists. Some friends were kind enough to review this book in manuscript form to offer suggestions.

I would like to thank my husband, Kirby Vosburgh, who as head gardener and occasional photographer has made this book possible. Through all my years as a flower arranger he has been supportive by driving, carrying, creating pottery and critiquing and encouraging. Kirby has created many containers for me and my students, in addition to his own work in the ceramics studio. My son, Kirby C., offered me drawings of flower bouquets when he was a child. I think he saw my future even before I did.

Finally, I want to thank my daughter, Jennett Murphy, whose education as a librarian and experience in publishing provided her with a good background to help me in all aspects of writing this book. We have kept each other company on Zoom through the pandemic time.

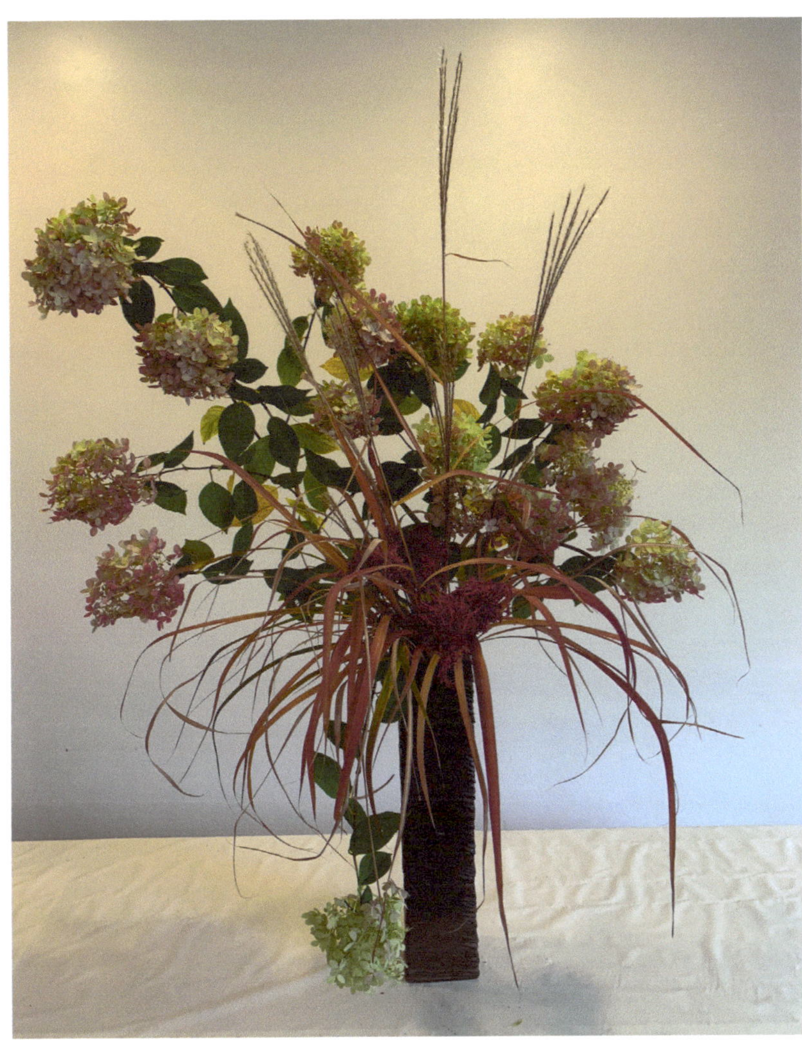

About the Author

Kaye began her ikebana studies in 1981. Her B.S. in biology and M.A.T. in teaching provided a good foundation. She holds the highest rank, Riji, in the Sogetsu School of Ikebana where she is an active teacher of Japanese flower arranging. Kaye is an Accredited Master Judge and a Flower Show School Design and Procedure Instructor for Judges in the National Garden Clubs, Inc.

From the beginning, Kaye has been involved in both Eastern- and Western-style arranging, with a goal of becoming proficient in creative design. Exhibiting in ikebana and garden club shows gave her experience as a designer. She joined Creative Floral Arrangers of the Americas (an organization which evolved from Bob Thomas' group) where she developed as a demonstrator.

She is a member and past Director of the Massachusetts Sogetsu Branch. She is a member of the New York Sogetsu Branch and workshop chairman of the New York State Capital District Sogetsu Study Group. She has twice been President of the Ikebana International Chapter #17 of Boston and is an Associate member of the NY Chapter of Ikebana International.

She has presented for the Creative Flower Arrangers of the Americas in Florida twice and given programs and workshops in all of New England and in New York, Pennsylvania, Ohio, Florida and in Quito, Ecuador.

She has chaired several Standard Flower Shows which have won National Awards and she has won numerous top awards for her design entries.

Kaye founded a Garden Club in Schenectady, Garden Explorers, with many friends from Master Gardener training. In Boston, she is a member of the Garden Club of the Back Bay and Noanett Garden Club. She enjoys demonstrating Western flower arranging as well as ikebana for garden clubs. Her favorite activity is sharing creative moments with other designers and students.

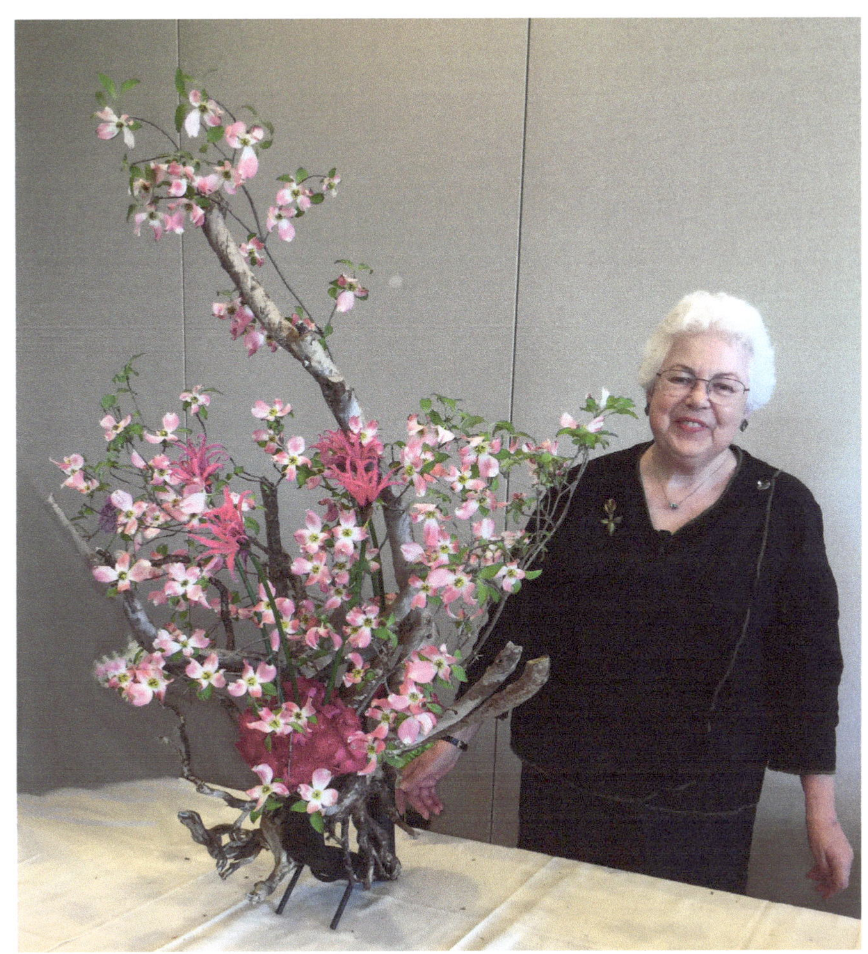

Additional Photo Descriptions

Front Cover: White container with spirea sheltering purple sweet peas. Container from Sogetsu School.

vi.   Kiwi vine creating space with spirea and forsythia creating mass.

ix.   Bamboo with its leaves removed placed upside down with peonies and astilbe.

97.   One branch of 'Unique' hydrangea with leaves of red grass, grass plumes, and amaranth.

99.   Large root balanced in an iron container embellished with dogwood branches, nerine lily, and hydrangea.

Back Cover: Garden scene: On the left, Japanese maple, and dogwood. Above the wall, the beautyberries.
               Left to right in the bed: Golden Spirit smoketree, forsythia, 'Unique' hydrangea, 'Royal Purple' smoketree, spirea, and enkianthus.

www.ingramcontent.com/pod-product-compliance
Lightning Source LLC
Chambersburg PA
CBHW042025050726

47602CB00010B/159